— the complete —

HOME BARTENDER'S

— guide —

REVISED AND UPDATED

the complete
HOME BARTENDER'S
guide
REVISED AND UPDATED

SALVATORE CALABRESE

Photography by
James Duncan

STERLING EPICURE
New York

To Sue, with love.

STERLING EPICURE
New York
An Imprint of Sterling Publishing
387 Park Avenue South
New York, NY 10016

STERLING EPICURE is a trademark of Sterling Publishing Co., Inc.
The distinctive Sterling logo is a registered trademark of Sterling Publishing Co., Inc.

ISBN 978-1-4027-8626-6

Created by Lynn Bryan,
The BookMaker, London, England.
Design: Mary Staples
Photography: James Duncan, except page 151, by Cameron Whitman, 213,
by CGissemann, and 246, by Ian O'Leary
Editor: Beverly LeBlanc
Updated design: Rachel Maloney

Distributed in Canada by Sterling Publishing
c/o Canadian Manda Group, 165 Dufferin Street
Toronto, Ontario, Canada M6K 3H6
Distributed in the United Kingdom by GMC Distribution Services
Castle Place, 166 High Street, Lewes, East Sussex, England BN7 1XU
Distributed in Australia by Capricorn Link (Australia) Pty. Ltd.
P.O. Box 704, Windsor, NSW 2756, Australia

For information about custom editions, special sales, and premium and corporate purchases,
please contact Sterling Special Sales at 800-805-5489 or specialsales@sterlingpublishing.com.

Printed in China

2 4 6 8 10 9 7 5 3 1

www.sterlingpublishing.com

CONTENTS

introduction

They call me the Maestro: I've been creating cocktails for nearly forty years. Bartending is in my blood!

When I first started working behind the bar, aged just eleven years old, I discovered the power a bartender can have and the way a bar can bring people together. I've been captivated ever since.

I've made drinks for the rich, for royalty and presidents—a *Who's Who* of the famous and the infamous. I've created drinks now known all over the globe, and I've traveled the world as a result of my passion for cocktails.

This book is my way of revealing some of the secrets to my success—it's my contribution to a bartending tradition that began in the mid-1800s, when the world's first mixologist, "Professor" Jerry Thomas, wrote the first ever book about cocktails. He would impress with drinks such as the Blue Blazer, setting whiskey on fire and passing it between two mixing glasses. It was his theatrics, charisma, personality, presence, and know how that has inspired countless bartenders, myself included.

Cocktails are hugely popular right now, probably more than ever before. Certainly, there has never been such a choice of great quality spirits, liqueurs, and fresh fruits and juices so freely available.

But for many people, cocktails remain obscure. For every enthusiastic drinker, there are ten more who think cocktails are just for the rich or the trendy. And of those who already enjoy certain cocktails, many don't know exactly what they are drinking or why.

The reason, as I see it, is that while there has clearly been an explosion in the quality of our food and drink, there's not actually so much good advice around on how to make cocktails.

Cocktails are not given the same popular status as wine or beer because they are either seen as intimidating, complicated, or too expensive.

That couldn't be further from the truth. To me, a well-made cocktail represents the pinnacle of sophisticated drinking. There's really no wider range of drinks that can rival the diversity in drink styles, the range of ingredients you can combine— hey, even in the range of glassware. And cocktails don't need to be complicated: sometimes the elegance of a great drink is in its simplicity.

Above all, cocktails can introduce you to a level of complexity in flavor—such as we've become used to in food—that's unmatched by any other type of drink. Tell me the time of day, the mood you're in, the reason you're drinking, and I can teach you whether to think about gin, cognac, vodka, whiskey—whatever!—and how to make the perfect cocktail.

If you're eating, and are looking for a drink that complements your meal, don't just think about wine. A single cocktail can introduce you to a realm of many different flavors, compared to a glass of wine that's essentially the same from start to finish.

We'll start with the basics. I'll teach you about Cobblers, Collins, Coolers, and Cups; Fizzes, Flips, and Flings. I'll teach you the difference between Martinis, Mules, Margaritas, and Mojitos; Smashes, Sours, and Slings. You'll be mixing and muddling, and shaking and stirring like a pro in no time.

And specially for this edition, I've selected a new collection of cocktails to really demonstrate the range of incredible taste sensations you can get from cocktails. Let it never be said that you hate gin or can't stand cognac. I'm confident you'll find something you like, whether a classic, such as a traditional Martini, Sazerac, or a Collins, or with something more contemporary.

As you get more experienced, you'll begin to understand why certain spirits, liqueurs, fruits, roots, herbs, and spices go so well together—and how they work together on the lips, the tongue, and around your mouth, before and after you've swallowed. Maybe you'll even be able to create a few flavor pairings of your own. That's

the secret to creating some memorable cocktails of your own, just like my own Breakfast Martini or Spicy Fifty—look out for my signature drinks.

I know it's easy to open a few bottles of beer and pass them around or to whip the corkscrew out of a bottle of wine. Too easy, in fact! You don't actually have to think to drink.

But to create something truly memorable, to really show your guests you care, and above all, to give them a drink that will knock their socks off—and I don't mean get them drunk!—we're really only talking about cocktails.

Just as it's a thrill to watch any professional at work, watching a great bartender make you a cocktail is fantastically entrancing. A bar is a stage, the bartender an actor or an entertainer, who impresses not just through the mastery of his drinks, but in his ability to put his audience at their ease and to keep them interested. Tell me you can do that with a bottle of wine!

So I invite you to join me on a fantastic journey. Just remember to bring your taste buds and an open mind.

Salute!

SALVATORE CALABRESE

BAR BASICS

tools & equipment

glassware

bar essentials

bar terms

general advice

easy techniques

flavors & garnishes

party planning

amalfi dream (left), page 248 and **fig supreme**, page 252

tools & equipment

There are certain tools and equipment that help you make delicious cocktails. Most can be found in the bar section of department stores.

BAR KNIFE
A small, sharp knife used for slicing fruit.

BARSPOON
It has a small bowl at the end of a handle.

BLENDER
Use to combine spirits, juice, fruit, and ice.

BOTTLE OPENER
Choose the least-complicated opener that feels good in your hand and is strong.

CHAMPAGNE STOPPER
Useful for saving the bubbles in a bottle.

CHOPPING BOARD
Use to slice fruit for garnishes.

COCKTAIL STICKS
Use for spearing pieces of cherries and other fruit for garnishes.

CORKSCREW
Use to open wine bottles.

DECORATIVE COASTERS
Use if you have tabletops that mark easily.

DASH POURER
Use for drops and dashes of bitters and some liqueurs when floating them.

GRATER
Use to dust a drink with chocolate or nutmeg.

ICE BUCKET AND TONGS
Make sure the bucket is wide enough to hold lots of ice. Use the tongs!

ICE SCOOP
Use to add ice to a shaker or blender.

JUICER
Important for making fresh grapefruit, orange, lemon, and lime juices.

MIXING GLASS
Used for mixing two or more ingredients with a barspoon.

MUDDLER
Use to mash sprigs of mint or berries into a pulp in the bottom of a mixing glass or an old-fashioned glass.

PONY-JIGGER
Use for correct measures to balance the flavors and strength of a cocktail.

SALT AND PEPPER GRINDERS
Use to add a spicy flavor in cocktails, such as Bloody Mary.

SHAKER
Use for mixing various spirits and juice together with ice.

STIRRERS
Stirrers can be made from glass or silver, with patterns and characters.

STRAWBERRY HULLER
Use to remove the stem and hull from a strawberry.

STRAWS
Use short straws for small glasses; for highballs and goblets, use two longer straws. Plain straws are best.

ZESTER
Use on lemon, orange, and lime peels to make garnishes.

1 *Clockwise from top:* Dash pourer, cloth for cleaning glasses, Angostura bitters, corkscrew and bottle opener, stirrers, and small grater

2 *Left to right:* Shaker, mixing glass with stirrer, two-piece silver shaker based on the Boston shaker, strainer, and pony-jigger

3 *Clockwise from top:* Juicer, lime squeezer, zester, and muddler

glassware

Fine, clear glasses with thin lips are best for showing off cocktails. Traditionally, each type of drink has a glass shape specifically for it. For instance, a long drink needs a highball; a Martini is served in a cocktail glass, and a Piña Colada loves a colada glass. A liqueur needs a small glass, as does a straight shot of a spirit.

When buying glasses, look for those with a design on the stem—it adds a visual interest to the presentation.

Always handle a stemmed glass by the stem, not the bowl, to keep the cocktail chilled. And keep a clean cloth nearby to "polish" glasses.

MAIN GLASS TYPES AND SIZES

Cocktail	4oz/12cl
Old-fashioned	5oz to 6oz/15cl to18cl
Shot	2oz to 3oz/6cl to 9cl
Liqueur	2oz to 3oz/6cl to 9cl
Highball	10oz/30cl
Wine	4oz to 9oz/12cl to 27cl

As you can see from the photograph, there are many glass styles. However, you need only a basic few. The cocktail glass is by far the most popular shape for almost any cocktail served without ice. A flute is essential for a champagne cocktail!

champagne flute

red wine

margarita

white wine

champagne saucer

CHAMPAGNE FLUTE

A flute is sophisticated and is preferred over those shaped like a saucer. (This shape was modeled on France's Empress Josephine's breast. However, it makes the champagne go flat quicker.)

COCKTAIL

A regular cocktail glass is best for the recipes in this book. A double cocktail glass is occasionally called for.

GOBLET

This is the original large glass and is best for exotic cocktails with lots of color, a few juices, and a big garnish on the side.

HIGHBALL

Used for long drinks and ideally should be wide at the rim. (If it's not, then you can catch your nose when you sip the drink!)

IRISH COFFEE

Designed to withstand the heat of coffee, it has a stem.

LIQUEUR

A small glass used for serving after-dinner digestifs.

OLD-FASHIONED

A short glass with a heavy base sits perfectly in the palm of your hand.

PORT

Designed for serving port or sherry.

PUNCH OR TODDY

Designed for holding hot drinks such as mulled wine; it usually has a handle.

SHOT

Designed for a measure of a strong spirit or spirits (pousse-café-style) that are downed in one gulp.

WHITE AND RED WINE

Wine glasses are good for cocktails that include fruit juices and a fancy garnish. White glass sizes range from 4oz/12cl to 6oz/18cl; red glass sizes range from 6oz/18cl to 9oz/27cl.

double cocktail

cocktail

goblet

highball

liqueur

old-fashioned

shot

bar essentials

SPIRITS

bourbon

brandy

gin

Pimm's No. 1 Cup

vodka

white (silver) and gold tequila

whiskey

white and dark rum

saké

LIQUEURS

amaretto

blue curaçao

crème de menthe (white and green)

crème de caçao (white and brown)

Cointreau

Grand Marnier

limoncello

WINES

champagne or sparkling wine

Dubonnet

dry and sweet vermouths

dry, medium, and sweet sherrys

red and white varieties

tawny port

BITTERS

Angostura bitters

Aperol

Campari

Cynar

Peychaud bitters

MIXERS

club soda

cola

ginger ale

mineral water (still and sparkling)

tonic water

7UP

JUICES

cranberry

lime

lemon

mango

orange

pineapple

tomato

white and pink grapefruit

EXTRAS

coconut cream

egg white*

fresh gingerroot

ground black pepper and salt

heavy (double) cream

superfine (caster) sugar

Tabasco sauce

Worcestershire sauce

SYRUPS

gomme syrup

grenadine

Orgeat (almond)

vanilla syrup

*A NOTE ABOUT EGG WHITE

Combining egg white with other ingredients and then shaking gives a drink a white frothy head. If you are concerned about using fresh egg white, use egg white powder, which is available from most food stores.

HOW TO MAKE A SYRUP

Many recipes call for gomme syrup, but you can make your own sugar syrup using granulated sugar. Gradually stir 1lb (½ kg) of granulated sugar into 13oz (1.3 liters) of boiling water in a saucepan. Bring to the boil and simmer. Skim it, leave to cool, and pour into small, clean bottles. Store in a dark cupboard.

ICE

Ice must be fresh and dry. Use the best filtered water to make ice or, if you prefer, use bottled spring water. Ice should only taste of water. Ice is used in a blender, a shaker, a mixing glass, or directly in a glass.

Why do you need ice? Ice is used to cool spirits as they are poured into a glass. Ice is available crushed, shaved, cracked, or cubed. The difference is that cracked and shaved ice are more watery than dry ice cubes. When added to a drink, the spirit is immediately diluted. With solid ice cubes, the ice holds its water for longer through the sipping. The average ice cube contains between 1 to 1½ozs (3 to 4.5cl) water, but the water melts very slowly.

The recipes in this guide use hard ice cubes and crushed ice. As a general rule, ice cubes are used for cocktails made in a shaker. Dry ice is important if you are making Martinis, because wet ice waters it down too much.

Crushed ice is used for drinks created in a blender. The crushed ice is only used in the blender, not the glass, unless the recipe specifically says to use crushed ice. Ice cubes are used in old-fashioned glasses and highballs, and never in cocktail glasses, unless you are using ice to chill them before pouring in the drink.

Many top-quality refrigerators make both ice cubes and crushed ice. If you do not own one of these luxury items, crush your own using a rolling pin. Or buy an ice-crusher. This is an added expense and only worthwhile if you intend to make a lot of cocktails over the coming years!

Some ice-cube trays produce fun shapes, such as stars, triangles, and hearts. These add an interesting visual touch to cocktails.

Remember, do not use the ice remaining in a shaker for the next drink, because the ice will be broken and will retain the flavor of the previous drink.

bar terms

It is best to use a double-ended pony-jigger when making cocktails because it helps you measure the specific amount of spirit, liqueur, or juice specified in a recipe.

One of its cups measures 1oz, the other 2oz. Some types have smaller ¼ and ½oz measurements marked inside the 2oz end.

The recipes in this book are given in ounces for American readers, and in centiliters for readers familiar with metric measurements.

The recipes in this guide are based on ⅓oz = 1cl, ⅔oz = 2cl, and ½oz = 1.5cl. Therefore 1oz = 3cl, 2oz = 6cl, and so on.

At first, use the jigger for exact amounts so you gain a good idea of what the cocktails *should* taste like. As your confidence grows, you might add more of this and a dash of that to change the taste to satisfy your palate. Always be consistent and retain the proportions.

The standard size of a cocktail is 3oz/9cl. Long drinks contain no more than 8oz/24cl; medium-sized cocktails are about 5oz/15cl; a spirit served on the rocks measures about 1½oz/4.5cl. Wine glasses hold from 4 to 5oz/12 to 15cl. A glass is always filled to a level of three-quarters, not all the way.

Following is a list of terms you might come across in the bar guide:

APERITIF
A cocktail served before dinner to stimulate the appetite.

BLEND
To use an electric blender to make a smooth liquid from fruit, juice, coconut cream, or cream.

BRUT
Dry (when referring to champagne)

BUILD
To pour the ingredients directly into a mixing or serving glass.

DASH
A small amount that flows when a bottle is quickly inverted once.

DIGESTIF
A cocktail served after dinner to aid digestion.

FLOAT
To float one spirit or liqueur over another, creating a layered drink.

FROSTED GLASS
A glass that's been chilled in the freezer.

FROSTED RIM
A glass which has a salted or sugared rim.

HOW MANY DRINKS CAN YOU GET FROM ONE BOTTLE?

If a bottle contains 23oz/70cl and a cocktail recipe calls for 1⅔oz/5cl, for example, you can make 14 of that particular cocktail.

MIXING GLASS

A large glass with measurements marked on the side.

MUDDLE

A term meaning to crush with vigor.

NEAT

Serving a drink "straight," without any ice, water, or mixer.

ON THE ROCKS

A drink poured over ice cubes.

PROOF

American description of alcohol content: 100 proof is 50 percent alcohol by volume (abv).

POUSSE-CAFÉ

A drink made of layers, created by floating a liqueur or spirit over a heavier one, followed by the next lightest.

SHAKE

To use a cocktail shaker to combine all the ingredients.

SHORT DRINK

Served in an old-fashioned glass.

STIR

To mix ingredients in a mixing glass.

SPIRAL

A thin peel of orange, lemon, or lime cut in an horizontal direction around the fruit to use as a garnish.

TALL DRINK

Served in a highball with ice and measures 8oz/24cl at the most.

TWIST

A thin, long strip of peel twisted in the middle and dropped into the drink.

ZEST

A strip of lemon or orange peel.

TYPES OF DRINKS

COBBLER A combination of spirit, fruit, and mixed berries with mint as a decoration. Served with a straw.

COLLINS A long and refreshing drink made with lots of ice. There are two versions: Tom Collins and John Collins.

COOLER Almost a Collins, but with a spiral of citrus peel trailing over the highball's rim. Contains soda or ginger ale, and perhaps bitters or grenadine. The soda to spirit ratio is 3 to 1.

CUP Traditionally British, wine-based cups are hot-weather drinks, the most famous being Pimm's No. 1 Cup.

FIZZ A Collins type, it is always shaken and served in a highball with straws.

FLIP Same family as eggnogs, it contains a fresh egg yolk but no milk. Served in a wine glass.

JULEP A long cocktail with fresh mint steeped in bourbon.

MOJITO Much like a julep, but with a rum base.

PUNCH Traditionally rum and water, hot or iced, with sugar and orange or lemon juice. Now made with spirits and mixers, and orange and lemon slices.

RICKEY An unsweetened cocktail of spirit, lime juice, and soda water first made in 1893.

SANGAREE A 19th-century American mix influenced by the Spanish red wine-based Sangria. Now made with soda, wines, ales, and spirits, and sweetened.

SLING A spirit-based cocktail with citrus juice and soda water, served in a highball with ice.

general advice

STORING CHAMPAGNE

Champagne should be kept in a rack in a horizontal position. This is how producers keep it in underground cellars. Champagne loves the dark and the coolness. It is important to maintain a consistent temperature of around 55°Fahrenheit (13°Celsius).

A warning: do not freeze champagne to chill it. This can ruin the contents.

Always use clean champagne flutes that have been wiped to remove any trace of residual dishwashing liquid.

OPENING CHAMPAGNE

Wrap a clean towel around the bottle and hold it firmly in one hand. With the other, undo the wire around the cork. Point the bottle away from you and any guests, and gently push the cork with both thumbs to release it. Turn the bottle as you do this. Or, you can hold the cork in one hand while you hold the bottle by the curved indentation in the other, and slowly turn the bottle—but not the cork—until the cork pops out.

When pouring champagne, aim for the middle of the flute and pour slowly. Pause after a few moments to let the bubbles subside, then start pouring again. Fill the glass to only three-quarters full. Do not waste a drop!

STORING WINE

Store red wine at room temperature. Do not place a bottle of claret or burgundy in the refrigerator. Store red wine on its side, so any sediment falls to the bottom when you stand the bottle upright.

White wines are best kept chilled, but do not place a bottle in the freezer to chill, because this has a detrimental effect.

STORING BRANDY, WHISKEY & OTHER SPIRITS

I recommend you store these bottles upright. If a spirit comes into contact with cork, an unwelcome effect is created.

OPENING WINE

There will be a seal around the neck of a wine bottle. Cut this with a sharp knife just below the top of the cork. Peel it off to expose the cork. Push the corkscrew into the cork and turn until the spiral is firmly inside. Pull out.

Modern corkscrews have different methods for extracting corks, so try a few to determine which is suitable for you.

If the cork breaks, carefully take out what's left in the neck of the bottle and re-insert the corkscrew. It will come out on the second attempt. If bits of cork bob in the wine, strain it into a decanter.

Always taste the wine before drinking it. If it is "corked" (tastes off), return the bottle to the store as soon as you can.

STORING SPIRITS & EAUX-DE-VIE IN THE FREEZER

The point of putting a bottle of the above in the freezer is to chill it so it remains chilled while you drink it. When you place spirits such as gin and vodka, and eaux-de-vie like Poire William, kirsch, framboise, and kummel in the freezer, you will see they do not freeze. This is because the spirit is 80 proof (40 percent alcohol by volume). Be careful not to put a bottle containing a spirit lower than this measurement, say, 74 proof (37 percent abv), or the spirit will actually freeze and the bottle might crack.

HOW TO CHILL A GLASS

Rule number one: always chill a cocktail glass before you pour any liquid into it. The chilled effect makes a drink look fabulous and appealing.

Put the required number of glasses in the freezer for a few hours before you need to use them. Or, fill them with crushed ice—this will chill the glass. Tip this ice away before the cocktail is poured.

FROSTING/CRUSTING THE RIM OF A GLASS

Part of the pleasure of a cocktail lies in its presentation. Classic cocktails, such as a Margarita and a Daiquiri, require the rim of the glass to be frosted (or crusted).

To achieve the crusty look, rub a wedge of lime, lemon, or orange around the rim of a glass and dip the rim in fine sea salt.

If a sugar-frost rim is required, pour superfine (caster) sugar in a saucer, rub the rim with a wedge of lemon, orange, or lime, and dip the rim in the sugar.

JUICING LIMES

Take one pale green lime and you have a cocktail. You may not know that there are two types of lime fruit: a large, seedless fruit and a smaller lime.

Which to use for a cocktail? Known in different countries under different common names, it is difficult to say which is the best type of lime. My advice to ensure a juicy lime is to look for the freshest one with a pale green skin. If its skin is dark green, you will get less juice from it.

Many bartenders roll a lime prior to juicing. The rolling action separates the juice from the pith inside the lime. You can also put the lime in hot water for about 30 seconds. This will release the juice inside. Then slice the lime with a sharp fruit knife.

Just squeezing the fruit in your hand is not enough to get the juice out. Use a hand-juicer—it also stops the seeds (if there are any) from escaping into the liquid. Use the juice immediately.

easy techniques

USING A SHAKER

Shake any recipe that contains spirits, juice, and heavy (double) cream. The most common shakers are the Boston shaker and the two-piece metal shaker you can buy from any quality home store.

THE BOSTON SHAKER is made of two pieces—one is metal, the other is clear glass. The ingredients are poured in the glass section so you can see what you are doing, then ice is added. The metal part covers the glass and is gently sealed with a slap of the palm. You will notice it nearly always sits at a sideways angle: this is normal.

Turn the shaker upside down. When the drink is shaken, the liquid will end up in the metal part. Let the drink settle for a moment before parting the two sections. If you can't open it easily, place your thumb under the middle section, where the metal and glass meet, and push gently. This will break the vacuum inside.

To serve the drink, pour it through a bar strainer, holding it firmly over the shaker's opening.

THE REGULAR SHAKER consists of a base, a small section with a fitted strainer, and a lid. It's usually compact, small, and easy to handle. Always be sure to hold the lid down firmly. If you get carried away, and it gets stuck, ease the lid up with both thumbs. Sometimes a quick, hard twist will also do the trick. If you have shaken it for a while, wipe the outside with a cloth to warm the sides slightly and loosen the vacuum.

USING A MIXING GLASS

Cocktails whose ingredients mix easily and must be served chilled are made (built) directly into a mixing glass, then poured into a cocktail glass. Always place about six ice cubes into the glass first and, using a barspoon, stir the ice around to chill the glass. Strain off any excess water. Add each spirit and stir the mixture well. Strain into a glass. Classics like Negroni and Manhattan are always stirred in a mixing glass.

HOW TO MUDDLE

This is a simple action requiring a little strength in the wrist. To muddle you need a muddler. Sometimes, the end of a barspoon has a muddler as part of its design.

More bartenders are using this method now—instead of bashing the fruits to a pulp, as in a blender.

Muddling brings out the essence, and most of the fruit remains intact.

Fruits or mint are muddled directly in the bottom of the glass. Choose a glass with a heavy base. Dice the fruit and place it in the glass or shaker. Add sugar (if stated) and/or a dash of spirit or wine (if stated) and muddle the fruit.

CREATING A LAYERED DRINK

Layered drinks are like magic. How do they do that! It's easy. The answer lies in the weight of each spirit in the recipe.

Generally, layered drinks are made in shot or liqueur glasses. All you need is a steady hand and a barspoon to float each liquid over the one already in the glass.

Read the label on the spirit or liqueur bottle to discover the alcohol volume—the lower it is, the more sugar it contains, and it will be heavier, like a syrup. If there are five ingredients in a recipe, such as in a Pousse-Café, begin with the first ingredient in the recipe, the heaviest.

To pour the second, less heavy ingredient, pick up the barspoon and place it in the glass on the edge of the first layer, with the back of the barspoon facing up.

Pour the next amount slowly onto the highest point of the spoon, and it will gradually flow down to create a second layer. Repeat the action for each of the successive lighter layers.

The beauty of a Pousse-Café is that it will hold for about 20 minutes if poured correctly. The sad thing is that your guest will gulp it down in one!

BLENDING COCKTAILS

Blended cocktails are delicious, combining the texture of fruit with the essence of the spirit. They're also the type of cocktail you can be exuberant with when creating a garnish. As a general rule, you blend any recipe that contains cream, fruit, and crushed ice.

How much to make? Usually a recipe is for one drink, but for the blender it is sometimes best to make two or more drinks at one time, especially if you are making the cocktails during a party.

Always wash, peel, and dice the fruit before adding it to the blender. And make sure there is enough liquid in the blender, too. Sometimes, you might have to add a dash of white wine or spirit to make the mixture easier to blend.

Some blended recipes also require the mixture to be poured through a strainer, giving the liquid a finer texture. This is easy to do: Place the strainer over the glass and pour small amounts of the mixture into it. With a teaspoon or barspoon, mash the mixture until you can see that most of the liquid has passed through the holes in the wire mesh. Then discard the remaining pips or flesh and pour in a further small amount, repeating the process.

Blended cocktails are best made and served immediately. You can blend the fruits and the spirits before an event, and place the mixture in the refrigerator, but do not add creamy ingredients until the last minute. And, as always, add the ice last.

flavors & garnishes

When making a cocktail, it is important to balance the flavors in the recipe. There are four basic flavors: sweet, sharp (sour), spicy, and bitter.

The perfect cocktail is the result of a harmony of one or more, or all four, flavors. Before you choose which cocktail to make, think about what you want from the drink. Each of us has taste buds that are satisfied by different flavors. For example, if you drink a Vodka Sour you might think it contains nothing but tartness. Yet sweetness underlies the flavor to balance the sharpness.

SWEETNESS in cocktails usually comes from ingredients such as liqueurs—Kahlua, Cointreau, Baileys, Grand Marnier, Galliano, and limoncello—that contain an intensity of sugar. These are low in alcohol volume, but high in sugar content. Some fruit juices also add sweetness. A Piña Colada tastes sweet because of pineapple juice and coconut cream.

SHARPNESS is a flavor that causes you to smack your lips after a sip. Sharpness refreshes your taste buds more than other flavors. Any recipe made with fresh lime or lemon juice will taste sharp, as will a recipe containing raspberries, which have a distinctly sharp taste. Cocktails with a sharp flavor include the Margarita.

SPICY COCKTAILS are those with a hint of cinnamon or nutmeg, or other such spices. A Bloody Mary is spicy because it features tomato juice and black pepper.

BITTERNESS is found in cocktails containing Campari and other bitters. Generally, bitterness comes with an ingredient made of herbal extracts, such as Fernet Branca (an excellent digestif). Bitter cocktails include the Negroni.

EXPERIMENT WITH FLAVORS

Consider which drinks you immediately like and make a note of the ingredients. Until you have mixed the recipe as given in this book, you will not know exactly how the drink should taste, so make it precisely the first few times, and then experiment. If you prefer a slightly tart taste, add more lemon or lime juice. Experiment until it is perfect for you. However, if you are making the cocktail for friends, ask them how they prefer it, and tailor the cocktail to please their palates.

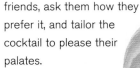

The following look good as a garnish:

APPLES (CUT IN A THIN WEDGE OR FAN)

BLACKBERRIES

BLUEBERRIES

CAPE GOOSEBERRIES

CUCUMBER PEEL (FOR A PUNCH, AND PIMM'S)

CELERY STICKS (OPTIONAL FOR BLOODY MARY)

KIWIFRUIT

LEMONS (IN A WEDGE OR SLICED)

LIMES (IN A WEDGE OR SLICED)

MARASCHINO CHERRIES (COCKTAIL CHERRIES)

MINT, FRESH

GREEN OLIVES (FOR A MARTINI)

ORANGES (IN A WEDGE OR SLICED)

PINEAPPLES

RED CURRANTS ON A STEM

RASPBERRIES

STAR FRUIT (THINLY SLICED)

STRAWBERRIES

Garnishes are the finishing touches. First, consider the flavor, then match the garnish with the dominate flavor.

Second, consider the color. A yellow garnish with a green drink would be visually disastrous.

Third, a garnish must be in proportion to the glass. Three red currants on a cocktail stick perched on the rim look lost, whereas a stalk of red currants cascading from the rim is perfect.

Strawberries can be dropped in the drink, particularly into a flute, or perched on the rim. Take out the green stem, and slice into as many pieces as you want without separating them. Fan out the slices and slip the strawberry over the rim. Or use a whole hulled strawberry, making a slit in the bottom and slipping it over the rim.

THREE-BERRY GARNISH

• Choose three blackberries or raspberries and a sprig of mint.

• Make a tiny incision in the top of one berry with a sharp knife.

• Select a leaf with a bit of a stem and push the stem into the incision. Spear all three berries with a cocktail stick. Add to the rim.

CAPE GOOSEBERRY GARNISH

• Hold a Cape Gooseberry (*Physallis*) in one hand. With the other, unfurl the layers one by one, working each fragile leaf into a shape. Make a small slit in the bottom of the fruit and sit it on the rim of the glass.

LIME/ORANGE/LEMON SPIRAL

• Using a zester and starting from the top, cut around a lime, making a long spiral.

• Hold the fruit firmly in your hand and press the zester firmly into the peel.

TIPS:

• *Choose fruit that is firm to the touch.*

• *Wash any fruit and dry it with a paper towel.*

• *Always use a sharp knife!*

party planning

TIMING

The organization for a cocktail party begins at least two weeks before the event. The evening will be more relaxing for you as the host or hostess if you do not have to worry about whether or not you have enough to drink—or have all the right ingredients for the drinks you wish to serve your guests.

THE COCKTAIL MENU

If you are having a celebratory cocktail party for, say, 20 people, it is best to decide before the event which cocktails to offer. Generally, a choice of six is fine. Read through some classic recipes and choose the ones you like most. If you know your guests like vodka, then choose two vodka recipes. If others prefer the taste of gin, add a gin-based recipe.

White rum and tequila (the spirit base of the classic Margarita) are also popular, and there are quite a few easy-to-make recipes using these spirits and various fruit juices.

Also, ask your guests in advance whether they prefer sweet or tart flavors.

However, the most important thing is to choose recipes you will feel comfortable making. Recipes that are mixed (built), muddled, and shaken are easiest; the blender is messy and noisy; however, it does result in some delicious cocktails.

When you have a definitive cocktail menu, make a list of spirits and mixers. If you are serving Margaritas, add fine salt for the rim to the list. And a saucer. Think about the garnish and make a second list of fruit required for this final touch.

Write a third list of the tools and equipment needed, including a small sharp knife and a cutting board, for making the drink and the garnish, and a clean tea towel to wipe up any spills.

ICE

The amount of ice you will need differs according to the types of cocktails you are going to make. Buy small bags of ice from the liquor store and place them in the freezer. Fill an ice bucket about five minutes before the guests arrive.

ADVANCE PREPARATION

You can prepare cocktails in advance without wasting ingredients. It is important to make sure that guests do not have to wait too long for their drinks when they arrive. For instance, you can salt the rim of several Margarita glasses beforehand. Then pour the recipe times the number of guests into a pitcher. Do not add ice at this stage. Place the pitcher in the refrigerator. As guests arrive, pour a measure for one cocktail into the shaker with ice.

You can also muddle fruit or fresh mint in advance and put it in the refrigerator. This saves time at the mixing stage.

Prepare each garnish in advance and place on a plate in the refrigerator and cover with a damp cloth to keep moist.

MIXERS

Tonic water, club soda, and sparkling water are essential. Buy smaller cans or bottles because the contents do not lose their fizz as quickly as larger bottles once opened.

JUICES

Make fresh orange, lemon, and lime juice if possible. Or try to buy freshly squeezed or natural pure juices for a better flavor.

HOW MUCH WINE FOR A DINNER PARTY?

This depends upon how much you know about the drinking habits of your guests.

However, as an average, assume each person will drink two to three glasses of wine during dinner. For four people you will need two or more 75cl bottles of wine. Find out whether your guests prefer red or white and buy extra of the type that is more popular. It is better to have more in the liquor cabinet than not enough.

• *If the recipe calls for a chilled cocktail glass, make sure you put several in the freezer hours before the event. If you don't have room in the freezer, put them in the refrigerator. Or fill them with ice cubes for 10 minutes.*

• *No martini cocktail glasses? Don't rush out and buy a dozen. It's not that expensive to rent glasses, so you could investigate the cost of renting.*

BUYING GUIDE

SPIRITS
Average number of drinks per bottle
Cocktails with a measure of 1½ oz

75cl bottle	16 cocktails
liter bottle	22 cocktails
1½ liter bottle	39 cocktails

WINE OR CHAMPAGNE
Average number of drinks per bottle
5oz serving per glass

75cl bottle	5 glasses
liter bottle	6 glasses
1½ liter bottle	10 glasses
3 liter bottle	20 glasses

HOW MANY COCKTAILS PER PERSON?

Cocktail party for 12 people:
Reckon on three cocktails per person. Therefore, 36 cocktails will suffice.

Pre-dinner cocktails:
Reckon on two drinks per person.

After-dinner cocktails:
Reckon on two drinks per person.

THE RECIPES

brandy

gin

rum

tequila

vodka

whiskey & bourbon

champagne & wine

bitters & other spirits

punches, cups & eggnogs

liqueurs

shooters

hot drinks

Calabrese classics

non-alcoholic

cosmopolitan, page 131

BRANDY

Brandy is a generic term for a spirit distilled from the juice, fruit, and pulp of any kind of fruit. It can be produced anywhere in the world. The name is from the Dutch brandewijn *("burnt wine"), and the creation of brandy was due almost entirely to the Dutch.*

Dutch demand for supplies of brandy meant the French were obliged to change the way they shipped wine to Holland to be used as raw material in the distilleries, called *wijnbranders* ("wineburners"). Distilled spirit was cheaper than wine to ship, so the French began to use the technique, and equipment, introduced by the Dutch for distillation, particularly in the Charente region (see Cognac).

What we call brandy is made from grapes that are distilled, aged in oak barrels, and transferred to glass jars after maturation. A two- to three-year-old brandy is young; ten to 15 years old is good. Forty to 60 years old is of excellent quality.

Countries that produce brandy include Armenia, France, Germany, Italy, Mexico, Portugal, South Africa, Spain (the largest consumer of brandy in the world), and the United States.

Two-thirds of the brandy for the American market comes from California. Over the past decade, a few small producers have been using cognac-style methods to make more exclusive and aromatic brandies for sipping after dinner.

South American brandy comes from Chile and is called *pisco*. It is made from Muscat grapes that are distilled and then aged in oak or in clay jars. A Pisco Sour cocktail is made only with this brandy.

happy world (left), page 39, and **cognac mint frappé**, page 36

GRAPPA AND MARC

Also called pomace brandy, these are regarded as "poor man's brandies" and are drunk as digestifs. The most well-known marcs, produced in France, are *marc de Champagne* (a delicate flavor) and *marc de Bourgogne* (aromatic and strong).

Grappa is produced in Italy and is not aged as such, but some brands may have been matured in wooden casks for between two to four years.

Both types of brandy are made from the remaining skins, husks, and stems of grapes that have been pressed to make wine.

COGNAC

Brandy from the Charente-Martime area in France is known as cognac. Grapes are grown in six regions: Grande Champagne, Petite Champagne, Les Borderies, Fins Bois, Bons Bois, Bois Ordinaires. The grapes used are Ugni Blanc, Folle Blanche, and Colombard. Maturation must take place in a *Jaune d'Or* and only in oak casks from the Limousin or Troncais forests. The minimum period it must be in the cask is 30 months.

Cognac is a blend of cognacs from different houses and vintages. Details on the label refer to the number of years the youngest cognac has been in the cask.

The following are the official cognac aging guidelines:

*****Three Star/V.S.** the youngest *eau-de-vie* is four-and-a-half years old.

V.S.O.P. or V.O. Very Special (or Superior) Old Pale the youngest is four-and-a-half to six years old.

Napoléon, Grande Réserve, X.O., and Extra Vieille the youngest is six-and-a-half years old.

SERVING TIPS

Serve both marc and grappa at room temperature in a balloon glass after dinner. A measure is about $1\frac{2}{3}$oz (5cl).

Almost all bars and restaurants serve brandy and cognac in a balloon glass. The makers of cognac, and connoisseurs, prefer to serve it in a tulip-shaped glass. Quarter-fill a glass, leaving space for the aroma to be released by the warmth of your hand.

Sip a cognac to experience the many flavors found in the finest cognacs.

> *Always chill a cocktail glass in the freezer before use.*

Adieu

Many fond farewells have been said after a few of these cocktails.

2oz/6cl	cognac
1oz/3cl	Grand Marnier
1/3oz/1cl	vanilla liqueur

Pour all ingredients into a mixing glass with ice. Stir. Strain into a cocktail glass. Garnish with a twist of orange.

Alexander No. 2

This is the 1920s pale relation to a Brandy Alexander made with brown crème de cacao.

1oz/3cl	brandy
1oz/3cl	white crème de cacao
1oz/3cl	heavy (double) cream

Pour all ingredients into a shaker with ice. Shake. Strain into a cocktail glass.

Amber Cloud

Sip this to get the aroma of the cognac and the fragrance of the Galliano.

1 1/3oz/4cl	cognac
2/3oz/2cl	Galliano

Pour all ingredients into a shaker with ice. Shake. Strain into an old-fashioned glass with crushed ice. Serve with a straw.

American Beauty

A classic cocktail with the full flavor of brandy and a hint of mint at the finish.

2/3oz/2cl	brandy
2/3oz/2cl	extra dry vermouth
2/3oz/2cl	fresh orange juice
1/2oz/1.5cl	ruby port
dash	white crème de menthe
dash	grenadine

Pour all ingredients into a shaker with ice. Shake. Strain into a wine glass.

Amour Sanglant (Bloody Love)

This cocktail is a deep orange color from the Sicilian variety of orange.

1 1/3oz/4cl	cognac
2/3oz/2cl	cherry brandy
1/3oz/1cl	vanilla liqueur
2 1/3oz/7cl	fresh blood-orange juice

Pour all ingredients into a shaker with ice. Shake. Strain into a wine glass. Garnish with a maraschino cherry.

Angel's Dream

Perfect for evenings when you've spent most of the day dreaming of angels.

1oz/3cl	maraschino liqueur
1oz/3cl	Parfait Amour
1oz/3cl	cognac

Pour the maraschino into a liqueur glass. Float the Parfait Amour over the back of a barspoon, and then the cognac.

Apple Car Martini

The apple flavor of calvados balances well with the orange and other ingredients.

1oz/3cl	calvados
1oz/3cl	triple sec/Cointreau
⅔oz/2cl	fresh lemon juice
⅓oz/1cl	gomme syrup

Pour all ingredients into a shaker with ice. Shake. Strain into a cocktail glass.

Banana Bliss

A creamy creation from the Southern Hemisphere that encapsulates all that is exotic.

1⅓oz/4cl	cognac
1oz/3cl	crème de bananes
	(banana liqueur)

Pour the cognac into a mixing glass with ice, then banana liqueur. Stir. Strain into an old-fashioned glass filled with ice.

B & B

A popular old classic drink that is sold premixed in many stores. Another version of this drink, called A & B, uses armagnac and Bénédictine.

| 1oz/3cl | brandy |
| 1oz/3cl | Bénédictine |

Pour the brandy directly into a brandy balloon and gently float the Bénédictine over a barspoon to lay on top.

Bentley

A classic drink that dates back to the 1920s and days of large prestige cars and glamorous women.

| 1⅔oz/5cl | applejack brandy |
| 1⅔oz/5cl | Dubonnet |

Pour the brandy and Dubonnet into a mixing glass with ice. Stir. Strain into a cocktail glass. Garnish with a twist of orange.

B P

This is a much-appreciated digestif, and a good medicine for a stomach upset.

| 1oz/3cl | brandy |
| ⅔oz/2cl | ruby port |

Pour the port into a port glass, followed by the brandy. Stir.

Between the Sheets

Created in the 1930s, this cocktail is the perfect one for a prelude to seduction.

1oz / 3cl	brandy
1oz / 3cl	Cointreau
1oz / 3cl	light rum
dash	fresh lemon juice

Pour all ingredients into a shaker with ice. Shake. Strain into a cocktail glass.

Block and Fall

This drink was created by a T. van Dycke at the Ciro Club, Deauville, France, in 1924. It was originally made with absinthe instead of Pernod.

⅔oz / 2cl	brandy
⅔oz / 2cl	Cointreau
½oz / 1.5cl	Pernod
½oz / 1.5cl	calvados

Pour all ingredients into a shaker with ice. Shake. Strain into a cocktail glass.

Bonita

If something is "bonito," it's nice. And this combination is very well-named.

2oz / 6cl	cognac
⅔oz / 2cl	fresh lemon juice
dash	gomme syrup
	apple juice

Pour all ingredients, except apple juice, into a highball filled with ice. Top up with apple juice. Stir. Garnish with a slice of apple.

Bosom Caresser

A 1920s classic first made by Harry Craddock at the American Bar in London's Savoy Hotel. Sweet Madeira can be added to this recipe.

1⅓oz / 4cl	brandy
⅔oz / 2cl	orange curaçao
dash	grenadine
1	free-range egg yolk

Pour all ingredients into a shaker with ice. Shake. Strain into a cocktail or small wine glass.

Bottoms Up

One from the late 1940s. A rich and powerful drink to sip, and when you see the bottom of the glass, it's time to retire to bed. Van der Hum, a tangerine-and-orange-flavored liqueur from South Africa, gives this drink a unique flavor.

1oz / 3cl	cognac
⅔oz / 2cl	Van der Hum liqueur
½oz / 1.5cl	heavy (double) cream
1	free-range egg yolk
dash	grenadine

Pour all ingredients into a shaker with ice. Shake. Strain into a cocktail glass.

Brandy Alexander

By far one of the most sophisticated after-dinner drinks, this was at the height of its popularity in the heady 1960s and 1970s and is still popular. When I visited the Mansion, at Turtle Creek in Dallas, I noticed they used the same spirit ingredients, but replaced the cream with a scoop of vanilla ice cream, and used a blender. While this is not strictly correct, it resulted in a chilled, creamy cocktail.

1oz / 3cl	brandy
1oz / 3cl	brown crème de cacao
1oz / 3cl	heavy (double) cream

Pour all ingredients into a shaker with ice. Shake. Strain into a cocktail glass. Garnish with a sprinkle of freshly grated nutmeg.

Brandy Cocktail

A 1920s classic drink. The original recipe did not use Angostura bitters.

1¾oz / 5cl	brandy
2 dashes	orange curaçao
2 dashes	Angostura bitters

Pour all ingredients into a mixing glass with ice. Stir. Strain into a balloon glass.

Brandy Crusta

Created in the 1850s by Joseph Santini of Jewel of the South, New Orleans. A true classic that is finding its way back!

1½ oz / 4.5cl	cognac
½oz / 1.5cl	orange curaçao
½oz / 1.5cl	fresh lemon juice
1 barspoon	gomme syrup
2 dashes	Angostura bitters

Crust a small goblet glass with sugar by wetting the edge with lemon juice and dipping it into sugar. Pour all the ingredients into a shaker filled with ice. Shake and strain into the glass. Add 1 ice cube and garnish by carefully placing a wide strip of pared lemon peel around the inside rim of the glass.

Charles' Nightcap

This combination gives an interesting, powerful, and fruity flavor.

1⅓oz/4cl	armagnac
1oz/3cl	pear schnapps

Pour both ingredients into a mixing glass with ice. Stir. Strain into a brandy balloon glass.

Chicago Cocktail

A classic after-dinner drink from the 1920s and 1930s, with its origins in the Speakeasy culture.

2oz/6cl	brandy
dash	Angostura bitters
dash	triple sec/Cointreau
	champagne

Rub a wedge of lemon around the rim of a glass. Dip it into a saucer of superfine (caster) sugar to create a frosted rim. Pour all ingredients, except champagne, into a mixing glass with ice. Stir. Strain into a cocktail glass. Top up with champagne.

Cognac Apple Snap

Ginger dominates the apple and lime flavors, while the earthiness of the cognac binds the flavors together.

1⅔oz/5cl	cognac
dash	fresh lime juice,
	apple juice,
	ginger beer

Pour the cognac and lime juice into a highball filled with ice. Fill the glass to about three-quarters with apple juice. Stir. Top up with ginger beer. Garnish with a slice of red apple.

Cognac Cosmopolitan

This is a wonderful drink! It has all the essence of the original Cosmopolitan, but with more body.

1⅔oz/5cl	cognac
½oz/1.5cl	Cointreau
½oz/1.5cl	fresh lemon juice
⅔oz/2cl	cranberry juice

Pour all ingredients into a shaker with ice. Shake. Strain into a cocktail glass. Garnish with a wedge of lime.

Cognac Mint Frappé

The fragrance of the cognac and the crème de menthe combines well with the aroma of the crushed mint leaves.

1oz/3cl	cognac
1oz/3cl	green crème de menthe
3 to 4	fresh mint leaves
½ teaspoon	superfine (caster) sugar

Place the mint leaves in an old-fashioned glass and add the sugar. Crush the leaves and sugar together with the back of a barspoon (or a wooden muddler) to bring out the essence of the mint. Add the spirits and stir. Fill the glass with crushed ice and stir again. Garnish with a mint leaf. Serve with a straw.

You can use any liqueur and more than one ingredient to make a frappé—a "frappé" is a drink that is served with finely crushed ice.

Convergence

Sweet, citrus, and strawberry flavors all converge into one utterly delectable cocktail!

1oz/3cl	cognac
1oz/3cl	pineau de Charente
⅓oz/1cl	crème de fraises (strawberry liqueur)
1oz/3cl	fresh orange juice

Pour all ingredients into a shaker with ice. Shake. Strain into a cocktail glass. Garnish with a strawberry set on the rim.

Corpse Reviver 1

Created by Frank Meier at the Ritz Bar, in Paris, in the 1920s. Take before 11 a.m. to revitalize the body!

1oz/3cl	brandy
1oz/3cl	sweet vermouth
1oz/3cl	calvados

Pour all ingredients into a mixing glass with ice. Stir. Strain into a cocktail glass.

Corpse Reviver 3

Created by Johnny Johnson at the Savoy's American Bar in London, in 1948.

1oz/3cl	brandy
1oz/3cl	white crème de menthe
1oz/3cl	Fernet Branca

Pour all ingredients into a mixing glass with ice. Stir. Strain into a cocktail glass.

Debut d'Eté

A robust cocktail with lots of fruit flavor to sip as you welcome the start of summer.

1⅔oz/5cl	cognac
⅔oz/2cl	maraschino liqueur
1oz/3cl	cranberry juice
1oz/3cl	fresh lime juice
⅓oz/1cl	passion fruit liqueur

Pour all ingredients into a shaker filled with ice. Shake. Strain into an old-fashioned glass filled with crushed ice. Garnish with a wedge of lime and a stem of red currants.

bosom caresser (left) and sidecar

Dirty Mother

A rich, coffee flavor with a strong finish. It is a soothing, opaque color.

1⅓oz / 4cl	brandy
1oz / 3cl	Kahlua

Pour the brandy into an old-fashioned glass with ice. Add the Kahlua. Stir.

Dream Cocktail

A 1920s classic full of promise. It's brandy, with an orange flavor and a hint of licorice. These combine well.

2oz / 6cl	brandy
1oz / 3cl	triple sec/Cointreau
dash	anisette liqueur

Pour all ingredients into a shaker with ice. Shake. Strain into a cocktail glass.

East India Cocktail

This truly is an old forgotten cocktail, first mentioned in Harry Johnson's New and Improved Bartender's Manual of 1882, popular with the Old Colonials of British East India.

2oz / 6cl	brandy
½oz / 1.5cl	raspberry syrup
dash	Angostura bitters
1 teaspoon	orange curacao
1 teaspoon	maraschino liqueur

Place all the ingredients in a shaker filled with ice. Shake and strain into a chilled cocktail glass. Garnish with a cocktail cherry.

First Night

To make sure this is not the only night, try a little of this divine drink.

1⅓oz / 4cl	brandy
½oz / 1.5cl	Van der Hum
½oz / 1.5cl	heavy (double) cream

Pour all ingredients into a shaker with ice. Shake. Strain into a cocktail glass.

Forbidden Cocktail

The brandy brings a strength to the smoothness of the vanilla-and-chocolate-flavored mixture. It's divine, and we've all done something forbidden, so sit back and sip.

1oz / 3cl	cognac
1oz / 3cl	crème de vanille (vanilla liqueur)
1oz / 3cl	white crème de cacao

Pour all ingredients into a shaker with ice. Shake. Strain into a cocktail glass and garnish with a chocolate stick.

Foreign Affair

A French and Italian affair, with the black sambuca emphasizing the dark side of the assignation!

1oz / 3cl	cognac
1oz / 3cl	black sambuca

Pour all ingredients into a brandy balloon. Swirl to mix.

French Connection

A classic after-dinner drink combining an almond flavor with the richness of brandy. One sip and you are back with actor Gene Hackman under that New York bridge.

1⅔oz / 5cl	cognac
1oz / 3cl	amaretto

Pour the brandy and amaretto into an old-fashioned glass filled with ice. Stir.

Happy World

With the combination of flavors and smooth texture, this is guaranteed to make your world seem a little happier, sip after sip after sip.

1oz / 3cl	brandy
½oz / 1.5cl	Cointreau
1oz / 3cl	fresh orange juice
½oz / 1.5cl	crème de bananes (banana liqueur)

Pour the brandy and Cointreau, then the orange juice and banana liqueur, into a shaker with ice. Shake. Strain into an old-fashioned glass. Garnish with a slice of orange and a maraschino cherry.

Hennessy Twist

Created by Fernando Castellon and voted best cognac cocktail of 2001 at Drink International, in London.

1oz / 3cl	cognac
⅔oz / 2cl	dry vermouth
⅓oz / 1cl	triple sec/Cointreau
⅓oz / 1cl	apricot brandy

Pour all ingredients into a mixing glass with ice. Stir. Strain into a cocktail glass. Garnish with a twist of orange.

Hold Up

So named because it grabs the attention of your taste buds with its coconut flavor.

1⅓oz / 4cl	cognac
⅔oz / 2cl	coconut rum
1oz / 3cl	fresh orange juice
⅓oz / 1cl	fresh lemon juice
dash	gomme syrup

Pour all ingredients into a shaker with ice. Shake. Strain into a cocktail glass.

Hoopla

All the fun of the fairground wrapped up in one sublime drink to hit the spot!

1oz/3cl	brandy
2⁄3oz/2cl	Cointreau
2⁄3oz/2cl	Lillet
2⁄3oz/2cl	fresh lemon juice

Pour all ingredients into a shaker with ice. Shake. Strain into a cocktail glass. Garnish with a spiral of lemon.

Horse's Neck

The original recipe was non-alcoholic, with lemon peel, ice, and ginger ale. In 1920, bourbon was added.

1 2⁄3oz/5cl	brandy
2 drops	Angostura bitters
	ginger ale

Pour all ingredients, except ginger ale, into a highball filled with ice. Top up with ginger ale. Stir. Garnish with a spiral of lemon.

Incognito

A classic aperitif with a nicely rounded flavor dominated by the softness of Lillet.

1oz/3cl	brandy
2oz/6cl	Lillet
1⁄3oz/1cl	apricot brandy
dash	Angostura bitters

Pour all ingredients into a mixing glass with ice. Stir. Strain into a cocktail glass.

Irish Beauty

It's a lovely drink, with smooth, earthy flavors. Makes the eyes go misty.

| 1 1⁄3oz/4cl | cognac |
| 2⁄3oz/2cl | Irish Mist |

Pour all ingredients into a brandy balloon. Swirl to mix.

Jack Rose

This is the one to have before—before anything wonderful!

1 2⁄3oz/5cl	applejack brandy
1⁄3oz/1cl	grenadine
2⁄3oz/2cl	fresh lime juice
dash	gomme syrup

Rub a wedge of lime around the rim of a cocktail glass and dip it in a saucer of superfine (caster) sugar.

Pour all ingredients into a shaker filled with ice. Shake. Strain into a cocktail glass.

Lancer Franc

A powerful cognac taste with a sweet strawberry note and a final orange flavor.

1 1⁄3oz/4cl	cognac
2⁄3oz/2cl	crème de fraises (strawberry liqueur)
	fresh orange juice

Pour the cognac and strawberry liqueur into a highball filled with ice. Top up with orange juice. Stir. Garnish with a slice of orange.

Last Drink Cocktail

Perhaps this is the one drink you would have if it was going to be your last—ever!

1oz / 3cl	cognac
½oz / 1.5cl	yellow Chartreuse
½oz / 1.5cl	cherry brandy
½oz / 1.5cl	kummel

Pour all ingredients into a shaker with ice and shake. Strain into a cocktail glass.

Limbo

This fruity concoction, with the dominance of peach, is a delicious long drink.

| 1oz / 3cl | peach brandy |
| 4oz / 12cl | pineapple juice |

Pour all ingredients into a highball filled with ice. Stir. Garnish with a wedge of pineapple and a maraschino cherry.

Lover's Delight

A mixture of cognac and Cointreau is guaranteed to bring tender emotions to the surface.

1⅓oz / 4cl	cognac
½oz / 1.5cl	Cointreau
½oz / 1.5cl	Chambord liqueur

Pour all ingredients into a shaker with ice. Shake. Strain into a cocktail glass.

Morning Glory

An intriguing cocktail of flavors that comes together to create a glorious surprise.

1⅔oz / 5cl	brandy
⅔oz / 2cl	orange curaçao
⅔oz / 2cl	fresh lemon juice
8 dashes	pastis
4 dashes	Angostura bitters

Pour all ingredients into a shaker filled with ice. Shake. Strain into a cocktail glass. Garnish with a twist of lemon.

Moulin Magic

A long and lingering flavor of pineapple is balanced by the dryness of the sparkling wine.

⅔oz / 2cl	brandy
4oz / 12cl	pineapple juice
	prosecco

Pour the brandy and pineapple juice into a shaker with ice. Shake. Strain into a highball filled with ice. Top up with prosecco. Stir. Garnish with a stem of red currants sitting on the rim.

Sidecar

Created by bartender Harry at Harry's New York Bar in Paris during the First World War and named after a motorcycle sidecar in which an army captain was chauffeur-driven to and from the bar. The name of this captain remains elusive, but one thing is for sure: The proportions of this cocktail are firmly laid down—two measures strong, one measure sweet, and one measure sour.

There are so many different recipes for this classic, but for me this is the real thing. Also, the cocktail glass must be ice cold, and a sugar-coated rim is optional.

1oz/3cl	brandy
²⁄₃oz/2cl	Cointreau
²⁄₃oz/2cl	fresh lemon juice

Pour all ingredients into a shaker with ice. Shake. Strain into a cocktail glass. Garnish with a maraschino cherry.

Playmate

All the different flavors play with the taste buds in a saucy way.

²⁄₃oz/2cl	apricot brandy
²⁄₃oz/2cl	brandy
²⁄₃oz/2cl	Grand Marnier
²⁄₃oz/2cl	fresh orange juice
1 teaspoon	egg white powder
4 dashes	Angostura bitters

Pour all ingredients into a shaker filled with ice. Shake. Strain into a cocktail glass. Garnish with a twist of orange.

Pisco Sour

Pisco is a South American brandy, distilled from Muscat grapes and matured in clay jars. It is named after the town of Pisco in Peru. It is drunk in small bars and cafés throughout Peru, Argentina, and other countries in South America. The egg white binds together all ingredients.

1²⁄₃oz/5cl	pisco
²⁄₃oz/2cl	fresh lime juice
dash	egg white powder
2 dashes	Angostura bitters
dash	gomme syrup

Pour all ingredients into a shaker with ice. Shake. Strain into a cocktail glass. Garnish with a wedge of lime.

Stinger

This smart-sounding cocktail was considered "a wholesome and well concocted" recipe by the respected American bartender Patrick Duffy, a legend during the 1920s and 1930s. The author Somerset Maugham was known to have imbibed one or two of these during his lifetime, as was Evelyn Waugh—the writer who, after drinking several of them, proclaimed it was to be his signature drink.

Usually served straight-up in pre-Prohibition days, most people request it on the rocks in an old-fashioned glass. It is perfect for late-night sessions when the allure of other cocktails has faded. At first, go easy on the crème de menthe. Remember, you can always add more if the palate demands.

1⅔oz / 5cl	brandy
⅔oz / 2cl	white crème de menthe

Pour the ingredients into a shaker filled with ice. Give it a good long shake to make the drink very cold. Strain into a chilled cocktail glass or, if you prefer on the rocks, in an old-fashioned glass with ice.

Smuggler

Given that some cognac houses were founded by descendants of smuggling dynasties, this is appropriately named!

2oz / 6cl	cognac
⅓oz / 1cl	apple juice
2oz / 6cl	white wine
slice	orange
½ slice	lemon
dash	gomme syrup

Muddle the orange and lemon slices, with the gomme syrup, in a shaker. Add the cognac and apple juice. Shake. Strain into a goblet filled with crushed ice. Top up with white wine. Serve with a straw.

Sundowner

This is a favorite cocktail in South African cocktail bars. Van der Hum, a tangerine-flavored liqueur, is famous as the national drink. Mixed with the fresh juices, it fairly hums.

1oz / 3cl	brandy
½oz / 1.5cl	Van der Hum
1oz / 3cl	fresh orange juice
½oz / 1.5cl	fresh lemon juice

Pour all ingredients into a shaker with ice. Shake. Strain into a cocktail glass. Garnish with a maraschino cherry and a slice of orange.

Sunny Dream

The best cocktail—a real smoothie with an apricot/ vanilla flavor.

⅔oz/2cl	Cointreau
1⅓oz/4cl	apricot brandy
1⅔oz/5cl	fresh orange juice
2 scoops	vanilla ice cream

Put the ice cream in the blender and add the remaining ingredients, along with half a scoop of crushed ice. Blend. Pour into a goblet. Garnish with a maraschino cherry and a sprig of mint. Serve with a straw.

Sweet Summer Breeze

Here is a refreshing, long drink with a bubbly finish and peach and orange flavors.

1oz/3cl	brandy
½oz/1.5cl	Cointreau
½oz/1.5cl	peach brandy
2oz/6cl	fresh orange juice
dash	grenadine
dash	champagne

Pour all ingredients, except champagne, into a shaker with ice. Shake. Strain into a highball filled with ice. Top up with champagne. Stir. Garnish with a wedge of peach and a stem of red currants.

The Coffee Cocktail

This drink is an old classic that was first introduced to the world by "Professor" Jerry Thomas in his bartender's guide published in 1887. The drink however has nothing to do with coffee; the only resemblance is the color!

1oz/3cl	brandy
1	egg
2oz/6cl	ruby port
1 teaspoon	sugar

Pour all the ingredients into a shaker filled with ice. Shake long and hard to allow the egg to combine with the other ingredients. Strain into a large liqueur glass or small wine glass. Garnish with grated nutmeg.

Three Miller

The Savoy Cocktail Book spells this as Miller, whereas others spell it as "Miler." Whatever, it is a great classic.

2oz / 6cl	brandy
1oz / 3cl	rum
dash	fresh lemon juice
2 dashes	grenadine

Pour all ingredients into a shaker with ice. Shake. Strain into a cocktail glass.

Valencia

A classic recipe dating from the late 1920s. Now, gin is used, but it is incorrect to add it if you want to make the original recipe.

2oz / 6cl	apricot brandy
1oz / 3cl	fresh orange juice
4 dashes	orange bitters

Pour all ingredients into a shaker with ice. Shake. Strain into a cocktail glass.

Wardman Park

The final cocktail tastes dry, with a great combination of rounded flavors. A taste of honey from the Drambuie makes this good to sip.

1oz / 3cl	brandy
⅔oz / 2cl	Drambuie
1⅓oz / 4cl	dry sherry

Pour all ingredients into a shaker with ice. Shake. Strain into a cocktail glass. Garnish with a twist of lemon.

GIN

Most of the well-known classic cocktails are made with gin as the base spirit. These include Martini, Gibson, Gimlet, Gin Fizz, Pink Gin, Singapore Sling, and White Lady.

Gin has been in existence for centuries. It is aromatic, yet has a delicate flavor ideal for mixing cocktails. For a refreshing drink, there's nothing better than a classic G & T (a gin and tonic).

Gin's secret is inexorably linked to the juniper berry and a 14th-century Flemish herbal drink made from its juice. Spirits made from cereals were combined with a restorative herb, juniper, and genever (a gin) was created. Old Tom was the favorite, a sweet, cordial-like spirit, but this style lost its sweetness over decades to become London Dry in style.

When you pour a measure of gin, you smell the "nose" immediately. Gin has character, it is herbal in its makeup (that's the genever ingredient), and each brand is carefully blended to give it an individual taste. The most common herbs and spices are juniper and coriander.

Some of the more recent brands released on the market list the botanicals on the label so you know exactly what you are buying. Bombay Sapphire, for instance, lists 10 botanicals, and juniper is the lesser fragrance in the heady mix: its aroma is musky, with hints of fresh citrus and licorice.

martini, page 62

The Dry Martini is a truly American gin cocktail. Without gin, the three-martini lunch would never have taken the place of nutritional food.

Legendary humorist H. L. Mencken described it as "the only American invention as perfect as the sonnet."

MAKING GIN

The best gin is recognized as that made from a grain, preferably corn, spirit and contains very few impurities. Any gin made with a molasses spirit will taste slightly sweeter.

Most gin is made in a continuous still to produce the 96 percent alcohol by volume ratio required. Once this is achieved, the spirit is redistilled. The second distillation involves the spirit being distilled along with natural botanicals to produce a subtle premium gin.

The most common botanicals include angelica, juniper berries, lemon peel, orange peel, licorice, orrisroot, cassia bark, calamus root, and the spices cardamon and cinnamon. Which botanicals are in which gin, and in what proportion, is a secret and is responsible for each brand's distinctive flavor.

For example, extra-dry gins usually contain more angelica or licorice whereas gins with a dominant citrus flavor contain more orange or lemon peel. The gin is then reduced to bottling strength, 75 proof in America and 35 percent alcohol by volume (abv) in Europe.

There are four types of gin as listed below:

• Dry gin (unsweetened)

• London Dry gin (unsweetened)

• Old Tom gin (slightly sweetened)

• Plymouth gin (slightly sweetened)

If you prefer a particular taste of one gin brand, always make the cocktail with the same brand, and it will taste the same each time. Singer Frank Sinatra and President John F. Kennedy both had their favorite brands. When you're ordering a cocktail in a bar, ask for your gin by brand name, too.

> *Always chill a cocktail glass in the freezer before use.*

Abbey

This cocktail is a delicious color and has a slightly bitter orange flavor.

1⅓oz/4cl	gin
1oz/3cl	fresh orange juice
⅔oz/2cl	maraschino liqueur
⅓oz/1cl	dry vermouth
4 drops	Angostura bitters

Pour all ingredients into a shaker with ice. Shake. Strain into a cocktail glass. Garnish with a maraschino cherry.

Alabama Fizz

A classic-style cocktail with the lip-smacking finish of fresh lemon juice.

2oz/6cl	gin
1oz/3cl	fresh lemon juice
dash	gomme syrup
	club soda

Pour all ingredients, except soda, into a shaker with ice. Shake. Strain into a highball with ice. Top up with soda. Garnish with a wedge of lemon in the drink.

Alaska

Writing in The Savoy Cocktail Book, *Harry Craddock commented: "So far as can be ascertained, this delectable potion is NOT the staple diet of the Esquimaux [sic]. It was probably first thought of in South Carolina—hence its name."*

1¾oz/5cl	gin
⅔oz/2cl	yellow Chartreuse
2 dashes	orange bitters

Stir the gin, Chartreuse, and bitters in a mixing glass until completely mixed. Strain into a cocktail glass. (Some recipes recommend shaking this drink, but this gives a cloudy effect to the drink.)

Alexander No. 1

A classic 1920s after-dinner drink that will spice up the hours after dinner.

1oz/3cl	gin
1oz/3cl	white crème de cacao
1oz/3cl	heavy (double) cream

Pour all ingredients into a shaker with ice. Shake. Strain into a cocktail glass. Sprinkle a fine layer of nutmeg on top of the drink—just enough to get the aroma of the nutmeg. It shouldn't overpower the flavor of the drink.

Alexander's Sister

This drink was considered risqué in the late 1920s and could possibly lead a young woman astray.

1oz / 3cl	gin
1oz / 3cl	green crème de menthe
1oz / 3cl	heavy (double) cream

Pour all ingredients into a shaker with ice. Shake. Strain into a cocktail glass. Garnish with a sprig of mint on the side of the glass.

Angel Face

In the 1950s you could find two or three recipes with this name that used different ingredients and were made in different ways. One used crème de cacao and cream, the other was similar to a pousse-café (layered) formula, made with crème de cacao and prunelle (sloe brandy). This recipe is the classic.

1oz / 3cl	gin
1oz / 3cl	apricot brandy
1oz / 3cl	calvados

Pour all ingredients into a shaker with ice. Shake. Strain into a cocktail glass.

Bella Taormina

This winning formula has a spicy flavor from the juniper and a hint of lemon.

1oz / 3cl	gin
⅔oz / 2cl	Aperol
½oz / 1.5cl	limoncello
½oz / 1.5cl	Mandarine liqueur
⅔oz / 2cl	fresh orange juice

Pour all ingredients into a shaker with ice. Shake. Strain into a cocktail glass. Garnish with a kumquat cut like a flower and a spiral of lime set on the rim.

Belmont Cocktail

In the 1920s the combination of gin and grenadine was seen as daring, like a flash of red lipstick.

1⅓oz / 4cl	gin
½oz / 1.5cl	grenadine
1oz / 3cl	heavy (double) cream

Pour all ingredients into a shaker with ice. Shake. Strain into a cocktail glass.

Blackfriars Punch

A truly delicate and refreshing combination, sweet and intense.

1oz/3cl	gin
1oz/3cl	Plymouth sloe gin
½oz/1.5cl	fresh lemon juice
1½oz/4.5cl	guava juice
1½oz/4.5cl	cranberry juice

Pour all ingredients into a shaker filled with ice. Shake, and strain into a highball glass filled with ice. Garnish with a slice of lemon folded over a raspberry and a blueberry on a cocktail stick.

Blue Bird

Not a hint of blue about this cocktail! However, it makes your heart sing like a bird.

1⅔oz/5cl	gin
1oz/3cl	triple sec/Cointreau
4 drops	Angostura bitters

Pour all ingredients into a shaker with ice. Shake. Strain into a cocktail glass. Garnish with a twist of lemon.

Blue Monday

This cocktail is a delicate shade of blue and has an orange flavor made effervescent with soda.

1oz/3cl	gin
1oz/3cl	Cointreau
dash	blue curaçao
	club soda

Pour the gin and Cointreau into a highball filled with ice. Top up with soda. Stir. Place a stirrer in the glass and, holding the bottle in the other hand, add a few drops of blue curaçao and stir quickly. The drink will become a delicate hue of blue. Serve with the stirrer.

Blue Wave

The best drink for a summer vacation taken by the ocean. The cocktail is a pale blue taste sensation.

1oz/3cl	gin
1oz/3cl	light rum
⅔oz/2cl	blue curaçao
3oz/9cl	pineapple juice
1oz/3cl	fresh lime juice
2 dashes	gomme syrup

Pour all ingredients into a shaker with ice. Shake. Strain into a colada glass filled with crushed ice. Garnish with a wedge of pineapple.

Boston

Here's an updated use for apricot brandy. (Remember the sweet '70s cocktails?) Combine it with fresh lemon juice for a surprise flavor.

1⅔oz/5cl	gin
1oz/3cl	apricot brandy
⅔oz/2cl	fresh lemon juice
2 dashes	grenadine

Pour all ingredients into a shaker with ice. Shake. Strain into a cocktail glass.

Bramble

A modern classic, this has all the luscious flavor of blackberry and lime juice balanced by the sugar and blackberry liqueur.

1½oz/4.5cl	gin
1oz/3cl	fresh lime juice
⅓oz/1.5cl	gomme syrup
⅓oz/1.5cl	crème de mure (blackberry liqueur)
	club soda

Pour all ingredients, except the blackberry liqueur, into a shaker filled with ice. Shake. Strain into a highball glass filled with crushed ice. Pour the blackberry liqueur over the top. Garnish with a blackberry and a sprig of mint. Serve with a straw.

Bronx

A predinner drink inspired by a visit to the Bronx Zoo in 1906 by Johnny Solon, renowned bartender at the Waldorf Astoria, New York.

1oz/3cl	gin
½oz/1.5cl	dry vermouth
½oz/1.5cl	sweet vermouth
1oz/3cl	fresh orange juice

Pour all ingredients into a shaker with ice. Shake. Strain into a cocktail glass. Garnish with a twist of orange.

Bronx Terrace

A new version of the classic cocktail, Bronx, with the tart flavor of lime.

1⅔oz/5cl	gin
1oz/3cl	dry vermouth
⅔oz/2cl	Rose's lime cordial

Pour all ingredients into a shaker with ice. Shake. Strain into a cocktail glass. Garnish with a spiral of lime.

Californie Palace

Here's a delicously dry cocktail with a hint of cherry from the maraschino liqueur.

1⅓oz/4cl	gin
⅔oz/2cl	dry vermouth
⅔oz/2cl	green Chartreuse
⅓oz/1cl	maraschino liqueur

Pour all ingredients into a mixing glass with ice. Stir. Strain into a cocktail glass. Garnish with a spiral of lime.

Caribbean Sunset

The best drink to take as you walk along the beach with the girl of your dreams, watching the sun go slowly down on the horizon . . .

1oz / 3cl	gin
1oz / 3cl	crème de bananes (banana liqueur)
1oz / 3cl	blue curaçao
1oz / 3cl	fresh lemon juice
1oz / 3cl	heavy (double) cream
dash	grenadine

Pour all ingredients, except grenadine, into a shaker with ice. Shake. Strain into a highball filled with ice. Add the grenadine, which will float to the bottom, creating a sunset effect. Garnish with a maraschino cherry and a slice of orange on a cocktail stick.

Caruso

This was created for the Italian tenor, Caruso, by the bartender at the Hotel Sevilla, Cuba, in the 1920s.

1oz / 3cl	gin
1oz / 3cl	dry vermouth
½oz / 1.5cl	green crème de menthe

Pour the ingredients into a mixing glass filled with ice. Stir with a barspoon. Strain into a cocktail glass. Drop a maraschino cherry into the drink.

Charlie N. Special

This cocktail is full of subtle flavors. Watch out for the spirited kick!

2oz / 6cl	gin
2oz / 6cl	cranberry juice
2oz / 6cl	guava juice
½oz / 1.5cl	fresh lemon juice
1oz / 3cl	coconut cream

Pour all ingredients into a shaker with ice. Shake. Strain into a highball filled with ice. Garnish with a stem of red currants and a slice of star fruit.

Clover Club

This was created around 1925 and takes its name from the famous American nightspot.

2oz / 6cl	gin
½oz / 1.5cl	grenadine
½oz / 1.5cl	fresh lemon juice
1 teaspoon	egg white powder

Pour the ingredients into a shaker with ice. Shake. Strain into a cocktail glass.

CLASSIC COCKTAIL

Collins

Usually a summer drink, a Collins is made with lots of ice in a highball.

The original Collins cocktail was a John Collins, and its origin can be traced back to John Collins, the headwaiter at a hotel and coffeehouse named Limmer's, in London, around 1790 to 1817. His original version used genever, a Dutch-style gin, club soda, lemon, and sugar. It wasn't until the 1880s that the drink found popularity in the United States—it was viewed as an upscale gin sling. When an enterprising bartender used Old Tom Gin, a London gin with a sweet flavor, the Collins became known as a Tom Collins.

Currently, bartenders serve a Collins made with London dry gin, and in America, if you are served a Collins made with bourbon or whiskey, it is a John Collins.

1⅔oz / 5cl	gin
⅔oz / 2cl	fresh lemon juice
2 dashes	gomme syrup
	club soda

Add the lemon juice, gomme syrup, and gin to a highball filled with ice. Top up with soda. Stir. Drop a slice of lemon in the drink. Serve with a stirrer.

Demon Martini

Let the devil take care of your palette—and I will be the angel to save you!

1⅔oz / 5cl	gin
½oz / 1.5cl	Lillet Blanc (French vermouth)
1 quarter	pomegranate pulp
2 barspoons	caster sugar
2 thin slices	sweet chili

Crust half of the rim of a chilled cocktail glass with sugar. Muddle the pomegranate in the bottom of the shaker. Add ice and remaining ingredients. Shake. Strain into the glass. Garnish with a thin slice of chilli on the rim of the glass.

Devil's Advocate

You'll become charming and convincing after two of these, to be sure.

2oz / 6cl	gin
1oz / 3cl	crème de framboise (raspberry liqueur)
2 dashes	dry vermouth

Pour the gin and vermouth into a mixing glass with ice. Strain into a cocktail glass. Add the liqueur—it sinks to the bottom.

Dirty Martini

So called because of its smudgy look, this Martini has an oily, bitter flavor.

2²⁄₃oz/8cl	gin
²⁄₃oz/2cl	brine from cocktail olives
⅓oz/1cl	extra dry vermouth

Pour all ingredients into a mixing glass with ice. Stir. Strain into a cocktail glass. Garnish with an olive on a cocktail stick.

E.Sencha.L

The subtle flavors of the Sencha Tea blended with the aromatics of the gin make a simple but full-flavored drink.

1½oz/4.5cl	frozen gin
1½oz/4.5cl	strong Sencha Tea (chilled)

Stir the gin and tea in a mixing glass. Do not stir with ice as this will dilute the drink. Serve in a chilled cocktail glass or a small tea cup. Garnish with a grapefruit twist.

Elise

This is a fine combination of almond and citrus flavors with the bite of juniper.

1⅓oz/4cl	gin
½oz/1.5cl	limoncello
½oz/1.5cl	peach schnapps
2⅓oz/7cl	fresh grapefruit juice
2⅓oz/7cl	mango juice
⅓oz/1cl	Orgeat (almond) syrup

Pour all ingredients into a shaker with ice. Shake. Strain into a highball filled with ice. Garnish with a small Cape Gooseberry. Serve with a straw.

Eddie Brown

Named after the boxer Eddie Brown, this cocktail has been around for 90 years, and I am sure it will be around for a lot longer. Some recipes call for this to be shaken, but I prefer to stir, as it gives a cleaner finish.

1½oz/4.5cl	gin
½oz/1.5cl	Lillet Blanc
½oz/1.5cl	apricot brandy

Stir into a mixing glass filled with ice. Strain into a chilled cocktail glass. Garnish with a twist of orange.

Everest

This drink was created by my good friend Gary Regan; it has a lot of personality, just like him!

2oz/6cl	gin
1oz/3cl	Coco Lopez
½ oz/1.5cl	fresh squeezed lemon juice
1 teaspoon	curry paste

Mix the curry paste with a few dashes of Coco Lopez to make a paste. Shake all ingredients vigorously with ice. Strain into a chilled cocktail glass.

Fino Martini

Like the classic Martini, only with a more rounded, full flavor of a fine dry sherry.

| 3oz/9cl | gin |
| 2 dashes | fino sherry |

Pour all ingredients into a mixing glass with ice. Stir. Strain into a cocktail glass. Garnish with a twist of lemon.

Gibson

Created for American artist Charles Dana Gibson at the Players Club, Manhattan, in the 1940s. Because olives were unavailable, the bartender used a white pearl onion.

| 3oz/9cl | gin |
| dash | dry vermouth |

Pour the gin into a mixing glass with ice. Add the dry vermouth and stir. Strain into a cocktail glass. Garnish with a white pearl onion in the drink.

singapore sling

Gimlet

Originally made with Plymouth gin, the recipe was printed in the 1930s. Rose's lime cordial is always used.

| 1⅔oz/5cl | Plymouth gin |
| ⅔oz/2cl | Rose's lime cordial |

Pour ingredients into an old-fashioned glass filled with ice. Stir. Garnish with a wedge of lime in the drink.

Gin and It

A perennially popular ladies' drink partaken at around 5 p.m. each day.

| 1⅓oz/4cl | gin |
| 1⅓oz/4cl | sweet vermouth |

Pour the gin and vermouth into an old-fashioned glass filled with ice. Stir. Garnish with a maraschino cherry and a twist of orange.

Gin and Tonic

This is the favorite gin mixed drink in the world. People always ask me how to make the perfect gin and tonic. Read below!

| 2oz/6cl | gin |
| 4oz/12cl | tonic water |

The correct proportion is one measure of gin and two of tonic. Use fresh tonic water from a small bottle or can. Do not drown the gin.

Pour the gin into a highball filled with ice. Add the tonic water. Stir. Garnish with a slice of lemon in the drink.

Gin Fizz

A long drink first mentioned in magazine articles published in the 1870s, the fizz is a close cousin of the Collins—only it is always shaken, not built. Many bartenders add egg white to give the drink more froth. This makes a Silver Fizz; add egg yolk to make a Golden Fizz.

1⅔oz/5cl	gin
1oz/3cl	fresh lemon juice
dash	gomme syrup
	club soda

Pour all ingredients, except soda, into a shaker with ice. Shake. Strain into a highball filled with ice. Top up with soda. Garnish with a slice of lemon. Serve with a stirrer.

Gina

A black-currant-flavored cocktail designed as a thirst quencher.

1⅔oz/5cl	gin
1oz/3cl	crème de cassis (black currant liqueur)
⅔oz/2cl	fresh lemon juice
	sparkling water

Pour all ingredients, except the sparkling water, into a shaker with ice. Shake. Strain into a highball filled with ice. Top up with sparkling water. Garnish with a slice of lemon.

Gin Rickey

The myth surrounding the original Gin Rickey concerns an American lobbyist, Joe Rickey, who, in 1893, liked to drink at Shoemaker's Restaurant, Washington, D. C. The bartender squeezed the juice of a few limes into gin and squirted a soda syphon over the concoction.

1⅔oz/5cl	gin
1oz/3cl	fresh lime juice
	club soda

Pour the gin and lime juice into a highball filled with ice. Top up with soda and stir. Garnish with a wedge of lime.

Golden Dawn

A predinner drink dating from 1930. Nine years later, Walter A. Madigan made a Golden Dawn without the calvados, and was runner-up at the International Cocktail Championship held in London. This version contains calvados.

⅔oz/2cl	gin
⅔oz/2cl	apricot brandy
⅔oz/2cl	calvados
⅔oz/2cl	fresh orange juice
dash	grenadine

Pour all ingredients, except grenadine, into a shaker with ice. Shake. Strain into a cocktail glass and add the grenadine to create a sunrise effect.

Jaded Lady

Advocaat, made from egg yolks and grape brandy, is a Dutch liqueur, just 30 proof.

1oz/3cl	gin
1oz/3cl	blue curaçao
1oz/3cl	advocaat
1⅓oz/4cl	fresh orange juice

Pour all ingredients into a shaker with ice. Shake. Strain into a cocktail glass.

Journalist

This is one of the recipes where you must follow the measurements exactly.

1⅔oz/5cl	gin
⅓oz/1cl	sweet vermouth
⅓oz/1cl	dry vermouth
dash	triple sec/Cointreau
dash	fresh lemon juice
2 drops	Angostura bitters

Pour all ingredients into a shaker with ice. Shake. Strain into a cocktail glass. Garnish with a twist of orange.

Kee-wee

One for those with a yearning for New Zealand, the land of milk and honey.

1⅔oz/5cl	gin
⅔oz/2cl	triple sec/Cointreau
1oz/3cl	kiwifruit purée
dash	gomme syrup

Pour all ingredients into a shaker with ice. Shake. Strain into an old-fashioned glass filled with crushed ice.

KGB

Be careful to whom you speak after one of these! Careless whispers are trouble!

1²⁄₃oz / 5cl	gin
½oz / 1.5cl	kummel
½oz / 1.5cl	apricot brandy
⅓oz / 1cl	fresh lemon juice

Pour all ingredients into a shaker with ice. Shake. Strain into a cocktail glass. Garnish with a twist of lemon.

Kiss in the Dark

Perhaps this makes you feel adventurous in the romance stakes. Try one and see!

1⅓oz / 4cl	gin
1oz / 3cl	cherry brandy
1oz / 3cl	dry vermouth

Pour all ingredients into a mixing glass with ice. Stir. Strain into a cocktail glass. Garnish with a maraschino cherry.

Kitten's Whiskers

The purr-fect harmony of sweet, dry, bitter, and spice in this great-tasting cocktail!

1oz / 3cl	gin
½oz / 1.5cl	dry vermouth
½oz / 1.5cl	sweet vermouth
½oz / 1.5cl	fresh orange juice
½oz / 1.5cl	Grand Marnier
dash	Angostura biters

Pour all ingredients into a shaker with ice. Shake. Strain into a cocktail glass. Garnish with a spiral of orange.

Knickerbocker

A heady mixture for gin drinkers with a passion for both sweet and dry vermouth.

1²⁄₃oz / 5cl	gin
⅔oz / 2cl	sweet vermouth
⅔oz / 2cl	dry vermouth

Pour all ingredients into a mixing glass filled with ice. Stir. Strain into a cocktail glass. Garnish with a twist of lemon.

Knockout

More than one of these and you will feel as if you have done a round or two with a boxer—with gloves off!

1oz/3cl	gin
1oz/3cl	dry vermouth
⅔oz/2cl	Pernod
⅓oz/1cl	white crème de menthe

Pour all ingredients into a shaker with ice. Shake. Strain into a cocktail glass. Drop a maraschino cherry into the drink.

Lady Diana

A classic cocktail with the sharpness of lime and the spicy flavor of juniper.

1oz/3cl	gin
1oz/3cl	Campari
⅔oz/2cl	fresh lime juice
dash	gomme syrup

Pour all ingredients into a shaker with ice. Shake. Strain into a cocktail glass. Garnish with a twist of orange.

La Habana

An intriguing combination of flavors to get you doing the salsa around the bar. Or dreaming of the Caribbean.

1oz/3cl	gin
1oz/3cl	apricot brandy
1oz/3cl	fresh lime juice

Pour all ingredients into a shaker with ice. Shake. Strain into a cocktail glass. Garnish with a wedge of lime.

Leave-It-To-Me

A confident cocktail from a bartender who was absolutely in charge of your taste buds.

1⅔oz/5cl	gin
⅔oz/2cl	dry vermouth
⅔oz/2cl	apricot brandy
dash	grenadine
⅓oz/1cl	fresh lemon juice

Pour all ingredients into a shaker with ice. Shake. Strain into a cocktail glass.

Maiden's Blush

This is the color of a warm blush and more than two will definitely bring a blush to a maiden's face!

2oz/6cl	gin
1½oz/1.5cl	triple sec/Cointreau
1½oz/1.5cl	fresh lemon juice
dash	grenadine

Place all ingredients into a shaker with ice. Shake. Strain into a cocktail glass.

Maiden's Prayer

Harry Craddock, in The Savoy Cocktail Book: *"If at first you don't succeed, cry, cry again."*

1oz/3cl	gin
1oz/3cl	Cointreau
½oz/1.5cl	fresh orange juice
½oz/1.5cl	fresh lemon juice

Place all ingredients into a shaker with ice. Shake. Strain into a cocktail glass. Garnish with a twist of orange.

The Martini

Today's Martini bears little resemblance to the original cocktail. Always an aspirational drink, imbibed by presidents and movie stars, the Martini has had a makeover. It's now mostly made with vodka.

The small town of Martinez, California, proclaimed that bartender Julio Richelieu mixed the first Martinez—a small drink with an olive dropped in it—which became the Martini. Richelieu left for San Francisco, making the Martinez his specialty. This was prior to 1887. In fact, "Professor" Jerry Thomas had included a Gin Cocktail that resembled the Martini in *The Bon Vivant's Guide*, published in 1862. By 1887, the gin cocktail had become the Martinez, and Thomas was claiming credit.

The myth continues: a traveler walked into the San Francisco Occidental Hotel bar and Thomas mixed him the first Martinez. But the people of Martinez claim the traveler was on his way to San Francisco from Julio's bar. Richelieu mixed the cocktail for him so he could get change from a gold nugget—to buy a bottle of whiskey. In 1929, the town erected a brass plaque stating that Martinez was the birthplace of the Martini.

My Martini

This is the classic Martini. There are just two ingredients: gin and dry vermouth. The only addition is an olive or a twist of lemon, depending upon your preference.

I keep the gin in the freezer, and a day or an hour before I know I have guests coming over, I put the glasses in the freezer to chill. A great Martini is one that stays very cold for as long as you drink it.

3oz/9cl	gin
1 to 2 drops	extra dry vermouth

Take the chilled cocktail glass from the freezer, handling it by the stem only. Pour the chilled gin directly into the glass. Fill a clean Angostura bitters bottle with dry vermouth so that you can shake a few drops of vermouth through its pourer into the gin. I do not mix the cocktail. I float two to three drops of vermouth over the top of the drink.

Cut a thin twist of lemon, then face the twist upside down over the glass and twist it to drop a few tears of juice in the drink. Rub the twist around the rim for the final touch to the perfect Martini. An olive is optional.

Mainbrace

This is a cocktail full of flavor, with the tart grapefruit juice balancing the triple sec.

1 oz / 3 cl	gin
1 oz / 3 cl	triple sec/Cointreau
1 oz / 3 cl	fresh grapefruit juice

Pour all ingredients into a shaker with ice. Shake. Strain into a cocktail glass. Garnish with a twist of lime.

Martinez

A classic first mentioned in O. H. Byron's 1884 book The Modern Bartender's Guide *now making a come back in the modern bar scene with the resurgence of the great classics. As a result of popular demand, many of the original spirits are being reproduced, like the Old Tom gin.*

1½ oz / 4.5 cl	Old Tom gin
1½ oz / 4.5 cl	Martini Rosso
½ oz / 1.5 c	Maraschino liqueur
2 dash	orange bitters
1 slice	fresh lemon

Place all ingredients, including the slice of lemon, into a shaker filled with ice. Shake sharply to extract the flavor from the lemon. Strain into a chilled small wine glass. Garnish with a small slice of lemon.

Million-Dollar Cocktail

Like the Singapore Sling, this cocktail was created at the beginning of the 20th century by Ngiam Tong Boon, at Raffles Hotel, in Singapore.

1 oz / 3 cl	gin
dash	sweet vermouth
dash	dry vermouth
4 oz / 12 cl	pineapple juice
1 teaspoon	egg white powder
dash	Angostura bitters

Pour the gin and both vermouths into a shaker filled with ice. Add the pineapple juice, egg white powder, and bitters. Shake sharply to create a froth. Strain into a highball filled with ice.

Nightmare

This drink is a pleasant red color and not at all nightmarish in flavor.

1 oz / 3 cl	gin
⅔ oz / 2 cl	Dubonnet
⅔ oz / 2 cl	cherry brandy
1 oz / 3 cl	fresh orange juice

Pour all ingredients into a shaker with ice. Shake. Strain into a cocktail glass. Garnish with a maraschino cherry.

Opal

If you like Cointreau, this is the cocktail for you since the orange flavor is enhanced by fresh orange juice.

1⅔oz/5cl	gin
⅔oz/2cl	Cointreau
1oz/3cl	fresh orange juice

Pour all ingredients into a shaker with ice. Shake. Strain into a cocktail glass. Garnish with a twist of orange.

Opera

Drink while relaxing at home as your favorite opera track plays on the sound system.

2oz/6cl	gin
½oz/1.5cl	Dubonnet
½oz/1.5cl	maraschino liqueur

Pour all ingredients into a shaker with ice. Shake. Strain into a cocktail glass. Garnish with a twist of orange.

Orange Blossom Special

When the orange trees come into flower, that's the time for this cocktail.

1⅔oz/5cl	gin
⅔oz/2cl	Cointreau
⅔oz/2cl	lychee liqueur
⅓oz/1cl	fresh lemon juice

Pour all ingredients into a shaker with ice. Shake. Strain into a cocktail glass. Garnish with a fresh lychee.

Oriental Passion

The delicacy of passion fruit flavor dominates this refreshing cocktail.

1⅔oz/5cl	gin
⅔oz/2cl	limoncello
1oz/3cl	passion fruit purée
dash	passion fruit syrup

Pour all ingredients into a shaker with ice. Shake. Strain into a cocktail glass. Garnish with a twist of orange.

Palm Beach Cocktail

This has all the glamor of an early evening Florida cocktail. Suitable for those who enjoy a hint of bittersweet flavor.

2oz/6cl	gin
½oz/1.5cl	sweet vermouth
½oz/1.5cl	fresh grapefruit juice

Pour all ingredients into a shaker with ice. Shake. Strain into a cocktail glass. Garnish with a maraschino cherry.

Paradise

Guaranteed to take you into the Garden of Eden with its delectable apricot and orange essences.

2oz/6cl	gin
½oz/1.5cl	apricot brandy
½oz/1.5cl	fresh orange juice

Pour all ingredients into a shaker with ice. Shake. Strain into a cocktail glass. Garnish with a twist of orange.

Perfect Lady

An elegant gin drink for an elegant lady with a taste for a hint of peach and citrus.

2oz / 6cl	gin
½oz / 1.5cl	peach schnapps
½oz / 1.5cl	fresh lemon juice
1 teaspoon	egg white powder

Pour all ingredients into a shaker with ice. Shake. Strain into a cocktail glass.

Peyton's Place

Here's a double hit of gin combined with citrus for those who like it tart.

1oz / 3cl	Plymouth gin
1oz / 3cl	sloe gin
2oz / 6cl	fresh grapefruit juice
	club soda

Pour all ingredients, except soda, into a shaker with ice. Shake. Strain into a highball filled with ice. Top up with soda. Garnish with a wedge of lime.

Pink Forest

This combination obviously did strange things to its creator on the way home.

1oz / 3cl	gin
1oz / 3cl	crème de fraises (strawberry liqueur)
⅔oz / 2cl	Cointreau
⅔oz / 2cl	heavy (double) cream

Pour all ingredients into a shaker with ice. Shake. Strain into a cocktail glass.

Pink Gin

Angostura bitters was perfected as a remedy for stomach complaints by Dr. Johann Siegert, a surgeon for the Prussian army at the Battle of Waterloo, for a military hospital at Angostura, on the Orinoco River, in Venezuela. He named it after the town.

Word of this herbal, plant-based remedy reached officers in the British Navy, who added it to the officers' medicine kit and their Plymouth gin rations. Hence, the spread in the upper echelons of the drink, "Pink Gin."

Some prefer their Pink Gin cocktail with a splash of iced water; others like it straight. Whichever way, this is a good aperitif, sending the drinker off in search of food in quick time. Always serve it ice cold.

1⅔oz / 5cl	gin
2 dashes	Angostura bitters

Pour the gin and bitters into a mixing glass with ice. Stir with a barspoon. Strain into a cocktail glass.

Pink Lady

An aperitif made with Plymouth gin named after a successful 1912 stage play.

1⅔oz / 5cl	Plymouth gin
⅔oz / 2cl	fresh lemon juice
1 to 2 dashes	grenadine
1 teaspoon	egg white powder

Pour all the ingredients into a shaker with ice. Shake. Strain into a cocktail glass. Garnish with a maraschino cherry dropped in the drink.

Ramos Fizz

In 1888, Henrico C. Ramos bought the Imperial Cabinet Saloon, New Orleans, where he created this cocktail. The recipe was a secret until the saloon closed at the start of Prohibition. Henrico's brother, Charles Henry Ramos, gave the recipe to the world.

1⅔oz / 5cl	gin
⅓oz / 1cl	fresh lime juice
⅓oz / 1cl	fresh lemon juice
3 dashes	orange-flower water
1 teaspoon	egg white powder
1⅔oz / 5cl	heavy (double) cream
1 teaspoon	superfine (caster) sugar
	club soda

Pour all ingredients, except soda, into a shaker with ice. Shake. Strain into an old-fashioned glass filled with ice. Top up with soda. Garnish with a wedge of lime.

Raspberry Collins

Here's a cocktail to quench your thirst on a hot day; full of rich raspberry flavor.

2oz / 6cl	gin
⅔oz / 2cl	crème de framboise (raspberry liqueur)
1⅔oz / 5cl	fresh lemon juice
⅓oz / 1cl	gomme syrup
3oz / 9cl	raspberry purée
	club soda

Pour all ingredients, except soda, into a shaker with ice. Shake. Strain into a highball filled with ice. Top up with soda. Garnish with two raspberries and half a slice of lemon on a cocktail stick.

Red Snapper

A pick-me-up drink, this is the original version of the Bloody Mary—made with gin, not vodka. Note it features the ubiquitous celery stalk.

2oz / 6cl	gin
4oz / 12cl	tomato juice
½oz / 1.5cl	fresh lemon juice
2 to 3 dashes	Worcestershire sauce
2 to 3 dashes	Tabasco sauce
pinch	celery salt
pinch	black pepper

Pour the gin, tomato juice, and lemon juice into a shaker with ice. Shake. Strain into a highball filled with ice. Add celery salt, pepper, and sauces. Stir. Garnish with a celery stalk and a wedge of lemon.

Ruby

Named for its superb ruby red color, this drink has a hint of plum flavor from the sloe gin.

1oz / 3cl	sloe gin
1oz / 3cl	sweet vermouth
1/3oz / 1cl	crème de framboise (raspberry liqueur)

Pour all ingredients into a mixing glass with ice. Stir. Strain into a cocktail glass. Garnish with two small raspberries on a cocktail stick set across the glass.

Salty Martini

A fascinating flavor, for the most demanding palates.

2oz / 6cl	frozen gin
1/2oz / 1.5cl	Tio Pepe sherry
1 teaspoon	caperberries brine

Stir into a mixing glass filled with ice. Strain into a chilled cocktail glass. Garnish with a single large caperberry, stalk on, dropped in the drink.

Showgirl

This is the ideal sweet cocktail for a feminine performer.

1 1/3oz / 4cl	gin
2/3oz / 2cl	lychee liqueur
2/3oz / 2cl	pineapple liqueur
2/3oz / 2cl	fresh peach purée

Pour all ingredients into a shaker with ice. Shake. Strain into a cocktail glass. Garnish with a wedge of peach.

Silver Bullet

A drink dating back before 1930. It has fennel and juniper flavors from the gin.

1 1/3oz / 4cl	gin
2/3oz / 2cl	kummel
1/3oz / 1cl	fresh lemon juice

Pour the ingredients into a shaker with ice. Shake. Strain into a cocktail glass.

Singapore Sling

By definition, a sling can be traced back to 1759, and its name is possibly derived from the German word *schlingen*, meaning to swallow quickly. Its origin is uncertain and there might be a connection to the Collins.

This original recipe, revered by British expatriots living in the Far East, is simple to make and refreshing. I back the legend that the Singapore Gin Sling was created at the Raffles Hotel, in Singapore, in 1915 by bartender Ngiam Tong Boon.

This long and exotic cocktail immediately appealed to women guests.

By 1930, when the name Singapore Sling arrived in Europe and the United States, it had lost its fruit juices and was distilled down to gin, cherry brandy, fresh lemon juice, and soda.

Raffles Singapore Sling

⅔ oz / 2cl	gin
⅔ oz / 2cl	cherry brandy
⅓ oz / 1cl	Cointreau
⅓ oz / 1cl	Bénédictine
⅓ oz / 1cl	fresh lime juice
2⅓ oz / 7cl	fresh orange juice
2⅓ oz / 7cl	pineapple juice

Pour all ingredients into a shaker with ice. Shake. Strain into a highball filled with ice. Garnish with a slice of pineapple and a maraschino cherry. Serve with a straw and a stirrer.

Singapore Sling

1⅓ oz / 4cl	gin
⅔ oz / 2cl	cherry brandy
⅔ oz / 2cl	fresh lemon juice
	club soda

Pour all ingredients, except soda, into a shaker with ice. Shake. Strain into a highball filled with ice. Top up with soda. Stir. Garnish with a slice of lemon and a maraschino cherry.

Sloe Gin Fizz

The original Fizz was mentioned in magazine articles in the 1870s and is a relative of the Collins. The difference being that the Fizz is always shaken. Many bartenders add egg white to give the cocktail a fizzy head.

1⅔oz /5cl	sloe gin
⅓oz / 1cl	fresh lemon juice
dash	gomme syrup
	club soda

Pour all ingredients, except soda, into a shaker with ice. Shake. Strain into a highball and top up with soda. Garnish with a slice of lime. Serve with a stirrer.

South Pacific

A stylish drink, with a graduation of fresh colors seen through the glass.

1oz / 3cl	gin
½oz / 1.5cl	Galliano
½oz / 1.5cl	blue curaçao
	7UP

Pour the gin and Galliano into a highball filled with ice. Stir. Add 7UP to almost three-quarters full. Pour the blue curaçao into the drink and let it sink to the bottom of the glass. Place a barspoon in the glass. Twist it just enough to disturb the curaçao, which will gently rise and merge with the Galliano. Garnish with a slice of lime on the rim. Serve with a straw.

Tea Ten Sidewalk

This drink has an interesting combination of unusual ingredients. It will tantalize your taste buds, with a powerful introduction on the lips from the crusted tea.

1½oz / 4.5cl	gin
½oz / 1.5cl	elderflower liqueur
1oz / 3cl	saké
½oz / 1.5cl	lemon juice
½oz / 1.5cl	gomme syrup
1	small pea-sized piece of wasabi

Coat the edge of a cocktail glass with clear honey and dip into crushed green tea leaves, giving a crusted effect. Pour all ingredients into a shaker with ice. Shake well. Pour into the prepared glass.

Texas Fizz

A welcome combination of orange and lemon flavors, with the lightness of soda.

1oz / 3cl	gin
½oz / 1.5cl	fresh orange juice
½oz / 1.5cl	fresh lemon juice
dash	grenadine
	club soda

Pour all ingredients, except soda, into a shaker with ice. Shake. Strain into a highball filled with ice. Top up with soda. Stir. Garnish with a twist of lemon.

The Buck

This is a fresh minty flavor with a bubbly, spicy finish from the ginger ale.

1⅔oz / 5cl	gin
1oz / 3cl	fresh lemon juice
⅔oz / 2cl	green crème de menthe
	ginger ale

Pour first three ingredients into a shaker with ice. Shake. Strain into a highball filled with ice. Top up with ginger ale.

The Sicilian

Imagine a hot red Mediterranean sun, and you have the color of this great drink, a great thirst quencher with a slightly bitter finish.

1oz / 3cl	gin
1oz / 3cl	Campari
½oz / 1.5cl	Cointreau
½oz / 1.5cl	cane syrup
1oz / 3cl	fresh lemon juice
2½oz / 7.5cl	fresh ruby grapefruit juice
2 dashes	orange bitters
	seltzer water

Build over ice in a 16oz highball glass. Stir. Top up with the seltzer water and garnish with an upturned wedge of fresh ruby grapefruit. Serve with a straw.

Tropical Butterfly

Close your eyes, sip, and you will find yourself in paradise!

1½oz / 4.5cl	gin
2½oz / 7.5cl	passion fruit juice
½oz / 1.5cl	elderflower cordial
½oz / 1.5cl	pear puree
3–4	fresh strawberries

Muddle the strawberries in a shaker. Add ingredients. Shake. Strain into a highball glass full of ice. Garnish with a strawberry sitting on the edge of the glass. Serve with a straw.

Tropical Dawn

A popular cocktail that takes the Campari and orange (the Garibaldi) one step further.

1oz / 3cl	gin
⅔oz / 2cl	Campari
1⅔oz / 5cl	fresh orange juice

Place all ingredients into a shaker with ice. Shake. Strain into an old-fashioned glass filled with crushed ice.

Twentieth Century

A cocktail with a chocolate flavor balanced by the citrus juice and the gin.

1⅔oz / 5cl	gin
⅔oz / 2cl	Lillet
⅔oz / 2cl	white crème de cacao
⅓oz / 1cl	fresh lemon juice

Pour all ingredients into a shaker with ice. Shake. Strain into a cocktail glass.

Venus

A great combination of sweet and bitters, this is dedicated to the Roman goddess of love.

2oz/6cl	gin
1oz/3cl	Cointreau
dash	gomme syrup
dash	Peychaud orange bitters
4	fresh raspberries

Pour all ingredients, including the raspberries, into a shaker with ice. Shake. Strain into a cocktail glass. Garnish with three raspberries.

Vesper

This is the cocktail that James Bond ordered in the movie Casino Royale, in memory of double agent Vesper Lynd.

2oz/6cl	gin
1oz/3cl	vodka
⅓oz/1cl	Lillet

Pour all ingredients into a shaker with ice. Shake. Strain into a cocktail glass. Garnish with a twist of orange.

White Lady

Created by legendary bartender Harry MacElhone while at Ciro's Club, London, in 1919. The perfect balance of sweet and sharp makes this an ideal aperitif.

1oz/3cl	gin
1oz/3cl	Cointreau
1oz/3cl	fresh lemon juice

Pour all ingredients into a shaker with ice. Shake. Strain into a cocktail glass.

Wibble

Created in response to a request to create a cocktail using Plymouth gin and Plymouth sloe gin. The bartender added a citrus note, balanced with sugar and crème de mûre.

1oz/3cl	Plymouth gin
1oz/3cl	Plymouth sloe gin
1oz/3cl	fresh grapefruit juice
⅓oz/1cl	crème de mûre (blackberry liqueur)
dash	fresh lemon juice
dash	gomme syrup

Pour all ingredients into a shaker with ice. Shake. Strain into a cocktail glass. Garnish with a twist of lemon.

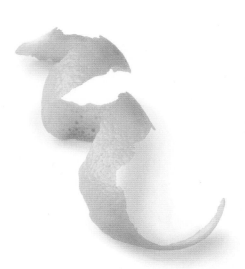

RUM

Rum is a Caribbean nectar made from sugar cane, the favorite tipple of many a pirate and buccaneer for centuries. Now, it is the base of many popular exotic cocktails, including Daiquiri, Piña Colada, Rum Punch, and Zombie.

Rum is produced from molasses and is the byproduct of manufacturing raw sugar from sugar cane. The molasses is then turned into alcohol by the process of fermentation. The alcohol is then distilled and becomes clear and colorless.

AGEING

Small oak barrels are used to age all rums, be they white or dark. Because wood is porous, it lets the rum spirit breathe, and with each breath, oxidation takes place. Light rum is matured in pale ash-wood barrels for just one year and then transferred to stainless-steel tanks to age longer. The dark types are in the barrel for three years and longer (up to 20 years, after which they start to lose flavor).

BLENDING

Most rums are blended from a variety of aged rums and different styles of rum. How much caramel and flavoring and which spices (giving the rum its

caipirinha (left), page 80, and **jade**, page 87

unique character) are to be added is the decision of the blender. Once the mixture has combined, it is diluted with water to the required bottling strength.

Rum is made all over the world, from Australia; the Caribbean islands; North, Central, and South America; and Africa to islands in the Indian Ocean, Asia, and even Europe.

The following is a list of the common names used to describe various rums:

WHITE Also called silver or light, this rum is clear, light, and dry. Most are not aged, but sometimes an aged type is available. White is a great base for many cocktails.

GOLD Also called *oro* or *ambré*, this style is sweeter, its color coming from the oak cask or perhaps caramel coloring.

DARK Also called black, this has been aged for a medium to long period in a charred barrel.

PREMIUM AGED/AÑEJO/RHUM VIEUX Mature rums, these are prized by aficianados.

FLAVORED AND SPICED These are usually served with fruit juice or a mixer.

OVERPROOF The white types are in demand for blending.

SINGLE MARKS These are rare, unblended rums from individual distilleries.

CACHAÇA

And then there is cachaça, a spirit distilled in Brazil. Also known as *aguardente de caña*, it is a spirit made from molasses, sugarcane juice, or a combination of both. This is the base spirit of a sensational, classic Caipirinha.

Rum was smuggled into America during Prohibition (1920 to 1933). A few bootleggers became wealthy. Records show that a consignment bought for $170,000 in the Bahamas had a street value of up to $2 million in Chicago.

Several folk heroes established their reputations during this era: people like Bill "King of Rum Row" McCoy, Gertrude Luthgoe, and "Scarface" Al Capone.

Always chill a cocktail glass in the freezer before use.

Ambassador

A delicate blend of apple and passion fruit flavor makes this a good thirst quencher.

1oz/3cl	white rum
1/3oz/1cl	apple schnapps
2 dashes	passion fruit liqueur
1oz/3cl	cranberry juice

Pour all ingredients into a shaker with ice. Shake. Strain into a cocktail glass.

Añejo Highball

Created by my good friend, Dale DeGroff. Añejo is the Spanish word for old, and in this case, it is applied to rum aged more than six years. This cocktail is his tribute to the great Cuban bartenders who tended both bar and souls during the 1920s and 1930s.

1 1/3oz/4cl	añejo rum
1/2oz/1.5cl	orange curaçao
1/2oz/1.5cl	fresh lime juice
2 dashes	Angostura bitters
4oz/12cl	ginger beer

Fill a highball with ice cubes. Pour the spirits in first, then add the ginger beer. Stir. Garnish with a slice of lime.

Apple Colada

The apple flavor is most refreshing. Blending the apple adds an extra texture.

1 1/3oz/4cl	white rum
2/3oz/2cl	apple schnapps
1oz/3cl	coconut cream
2 1/3oz/7cl	apple juice
1/2 teaspoon	superfine (caster) sugar
half	apple, peeled

Place all ingredients into a blender and blend for 10 seconds. Add a scoop of crushed ice and blend again until smooth. Pour into a colada glass. Garnish with a wedge of apple in a fan shape and a maraschino cherry on a cocktail stick. Serve with a straw.

Apple Daiquirí

A new version of the classic Daiquiri, this has a spicy flavor from both the rum and cinnamon with a crisp apple finish.

1 2/3oz/5cl	white rum
2/3oz/2cl	apple schnapps
1/2oz/1.5cl	cinnamon schnapps
1/2oz/1.5cl	fresh lime juice
dash	gomme syrup

Pour all ingredients into a shaker with ice. Shake well. Strain into a cocktail glass. Garnish with a wedge of apple.

Artlantic

Designed to recreate a luxurious trans-Atlantic crossing—true blue waters with plenty of sophistication.

1oz/3cl	spiced rum
⅔oz/2cl	amaretto
⅔oz/2cl	blue curaçao
⅔oz/2cl	fresh lime juice
3oz/9cl	apple juice

Pour all ingredients into a shaker filled with ice. Shake. Strain into a highball filled with ice. Garnish with a slice of orange and a sprig of mint.

Atlantic Breeze

A refreshing long drink with a fruity flavor topped off by a hint of herbs from the Galliano. A golden color.

1⅓oz/4cl	white rum
½oz/1.5cl	apricot liqueur
2⅓oz/7cl	pineapple juice
½oz/1.5cl	fresh lemon juice
⅓oz/1cl	Galliano

Pour all ingredients, except Galliano, into a highball filled with ice. Stir well. Float the Galliano on top. Garnish with a slice of orange.

Bacardi Classic

Only Bacardi rum should be used to make this drink. In 1936, a temporary injunction to restrain a New York hotel and restaurant from selling Bacardi cocktails unless they contained Bacardi rum was denied. The company then won a permanent injunction at the New York Supreme Court later that year.

1⅔oz/5cl	Bacardi white rum
1oz/3cl	fresh lime juice
1teaspoon	grenadine

Pour all ingredients into a shaker with ice. Shake. Strain into a cocktail glass. Garnish with a cherry on a cocktail stick across the glass.

Barracuda

This drink is not half as dangerous as a close encounter with an actual barracuda! After one or two you might feel brave enough to step into the sea.

1⅓oz/4cl	gold rum
⅔oz/2cl	Galliano
3⅓oz/10cl	pineapple juice
⅔oz/2cl	fresh lime juice

Pour all ingredients into a shaker with ice. Shake. Strain into a highball filled with ice. Garnish with a wedge of lime. Serve with a stirrer.

Bahama Mama

This drink has strength, sweetness, and a delicate coffee flavor, and the lemon gives it a hint of sharpness.

1⅓oz/4cl	dark rum
⅔oz/2cl	151 proof Demerara rum
½oz/1.5cl	coconut liqueur
½oz/1.5cl	coffee liqueur
4oz/12cl	pineapple juice
⅓oz/1cl	fresh lemon juice

Pour all ingredients, except 151 proof rum, into a shaker with ice. Shake. Strain into a highball filled with ice. Gently float the Demerara rum over the top. This will give it a strong nose and taste at the first sip. Garnish with a wedge of pineapple and a cherry. Serve with a straw.

Banana Boat

This is a wonderful creamy cocktail with lots of flavor. It's also invigorating and a real smoothie with a hint of chocolate.

1oz/3cl	white rum
1oz/3cl	white crème de cacao
half	banana, peeled
2 scoops	vanilla ice cream

Pour all ingredients into a blender with crushed ice. Blend until smooth. Pour into a highball. Garnish with a small slice of banana set on the rim.

Batida Morango

A batida is a traditional Brazilian workingman's drink and can be made with any fruit. Cachaça remains the spirit base.

2oz/6cl	cachaça
1oz/3cl	fresh lime juice
4	fresh strawberries, diced
2 teaspoons	superfine (caster) sugar

Pour all ingredients into a blender with crushed ice. Blend until smooth. Pour into a highball. Serve with a straw.

Beja Flor

A delicious Brazilian cocktail served ice cold for the full effect. It's very fruity.

2oz/6cl	cachaça
1oz/3cl	triple sec/Cointreau
1oz/3cl	crème de bananes (banana liqueur)

Pour all ingredients into a shaker filled with ice. Shake. Strain into a cocktail glass. Garnish with a slice of banana set on the rim.

WHY DID HAVANA'S GENIUS BARTENDER CONSTANTINO RIBALAIGUA ROLL HIS LIMES?

The rolling of the lime separates the juice from the pith inside the lime. You can also try putting the lime in hot water for about 30 seconds; this action releases the juice inside. Then cut with a sharp fruit knife.

Berry Nice

This is a an updated version of the Caiprinha, using the same spirit but using different fruits. This recipe is for two.

2oz/6cl	cachaça
2	small limes
few	raspberries
few	blueberries
6	strawberries diced, and hulled
1 tablespoon	brown sugar

Wash each lime, remove the top and the bottom, and cut into small segments, from top to bottom. Add the sugar and pieces of lime to the bottom of a small mixing bowl. Muddle the lime, releasing the juices, then add the berries. Continue to muddle until the juices run freely from the fruit. The juice will be red from the strawberry, green, and purple from the blueberries. Place one scoop into a old-fashioned glass or small tumbler. Add the cachaça and cracked ice and stir. Serve with a stirrer and a short straw.

Blue Amour

A cocktail designed to recreate the mood of the deep blue ocean.

1oz/3cl	spiced rum
⅔oz/2cl	amaretto
⅔oz/2cl	blue curaçao

Pour all ingredients into a shaker filled with ice. Shake. Strain into a highball filled with ice.

Blue Hawaiian

This is a classic drink from the original holiday isle of Hawaii in the Pacific. Made even more famous by Elvis Presley in the 1970s, this drink will always be associated with his hip-shaking sensuality.

1oz/3cl	white rum
1oz/3cl	blue curaçao
1oz/3cl	coconut cream
2oz/6cl	pineapple juice

Pour all ingredients into a blender with a scoop of dry crushed ice. Blend until smooth. Pour into a goblet. Garnish with a slice of pineapple and a maraschino cherry.

Blue Heaven

The hint of spice from the rum, the sweet almond of the amaretto, and the freshness of the lime and pineapple juice combination sends your palate a-knock-knock-knocking on heaven's door.

1oz/3cl	white rum
½oz/1.5cl	amaretto
½oz/1.5cl	blue curaçao
½oz/1.5cl	fresh lime juice
3⅓oz/10cl	pineapple juice

Pour all ingredients into the shaker with ice. Shake. Strain into a highball filled with ice. To garnish, place a maraschino cherry, a wedge of pineapple, and a small pineapple leaf on a cocktail stick and place it on the rim.

Blue Mist

A great creamy drink to sip on the beach late at night. It has a fresh orange flavor.

1⅓oz/4cl	white rum
½oz/1.5cl	blue curaçao
½oz/1.5cl	heavy (double) cream
1oz/3cl	fresh orange juice

Pour all ingredients into a shaker with ice. Shake. Strain into a cocktail glass.

Blue Passion

For those who are passionate about blue, this is the perfect cocktail—it's also strong and tangy.

1oz/3cl	white rum
1oz/3cl	blue curaçao
1oz/3cl	fresh lime juice
dash	gomme syrup

Pour all ingredients into a shaker with ice. Shake. Strain into a cocktail glass.

Bolero

One with an earthy apple flavor and a hint of sweetness from the vermouth.

1⅔oz/5cl	white rum
1oz/3cl	apple brandy
½oz/1.5cl	sweet vermouth

Pour all ingredients into a shaker with ice. Shake. Strain into a cocktail glass. Garnish with a twist of orange in the drink.

Bossa Nova

A long drink with all of the excitement of the South American rhythm from which it takes its name.

1oz/3cl	white rum
1oz/3cl	Galliano
½oz/1.5cl	apricot brandy
2oz/6cl	pineapple juice
½oz/1.5cl	fresh lemon juice
1 teaspoon	egg white powder

Pour all ingredients into a shaker with ice. Shake. Strain into a highball filled with ice. Garnish with a small slice of pineapple and a sprig of mint on the rim. Serve with a straw and a stirrer.

Bossa Nova II

A newer version of the above recipe, with a cleaner taste from the apple juice.

1oz/3cl	white rum
½oz/1.5cl	Galliano
½oz/1.5cl	apricot brandy
3oz/9cl	clear apple juice
⅔oz/2cl	fresh lime juice
1 teaspoon	egg white powder

Pour all ingredients into a shaker filled with ice. Shake. Strain into a highball filled with ice. Garnish with a wedge of lime. Serve with a straw.

Caipirinha

Possibly the best-loved Brazilian cocktail, full of lip-smacking flavor. Literally translated it means "peasant's drink," and it has a reputation as the cocktail that could replace the malaria shot! It gets its kick from the cachaça, a Brazilian spirit distilled from sugarcane juice. In the 1920s and 1930s car king Henry Ford outlawed the Caipirinha in Fordlandia, his company town located in Brazil.

Serious bartenders will make this drink with a long wooden pestle, larger than the usual muddler, to bring out the full flavor of the lime, just as the Brazilians did. Just the cocktail for flaunting on the beach, on the yacht out to sea . . . wherever your heart takes you.

1²⁄₃oz / 5cl	cachaça
1	small fresh lime
1½ teaspoons	superfine (caster) sugar

Wash the lime and slice off the top and bottom, and cut into small segments from top to bottom. Add the lime slices and the sugar to an old-fashioned glass. Crush the lime to make juice, and muddle to make sure the sugar has dissolved. Add ice cubes and the cachaça and stir. Serve with a stirrer. A straw is optional.

Caribbean Breeze

Shooting the breeze out on the ocean with this long drink is a not-to-be-forgotten experience.

1¹⁄₃oz / 4cl	dark rum
¹⁄₃oz / 1cl	crème de bananes (banana liqueur)
2¹⁄₃oz / 7cl	pineapple juice
1³⁄4 /5cl	cranberry juice
¹⁄₃oz / 1cl	Rose's lime cordial

Pour all ingredients into a shaker with ice. Shake. Strain into a highball filled with crushed ice. Garnish with a slice of lime. Serve with a straw.

Choco Colada

This is a deliciously smooth colada for those who love the taste of chocolate.

1¹⁄₃oz / 4cl	white rum
¹⁄₃oz / 1cl	dark rum
1¹⁄₃oz / 4cl	milk
²⁄₃oz / 2cl	chocolate syrup
¹⁄₃oz / 1cl	Tia Maria
1oz / 3cl	coconut cream

Pour all ingredients into a blender with crushed ice. Blend for 10 seconds. Pour into a goblet or colada glass. Sprinkle with a few fine chocolate shavings. Serve with a straw.

Cocobanana

A Caribbean cocktail with lots of energy from the banana and a hint of almond.

1²⁄₃oz / 5cl	gold rum
1oz / 3cl	amaretto
2oz / 6cl	pineapple juice
1oz / 3cl	coconut cream
2 scoops	vanilla ice cream
1	ripe banana, peeled

Place all ingredients into a blender with crushed ice. Blend. Strain into a highball. Garnish with a slice of banana set on the rim. Serve with a straw.

Cococabana

A combination of rum, coconut, and melon gives this drink a full flavor.

1oz / 3cl	coconut rum
1oz / 3cl	melon liqueur
3¹⁄₃oz / 10cl	pineapple juice
1oz / 3cl	coconut cream

Place all ingredients into a blender with a scoop of crushed ice and blend. Pour into a goblet. Garnish with a slice of star fruit. Serve with a straw.

Citrus Rum Cooler

A typically tropical weather drink designed to quench the thirst. A traditional cooler, with a lip-smacking flavor.

1¹⁄₃oz / 4cl	white rum
²⁄₃oz / 2cl	triple sec/Cointreau
1²⁄₃oz / 5cl	fresh orange juice
¹⁄₂oz / 1.5cl	fresh lime juice
few dashes	gomme syrup
	7UP

Pour all ingredients into a shaker with ice. Shake. Strain into a highball filled with ice. Top up with 7UP. Garnish with a wedge of lime wrapped in a spiral of orange peel that trails a little way down the outside of glass. Serve with a straw.

Cuba Libre

The advent of Coca-Cola in 1886 was integral to the creation of this drink. In 1893 an Army lieutenant based in Cuba mixed Bacardi rum with the new soft drink, Coca-Cola (it being the soft drink the troops brought with them), and proclaimed it Cuba Libre.

1²⁄₃oz / 5cl	white rum
1oz / 3cl	fresh lime juice
	Coca-Cola

Pour the juice, then the rum into a highball filled with ice. Top up with Coca-Cola. Garnish with a wedge of lime. Serve with a stirrer.

Cuban Heat

This is a delicate red cocktail, full of spice, a hint of almond, and cranberry.

2oz/6cl	white rum
1oz/3cl	amaretto
	cranberry juice

Pour the rum and the amaretto into an old-fashioned glass with ice. Top up with cranberry juice. Garnish with a stem of red currants on the rim.

Cuban Passion

Anyone who has had the chance to go to Cuba will know what passion means.

1⅓oz/4cl	white rum
⅔oz/2cl	passion fruit juice
2⅔oz/8cl	grenadine
3oz/9cl	fresh orange juice

Pour all ingredients into a shaker with ice. Shake. Strain into a highball filled with ice. Garnish with a wedge of lime.

Cute Rose

This is a delicate pale pink cocktail, full of spice and the intrigue of a Caribbean island.

2oz/6cl	white rum
1⅓oz/4cl	pineapple juice
1oz/3cl	coconut cream
2 dashes	grenadine

Pour all ingredients into a blender with crushed ice. Blend. Pour into a goblet. Garnish with a wedge of pineapple and a maraschino cherry.

CLASSIC COCKTAIL

Daiquiri

The most-repeated myth about its origins concerns American engineer Jennings Cox, working near the East Coast town of Daiquiri in Cuba. In the long, hot summer of 1896 Jennings Cox is said to have run out of his gin supplies when expecting important guests. His local colleagues drank a mixture of rum and lime juice and it was this, with the addition of granulated sugar, that he offered his guests, naming it a Daiquiri after the town.

Admiral Lucius W. Johnson had met Jennings Cox and introduced the cocktail to the Army & Navy Club in Washington, D.C. A plaque hangs in the club's Daiquiri Lounge. Additional fame came to the humble daiquiri when President John F. Kennedy proclaimed it his favorite predinner drink. The German actress Marlene Dietrich, when in London, liked to sip a daiquiri at the Savoy's American Bar.

1⅔oz/5cl	white rum
⅔oz/2cl	fresh lime juice
2 to 3 dashes	gomme syrup

Pour all ingredients into a shaker with ice. Shake. Strain into a cocktail glass. Garnish with a wedge of lime.

Daiquiri Blossom

A refreshing version of the daiquiri with the delicate taste of orange.

2oz/6cl	white rum
1oz/3cl	fresh orange juice
dash	maraschino liqueur

Pour all ingredients into a shaker with ice. Shake. Strain into a cocktail glass. Garnish with a twist of orange.

Grapefruit Daiquiri

A refreshing version of the daiquiri with the slightly bitter taste of grapefruit.

2oz/6cl	white rum
1oz/3cl	fresh grapefruit juice
dash	gomme syrup

Pour all ingredients into a shaker with ice. Shake. Strain into a cocktail glass. Garnish with a twist of grapefruit.

Raspberry Mint Daiquiri

This has a fresh fragrance from the combination of mint and raspberries.

1⅔oz/5cl	white rum
handful	fresh raspberries
6 leaves	fresh mint

Place all ingredients into a shaker with ice. Shake. Strain into a double cocktail glass. Garnish with three raspberries and a sprig of mint on a cocktail stick.

Vanilla Daiquiri

Flavored rum has a unique flavor and you can easily make it yourself at home.

2oz/6cl	vanilla-flavored white rum
⅔oz/2cl	fresh lime juice
⅓oz/1cl	gomme syrup

Scrape the inside of three vanilla pods into a bottle of rum. Replace the cap and leave for a week. Shake occasionally. Pour all ingredients into a shaker with ice. Shake. Strain into a cocktail glass.

FROZEN DAIQUIRI

The blender has reinvented this classic. Crushed ice is used to give the drink frostbite. You can make one with any soft fruit that can be liquidized to create flavor.

Whichever fruit you use, add the same flavor in a liqueur. Serve these cocktails with a straw.

Ernest Hemingway Special

Created by Constantino Ribalaigua for Ernest Hemingway, who loved it.

1¾oz/5cl	white rum
⅔oz/2cl	fresh grapefruit juice
⅓oz/1cl	maraschino liqueur
⅔oz/2cl	fresh lime juice

Put all ingredients into a shaker with crushed ice. Shake. Strain into an old-fashioned glass filled with ice. Add a wedge of lime. Serve with a straw.

La Floridita

The original cocktail created at Havana's famous bar of the same name.

1¾oz / 5cl	Havana white rum
dash	maraschino liqueur
⅔oz / 2cl	fresh lime juice
dash	gomme syrup

Pour all ingredients into a shaker with crushed ice. Shake. Strain into a cocktail glass filled with dry crushed ice; this instantly freezes the liquid. Garnish with a wedge of lime. Serve with a straw.

Peach Daiquiri

This has the delicious flavor of peaches with the strength of rum.

1⅓oz / 4cl	white rum
⅔oz / 2cl	peach schnapps
1oz / 3cl	fresh lime juice
1	fresh peach, skinned and diced

Put all ingredients into a blender. Blend. Add crushed ice. Blend again. Pour into a cocktail glass. Garnish with a wedge of peach. Serve with a straw.

Pear Daiquiri

The light and refreshing flavor of chilled pear fills the mouth with every sip.

1⅓oz / 4cl	white rum
⅓oz / 1cl	pear schnapps
1oz / 3cl	fresh pear purée
1oz / 3cl	fresh lime juice
dash	gomme syrup

Pour all ingredients into a blender with crushed ice. Blend. Pour into a double cocktail glass.

Dark and Stormy

Originating in Bermuda, this cocktail is made with local Gossens dark rum.

1⅔oz / 5cl	Gossens dark rum
½oz / 2cl	fresh lime juice
	ginger beer

Pour the rum and lime juice into a highball with ice. Top up with ginger beer. Stir. Garnish with a twist of lime.

Diavolo Nero

Created by my dear friend and living legend Peter Dorelli, who performed for 40 years at the Savoy Bar. Like Peter, it's in a class of its own!

1½oz/4.5cl	aged rum
⅔oz/2cl	Grand Marnier
⅔oz/2cl	blackberry liqueur
⅔oz/2cl	balsamic vinegar
2 thin slices	chili pepper

Pour all the ingredients in a shaker filled with ice. Shake sharply and strain into a chilled cocktail glass. Garnish with a twist of orange and 3 blackberries.

Dolce Havana

A mild, smooth cocktail with the fragrance of oranges and limes and a hint of rhubarb.

1⅓oz/4cl	white rum
⅔oz/2cl	Aperol
½oz/1.5cl	Cointreau
1oz/3cl	fresh orange juice
⅔oz/2cl	fresh lime juice

Pour all ingredients into a shaker with ice. Shake. Strain into a cocktail glass. Garnish with a Cape Gooseberry.

Dragnet

Remember the television series of the same name? Drink as you watch reruns.

2oz/6cl	cachaça
3oz/9cl	red grape juice
1oz/3cl	fresh lime juice

Pour all ingredients into a shaker with ice. Shake. Strain into a highball filled with ice.

El Burro

A rich and creamy exotic drink with a hint of coffee at the finish.

1oz/3cl	dark rum
⅔oz/2cl	Kahlua
1oz/3cl	coconut cream
1oz/3cl	heavy (double) cream
½	banana

Pour all ingredients into the blender. Blend. Add crushed ice. Blend again. Pour into a colada glass.

El Presidente I

*Take your pick of South
American presidents past
and present as you raise
your glass.*

2oz/6cl	white rum
⅔oz/2cl	Dubonnet
⅓oz/1cl	grenadine

Pour all ingredients into a shaker with ice.
Shake. Strain into a cocktail glass.

El Presidente II

*This version has the sweet
flavor of oranges combined
with the strength of the rum.*

2oz/6cl	white rum
½oz/1.5cl	orange curaçao
½oz/1.5cl	dry vermouth
dash	grenadine

Pour all ingredients into a shaker with ice.
Shake. Strain into a cocktail glass.

Fancy Drink

*A good drink for when you
are really thirsty. It has a
bitter, sparkling finish.*

1oz/3cl	white rum
1oz/3cl	Grand Marnier
2oz/6cl	fresh grapefruit juice
	bitter lemon

Pour all ingredients, except bitter lemon, into
a shaker with ice. Shake. Strain into a highball
filled with ice. Top up with bitter lemon.

Fluffy Duck

*An amusing name for a
smooth-tasting, creamy
cocktail.*

1oz/3cl	white rum
1oz/3cl	advocaat
⅓oz/1cl	heavy (double) cream

Pour the rum and advocaat into a highball
filled with ice. Stir. Float the cream on top
of the drink. Garnish with a strawberry and a
sprig of mint set in its top. Serve with a straw
and a stirrer.

French Tear

*A sweet and strong little
number with the taste of
pineapple dominating.*

1oz/3cl	spiced rum
1oz/3cl	Grand Marnier
1oz/3cl	pineapple juice

Pour all ingredients into a shaker with ice.
Shake. Strain into a cocktail glass.

Hurricane

A classic cocktail made to present a whirlwind of tastes in one glass, to be drunk while listening to the wind wailing around outside.

1oz/3cl	white rum
1oz/3cl	dark rum
⅔oz/2cl	triple sec/Cointreau
1oz/3cl	fresh lime juice
⅔oz/2cl	gomme syrup
⅓oz/1cl	grenadine
3oz/9cl	fresh orange juice
3oz/9cl	pineapple juice

Pour all ingredients into a shaker with ice. Shake. Strain into a highball with ice. Garnish with a small wedge of pineapple set on the rim.

Hurricane Cooler

The original Hurricane was a short drink, served in a cocktail glass–a combination of dark and white rum, passion fruit syrup, and lime juice.

1⅓oz/4cl	dark rum
⅔oz/2cl	white rum
⅔oz/2cl	fresh lime juice
1⅔oz/5cl	passion fruit juice
1oz/3cl	pineapple juice
1oz/3cl	fresh orange juice
⅓oz/1cl	black-currant syrup

Pour all ingredients into a shaker with ice. Shake. Strain into a colada glass filled with crushed ice. Garnish with a slice of pineapple and a cherry. Serve with a straw.

Jade

This cocktail is an elegant shade of green and is equally delicious to drink. The finish has a sharp hint of lime.

1⅓oz/4cl	white rum
½oz/1.5cl	green crème de menthe
½oz/1.5cl	blue curaçao
⅔oz/2cl	Rose's lime cordial
dash	gomme syrup

Rub a wedge of lime around the rim of the glass to moisten it. Dip it into a saucer of superfine (caster) sugar to create a frosted rim. Pour all ingredients into a shaker with ice. Shake. Strain into a cocktail glass.

Jamaican Mule

An exotic version of the Moscow Mule, traditionally made with vodka.

1⅔oz/5cl	dark Jamaican rum
⅔oz/2cl	fresh lime juice
	ginger beer

Pour the rum and lime juice into a highball filled with ice. Top up with ginger beer. Stir. Garnish with a wedge of lime dropped in the drink.

Jamaican Sangria

A heavenly balance of flavors for a Sangria with a Caribbean twist.

1½oz / 4.5cl	dark rum
1oz / 3cl	red wine
½oz / 1.5cl	apricot brandy
½oz / 1.5cl	strawberry liqueur
1½oz / 4.5cl	orange juice
1 barspoon	honey syrup

Pour all ingredients into a shaker filled with ice. Strain into a highball glass filled with ice. Garnish with a slice of orange, a raspberry, and mint tip. Serve with a straw.

Jerry's Special

An exotic combination of fruit juices and the strong flavor of dark rum.

1oz / 3cl	dark rum
⅓oz / 1cl	Cointreau
⅔oz / 2cl	cranberry juice
⅓oz / 1cl	passion fruit juice
dash	grenadine

Pour all ingredients into a shaker with ice. Shake. Strain into a cocktail glass.

King Creole

As dark as the soul music that gave birth to the blues, here's a rock 'n' roll flavor to savor.

1oz / 3cl	dark rum
½oz / 1.5cl	crème de banana (banana liqueur)
½oz / 1.5cl	Kahlua
1oz / 3cl	heavy (double) cream

Pour all ingredients, except cream, into a shaker with ice. Strain into a cocktail glass. Gently float the cream over the top.

Knickerbocker Special

A new version of the classic cocktail, which was originally created in New York.

2oz / 6cl	white rum
½oz / 1.5cl	crème de framboise (raspberry liqueur)
⅓oz / 1cl	fresh lemon juice
½oz / 1.5cl	orange curaçao

Pour all ingredients into a shaker with ice. Shake. Strain into a cocktail glass. Garnish with a wedge of pineapple.

Lemon Beat

A cute Brazilian number with a tart flavor from the lemon juice balanced by the honey.

2oz / 6cl	cachaça
1oz / 3cl	fresh lemon juice
1 teaspoon	clear honey

Pour all ingredients into a shaker with ice. Shake. Strain into an old-fashioned glass filled with ice. Garnish with a slice of lemon.

Liberty

The rum and calvados combination creates a strong vanilla and apple flavor.

1oz / 3cl	white rum
1oz / 3cl	calvados
⅓oz / 1cl	fresh lemon juice
⅔oz / 2cl	gomme syrup

Pour all ingredients into a mixing glass with ice. Stir. Strain into a cocktail glass. Garnish with wedge of apple.

Loco

An interesting name (loco is Spanish for mad)—as there is nothing mad about this!

1⅔oz / 5cl	white rum
⅔oz / 2cl	peach schnapps
5oz / 15cl	cranberry juice
⅓oz / 1cl	fresh lime juice

Pour all ingredients into a shaker with ice. Shake. Strain into a highball filled with ice. Garnish with a lime wedge.

Long Island Iced Tea

This is the drink that guarantees you will have a hangover the next day. Extremely alcoholic, it makes you tipsy quickly. Dating from the Prohibition era, this delicious long cocktail was originally made with any available spirit, hence there are many different recipes around today.

Basically, it was made with five spirits: light rum, vodka, gin, tequila, and Cointreau. It is simple to make, too. Measure each spirit exactly to maintain the correct balance of flavor. Some recipes leave out the vodka, others omit the tequila. This has them all! If triple sec is omitted, this is a Texas Tea; if blue curaçao is used in place of triple sec, this is a Miami Iced Tea.

⅓oz / 1cl	light rum
⅓oz / 1cl	vodka
⅓oz / 1cl	gin
⅓oz / 1cl	tequila
⅓oz / 1cl	Cointreau
⅔oz / 2cl	fresh lime juice
	cola, chilled

Pour all ingredients, except cola, into a highball filled with ice. Stir. Top up with chilled cola. Garnish with a wedge of lime. Serve with a straw and a stirrer.

Louisa

A cute lilac color, this drink has a hint of sweetness from the pineapple juice.

1⅓oz/4cl	white rum
⅔oz/2cl	Parfait Amour
1oz/3cl	pineapple juice

Pour all ingredients into a shaker with ice. Shake. Strain into a cocktail glass. Garnish with a slice of orange and a maraschino cherry.

Louisiana Lullaby

A dark rust color, this drink has a hint of sweetness on the finish.

2oz/6cl	dark rum
½oz/1.5cl	Dubonnet
½oz/1.5cl	Grand Marnier

Pour all ingredients into a mixing glass with ice. Stir. Strain into a cocktail glass. Garnish with a twist of lemon.

Love in the Afternoon

Luscious, languid strawberry flavor incites you to indulge in great passion in the heat of the afternoon.

1oz/3cl	dark rum
1oz/3cl	fresh orange juice
1oz/3cl	coconut cream
½oz/1.5cl	crème de fraise (strawberry liqueur)
½oz/1.5cl	heavy (double) cream
5	strawberries

Place all ingredients into a blender. Add a scoop of crushed ice. Blend. Pour into a goblet. Garnish with a strawberry with a sprig of mint. Serve with a straw.

Madagascar Sour

An unusual sour recipe with a dominance of vanilla flavor over the rum and lime juice.

1⅔oz/5cl	white rum
½oz/1.5cl	vanilla liqueur
½oz/1.5cl	vanilla sugar syrup
⅔oz/2cl	fresh lime juice

Pour all ingredients into a shaker with ice. Shake. Strain into a cocktail glass. Garnish with a wedge of lime.

Mary Pickford

A genuine classic cocktail immortalized in many recipe books. The cocktail was created at the Hotel Sevilla Bar in Cuba, in the 1920s when the elegant Mary Pickford was at the height of her fame as an actress—a true classic.

1½oz / 4.5cl	white rum
½oz / 1.5cl	maraschino liqueur
1oz / 3cl	pineapple juice
1 barspoon	grenadine

Pour all ingredients in a shaker with ice. Strain into a cocktail glass. Garnish with a red maraschino cherry.

Mai Tai

The origin of this cocktail is a tale of two bartenders: Don Beach at the Beachcomber restaurant in Hollywood in the early 1930s; and Victor "Trader Vic" Bergeron of his Emeryville bar, Hinky Dinks, in 1944. Trader Vic mixed a cocktail of 17-year-old dark Jamaican rum, the juice of a fresh lime, a few dashes of orange curaçao, Orgeat, and rock candy syrup. After shaking it, he poured it into a glass filled with shaved ice, garnished it with a wedge of lime and a sprig of mint, and presented it to Eastham and Carrie Guild, friends from Tahiti. After a sip, they pronounced it: "Mai tai—Roa Ae," which meant: "Out of this world. The best."

⅔oz / 2cl	dark rum
⅔oz / 2cl	golden rum
⅓oz / 1cl	triple sec/Cointreau
⅓oz / 1cl	Orgeat (almond syrup)
⅔oz / 2cl	fresh lime juice
3 dashes	grenadine

Pour all ingredients into a shaker with ice. Shake. Strain into a goblet. Garnish with a tropical orchid or a wedge of lime. Serve with a straw and a stirrer.

CLASSIC COCKTAIL

Mojito

This is a classic Cuban cocktail, revived during the Prohibition era. The Bodeguita del Medio Bar in Havana is famous for its Mojitos. It's all they serve. The barman lines up 10 to 15 glasses and it is a neverending parade of Mojitos from dawn until late. The bar is unchanged from the day it opened. All the walls are signed—my signature is above the bar in the only tiny space left.

1²⁄₃oz / 5cl	white rum
1 teaspoon	superfine (caster) sugar
²⁄₃oz / 2cl	fresh lime juice
bunch	fresh mint on the stem
	sparking water or club soda
2 dash	Angostura bitters (optional)

Put the sugar and lime juice in the bottom of a highball with a thick base. Add the mint leaves and gently release the flavor, without bruising it, with the back of a barspoon. Mint is a delicate herb and needs to be handled gently. Add the rum and fill the glass with crushed ice. Stir. Top up with sparkling water or club soda. Stir again. Add bitters if you prefer, to cut through the sweetness. Garnish with a sprig of mint. Serve with a straw.

Mojito Martini

An unusual dry, minty flavor with a spicy rum flavor. Not the usual Martini!

1²⁄₃oz / 5cl	white rum infused with fresh mint
²⁄₃oz / 2cl	fresh lime juice
dash	gomme syrup

Place a few large sprigs of mint in a bottle of white rum to infuse for just a day. Then remove the mint or it will spoil and taint the rum.

Pour all ingredients into a shaker with ice. Shake. Strain into a cocktail glass. Gently press a leaf of mint on the inside of the glass by the rim. Don't worry—it will stay in place.

Pink Mojito

The addition of cranberry juice gives this its color and a tart flavor over the mint.

1³⁄₄oz / 5cl	white rum
1 teaspoon	superfine (caster) sugar
1oz / 3cl	fresh lime juice
sprig	fresh mint leaves
dash	cranberry juice
dash	sparkling water

Put the sugar and lime juice in the bottom of a highball. Add the mint leaves and muddle. Add the rum and fill the glass with crushed ice. Add a dash of cranberry juice. Top up with sparkling water. Stir. Serve with a stirrer.

daiquiri (left) and frozen daiquiri

Mojito Special

A great combination of ginger and mint creating a refreshing long drink.

1oz / 3cl	dark rum
few	sprigs of mint
1 teaspoon	brown sugar
3⅓oz / 10cl	ginger beer

Put the sugar and lime juice in the bottom of a highball. Add mint leaves and muddle. Add the rum and fill the glass with crushed ice. Top it up with ginger beer. Stir. Serve with a stirrer.

Mulata

A delicious cold cocktail with a smooth, chocolate flavor and a citrus overlay.

2oz / 6cl	white rum
⅔oz / 2cl	brown crème de cacao
⅔oz / 2cl	fresh lemon juice
⅓oz / 1cl	gomme syrup

Place all the ingredients into a blender with crushed ice. Blend until smooth. Serve in a cocktail glass.

Mulata Daisy

Taking his inspiration from a beautiful Latina flower seller from the streets of Cuba, this was a winning recipe for a new star of the bar world, Agostino Perrone.

1⅓oz / 4cl	Bacardi rum
¾oz / 2.5cl	crème de cacao brown
⅔oz / 2cl	lime juice
2 teaspoons	castor sugar
1½ teaspoon	fennel seeds
⅓oz / 1cl	Galliano L'Authentico

Dust the rim of a champagne flute with chocolate powder and carefully rinse it with the Galliano L'Authentico. In a shaker, muddle the fennel seeds. Add the other ingredients with cubed ice. Shake hard. Fine-strain into the glass.

Nevada

A combination of bitter and sour flavors, with the strength of dark rum.

1⅔oz / 5cl	dark rum
1oz / 3cl	fresh grapefruit juice
⅔oz / 2cl	fresh lime juice
dash	gomme syrup

Pour all ingredients into a shaker with ice. Shake. Strain into a cocktail glass.

Painkiller

Charles Topias, proprietor of Pusser's at the Beach Bar in Fort Lauderdale, discovered this at the Soggy Dollar Bar, British Virgin Islands. Most of the bar's customers were sailors and there was no dock. They had to swim ashore and paid for drinks with wet dollars.

2oz/6cl	white rum
4oz/12cl	pineapple juice
1oz/3cl	fresh orange juice
1oz/3cl	coconut cream

Pour all ingredients into a shaker with ice. Shake. Strain into a highball filled with ice. Garnish with a wedge of pineapple and a maraschino cherry on a cocktail stick.

Passion Fruit Batida

A brilliant combination of sweet and sour, with the texture of passion fruit purée.

1⅔oz/5cl	cachaça
1oz/3cl	passion fruit purée
⅓oz/1cl	gomme syrup

Pour ingredients into an old-fashioned glass over crushed ice. Stir. Garnish with a wedge of lime. Serve with two straws.

Piña Colada

The most infamous of the coladas is the Piña Colada—its title means "strained pineapple." There are fans who will drink no other summer cocktail. This exotic number originated in Puerto Rico, and there are two contenders who claim to have invented the recipe. Ramón Marrero Perez of the Caribe Hilton is adamant he mixed the first in 1954; Don Ramón Portas Mingot of La Barrachina Restaurant Bar staked his claim a decade later—1963.

You can use pineapple juice from a can, or you can use the juice and the fiber from pineapple crushed in a blender. Use the freshest, top-quality fruit you can buy. When made, all of the drink should be milky white, not separated into clear liquid and froth.

1⅔oz/5cl	white rum
3⅓oz/10cl	pineapple juice
1⅔oz/5cl	coconut cream
	crushed ice

Pour the pineapple juice into the blender. Add the coconut cream and the rum. Blend. Add the crushed ice and blend. Pour into a colada glass. Garnish with a wedge of pineapple and a maraschino cherry. Serve with a straw.

P.S. I Love You

It is impossible not to like this creamy cocktail, with its good intentions.

⅔oz/2cl	dark rum
⅔oz/2cl	Irish Cream liqueur
⅔oz/2cl	amaretto
⅔oz/2cl	coffee liqueur
1⅔oz/5cl	heavy (double) cream
1⅔oz/5cl	milk

Pour all ingredients into a shaker with ice. Shake. Strain into a highball filled with ice. Serve with a straw. Garnish with a Cape Gooseberry. Sip. Lick lips.

Petake Cocktail

Van der Hum is a Dutch-made aromatic liqueur with a tangerine flavor. A great combination of flavors!

2oz/6cl	golden rum
1oz/3cl	Cointreau
dash	Van der Hum
dash	pineapple juice
dash	papaya juice
dash	fresh lime juice

Pour all ingredients into a shaker with ice. Shake. Strain into a double cocktail glass. Garnish with a Cape Gooseberry on the rim.

Reef Juice

A recipe from the Beach Bar in Fort Lauderdale, Florida, this is full of pineapple flavor with a hint of banana.

1⅔oz/5cl	rum
⅔oz/2cl	vodka
1oz/3cl	crème de bananes (banana liqueur)
⅔oz/2cl	fresh lime juice
2oz/6cl	pineapple juice

Pour all ingredients into a shaker with ice. Shake. Strain into a highball filled with ice. Garnish with a wedge of pineapple and a maraschino cherry on a cocktail stick set across the glass.

Rum Crush

A brilliant combination of flavors crushed together in one cocktail! Apple and mint flavors dominate.

1⅔oz/5cl	dark rum
⅓oz/1cl	peach schnapps
⅓oz/1cl	apple juice
⅓oz/1cl	fresh lime juice
3	mint leaves
dash	gomme syrup

Pour all ingredients into a shaker with ice. Shake. Strain into an old-fashioned glass filled with ice. Garnish with a wedge of lime and a sprig of mint.

Scorpion

One of the delicious cocktails invented by Trader Vic Bergeron in his Oakland, California, bar. I'm not sure of the name's origins—but maybe it refers to a close encounter with the real thing.

1oz / 3cl	dark rum
½oz / 1.5cl	white rum
½oz / 1.5cl	brandy
⅓oz / 1cl	triple sec/Cointreau
1⅔oz / 5cl	fresh orange juice
⅔oz / 2cl	fresh lime juice

Pour all ingredients into a shaker with ice. Shake. Strain into a highball filled with crushed ice. Squeeze a wedge of lime directly in the drink and drop it in. Serve with a straw.

Spiced Swizzle

This has a wonderful almond flavor at the finish, and just a hint of citrus flavor

2oz / 6cl	spiced rum
1oz / 3cl	fresh lime juice
⅓oz / 1cl	gomme syrup
⅔oz / 2cl	amaretto

Pour all ingredients, except amaretto, into a shaker with ice. Shake. Strain into an old-fashioned glass filled with ice. Float the amaretto over the top. Garnish with a slice of lime. Serve with a straw.

CLASSIC COCKTAIL

Smokey Rum Fashioned

To make tobacco syrup: take 4 medium sized mild cigars (ideally use up damaged ones if you have any), 10oz/300ml water, and 1lb./450 grams white sugar.

Heat the water and sugar until the sugar has dissolved, simmer gently until it has thickened slightly, and remove from the heat. Break the cigars and stir them into the syrup, then cover and leave overnight to infuse. The next day, strain out the cigars and gently simmer the syrup once more until it thickens. Strain and allow to cool.

1 barspoon	Scotch whiskey
1 barspoon	tobacco syrup
1 wedge	orange squeezed
2oz / 6cl	Zacapa 23 rum

Add whiskey, tobacco syrup, and a squeeze of orange to an old-fashioned glass and mix together. Slowly add the rum along with some ice cubes and build as you would with an old fashioned. Garnish with a large twist of orange.

Special Cachaça

With a base spirit distilled from the juice of Brazilian sugar cane, and at 82 proof, this is a great cocktail!

2oz/6cl	cachaça
2oz/6cl	Punt e Mes
⅔oz/2cl	Grand Marnier

Pour all ingredients into a shaker with ice. Shake. Strain into an old-fashioned glass filled with ice. Garnish with a slice of orange.

St. James's

A punchy fruit-flavored treat in a glass with a fresh hint of tartness on the finish.

1½oz/4.5cl	aged rum
1½oz/1.5cl	Campari
2½oz/7.5cl	guava juice
⅔oz/2cl	fresh lime juice
⅓oz/1cl	gomme syrup

Pour all ingredients into a shaker filled with ice. Strain into a highball glass filled with ice. Garnish with a wedge of lime and a raspberry and a blackberry on a cocktail stick.

Sydney Sling

An exotic cocktail that brings to mind the sun, and the razzamatazz of that great Australian city, Sydney.

1¾oz/5cl	white rum
⅔oz/2cl	fresh lemon juice
⅔oz/2cl	cherry brandy
2⅓oz/7cl	guava juice
2⅓oz/7cl	pineapple juice
few dashes	peach schnapps
half	banana

Place all ingredients into the blender and blend for a few moments to let the banana blend. Then add two scoops of crushed ice and blend until smooth. Pour into a goblet. Garnish with a Cape Gooseberry. Serve with a straw.

Tidal Wave

Two of these and you may well be swept off your feet with a rush of spicy flavors.

1oz/3cl	spiced rum
2oz/6cl	Grand Marnier
1oz/3cl	fresh lemon juice
	bitter lemon

Pour all ingredients, except the bitter lemon, into a shaker with ice. Shake. Strain into a highball filled with ice. Top up with bitter lemon. Garnish with a wedge of lemon.

Tropical Cachaça

The fresh flavors of mango and pineapple fill each mouthful with exotic flavors.

1oz/3cl	cachaça
1oz/3cl	mango juice
1oz/3cl	pineapple juice
dash	coffee liqueur

Pour the first three ingredients into a shaker filled with ice. Shake. Strain into a cocktail glass. Gently float the coffee liqueur on top of the drink.

Tangy Cachaça

The fresh, lip-smacking taste of fresh passion fruit is superb with the cachaça.

2oz/6cl	cachaça
pulp 1	passion fruit

Pour ingredients into a shaker with ice. Shake. Strain into an old-fashioned glass filled with crushed ice.

Tropical Cream

A fruity combination with a hint of nuttiness present in the creamy finish.

1oz/3cl	white rum
⅔oz/2cl	melon liqueur
⅓oz/1cl	hazelnut liqueur
⅓oz/1cl	peach schnapps
⅓oz/1cl	coconut rum
½oz/1.5cl	fresh orange juice
½oz/1.5cl	heavy (double) cream

Pour all ingredients into a shaker with ice. Shake. Strain into a cocktail glass.

Tropical Delight

This cocktail combines two popular flavors—banana and coconut—with rum.

1oz/3cl	gold rum
1	banana, peeled
1oz/3cl	coconut cream
3oz/9cl	pineapple juice
3oz/9cl	fresh orange juice
2 scoops	vanilla ice cream

Place all ingredients into a blender with crushed ice. Blend until smooth. Pour into a highball. Serve with a straw. Garnish with a slice of banana.

Tropical Spice

Here is an exotic combination of spicy rum and fruit juices. One sip of this and you'll find yourself in limbo land.

1⅓oz / 4cl	spiced rum
⅔oz / 2cl	triple sec/Cointreau
1⅓oz / 4cl	fresh orange juice
1⅓oz / 4cl	papaya juice
⅔oz / 2cl	fresh lime juice

Place all ingredients into a shaker with ice. Shake. Strain into a highball filled with ice. Garnish with a slice of orange, a slice of lime, and a cherry in the middle on a cocktail stick across the glass. Serve with a straw.

Turquoise Blue

This cocktail is the color of an ocean not far away from the memory after a vacation.

1oz / 3cl	white rum
⅓oz / 1cl	triple sec/Cointreau
⅓oz / 1cl	blue curaçao
1oz / 3cl	fresh lime juice
⅓oz / 1cl	gomme syrup
2oz / 6cl	pineapple juice

Pour all ingredients into a shaker with ice. Shake. Strain into a highball filled with ice. Garnish with a slice of star fruit.

West Indian Colada

The addition of papaya adds a taste of the exotic to this creamy, rum-based cocktail. It's a typical colada-style cocktail from the Caribbean.

1⅔oz / 5cl	white rum
⅔oz / 2cl	coconut rum
2oz / 6cl	pineapple juice
half	fresh papaya
⅔oz / 2cl	coconut cream
1oz / 3cl	heavy (double) cream

Peel and dice the papaya and put it in the blender. Add the other ingredients and a scoop of crushed ice. Blend until smooth. Pour into a colada glass. Garnish with a wedge of pineapple.

Yellow Bird

A classic cocktail that has caught the imagination of generations of cocktail drinkers. It's popular in the Caribbean islands at any time of day.

1oz / 3cl	white rum
½oz / 1.5cl	Cointreau
½oz / 1.5cl	Galliano
½oz / 1.5cl	fresh lime juice

Pour all ingredients into a shaker with ice. Shake. Strain into a cocktail glass. Garnish with a spiral of lime on the rim and a slice of orange in the drink.

Zombie

There is a record of this recipe dating back to 1935. One story from the 1930s involves Don Beach of the Beachcomber bar, who created the drink to cure a guest's hangover. When asked if he liked the drink, he claimed it had turned him into a zombie.

The second involves a Christopher Clark, who had returned to America with the recipe. The third report claims it was served at the 1939 World's Fair in New York.

½oz / 1.5cl	white rum
½oz / 1.5cl	golden rum
½oz / 1.5cl	dark rum
⅓oz / 1cl	cherry brandy
⅓oz / 1cl	apricot brandy
1¾oz / 5cl	pineapple juice
1oz / 3cl	fresh orange juice
⅓oz / 1cl	fresh lime juice
dash	Orgeat (almond syrup)
⅓oz / 1cl	151 proof Demerara rum

Pour all ingredients, except Demerara rum, into a shaker with ice. Shake. Strain into a highball filled with crushed ice. Float the Demerara on top. Garnish with a slice of orange, a slice of lime, and a sprig of mint. Serve with a straw and a stirrer.

TEQUILA

⸎

A Mexican spirit with magical taste properties, tequila is distilled from the fermented juice of the blue agave, a succulent plant found all over the country. Tequila is a specific mezcal (this is the drink with the worm in it, not tequila), and by law is produced in designated regions, mostly in Jalisco, home of the magnificent mariachi, the musicians with those elegant, wide-brimmed hats.

Popular tequila cocktails include the magnificent Margarita, which came to the world's attention in the 1950s; Brave Bull, La Bomba, and Tequila Mockingbird. All of those names conjure up an exotic lifestyle and tequila delivers this fantasy brilliantly! And who can forget those alcoholic tequila slammers, guaranteed to bring on a night of indulgent fun.

In 1795, Don Jose Maria Guadalupe Cuervo, a Spaniard, set up a distillery in Tequila, Mexico, that used cultivated, as opposed to wild, agave to produce the spirit. Hence tequila was born.

Mature agaves are harvested all year round, and its piña (the heart of the plant) is taken to the distillery and cooked, which converts the high starch levels into fermentable sugars. These are extracted from the cooled piña by crushing the pulp and stringy fibers and washing them with cold water to separate the sugars from the pulp. Fermentation takes place in large stainless steel vats, and most distillers remain secretive about the strain of yeast they introduce at this stage. Tequila is double-distilled in pot stills, and it is the strength to which it is distilled that creates the character of the spirit.

rude cosmopolitan (left), page 116, and **blackberry margarita**, page 109

AGEING

The strength, type of barrel, and the length of the ageing period each have an effect on the resulting tequila. Regulations state that only oak barrels (usually old bourbon barrels) can be used, and the alcohol by volume (abv) must remain between 30 to 55 percent and is usually 40 percent (80 proof). Tequila, like cognac, whiskey, and other high-end spirits, gains color, aroma, and flavor from ageing in wood for between one and three years.

TYPES OF TEQUILA

There are two basic types of tequila: 100 percent agave and mixed tequila (mixto). Look at a label; if it does not say "100 percent agave," then it is sure to be mixto. The 100 percent agave is distilled entirely from fermented juice from the plant. Mixto is distilled from a combination of agave juice and a variety of other sugars.

BLANCO OR PLATA (WHITE OR SILVER): The original style, it is clear and usually bottled immediately after distillation or left for no more than 60 days in the tank. It can be 100 percent agave or mixto. Used mainly for mixing with juices or liqueurs.

REPOSADO (RESTED): Is aged for between two and 11 months in tanks or an oak barrel. Can be 100 percent agave or mixto.

AÑEJO (AGED): Produced from 100 percent agave and left for a minimum of one year in the wooden barrel. The finest stay for up to four years. Can be 100 percent agave or mixto.

JOVEN ABOCADO (OFTEN CALLED GOLD): This style has the characteristics of an aged tequila, but the golden color is merely an additive such as caramel. This type is nearly always mixto.

> Remember to make the best cocktails you must always use the best ingredients, so look for the words "100 percent agave tequila" on the label.

Always chill a cocktail glass in the freezer before use.

Acapulco

A strong and fruity party time cocktail to match the pulse of the fascinating Mexican city.

1oz/3cl	gold tequila
1oz/3cl	gold rum
1⅔oz/5cl	fresh grapefruit juice
3⅓oz/10cl	pineapple juice

Pour all ingredients into a shaker with ice. Shake. Strain into a highball filled with ice. Garnish with a wedge of pineapple.

Alba Rosso

A refreshing short drink that smacks of citrus flavors and a hint of mint.

2oz/6cl	tequila
2oz/6cl	cranberry juice
dash	gomme syrup
3	lime wedges, diced
6 sprigs	fresh mint

Muddle the mint, lime wedges, and the gomme syrup in a shaker. Add the tequila, cranberry juice, and ice. Shake. Strain into an old-fashioned glass filled with crushed ice. Garnish with a sprig of mint. Serve with a straw.

Bloody Maria

A classic cocktail, a close relative of the Bloody Mary, and just as restorative to the system.

2oz/6cl	silver tequila
5oz/15cl	tomato juice
⅓oz/1cl	fresh lemon juice
1 pinch	celery salt
1 pinch	black pepper
4 dashes	Tabasco sauce
4 dashes	Worcestershire sauce

Pour all ingredients into a shaker with ice. Shake. Strain into a highball filled with ice. Garnish with a celery stick and a wedge of lime.

Brave Bull

A classic drink with a kick from the tequila disguised by the softness of the Kahlua.

1⅓oz/4cl	silver tequila
⅔oz/2cl	Kahlua

Pour all ingredients into an old-fashioned glass filled with ice. Stir.

Cherry Picker

This has a sour apple flavor with a cherry finish and strength from the tequila.

1oz/3cl	gold tequila
1oz/3cl	cherry brandy
⅓oz/1cl	fresh lime juice
1oz/3cl	clear apple juice

Pour all ingredients into a shaker with ice. Shake. Strain into a cocktail glass. Garnish with a twist of lime.

Clam Digger

You can make this drink to suit your palate by adding more spice or making it with less. It depends on how you, or your guests, like it.

1²⁄₃oz / 5cl	silver tequila
3oz / 9cl	tomato juice
3oz / 9cl	clam juice
2 teaspoons	horseradish
dash	Tabasco sauce
dash	Worcestershire sauce
½oz / 1.5cl	fresh lime juice

Pour all ingredients into a shaker with ice. Shake. Strain into a highball filled with ice. Garnish with a wedge of lime.

Coconut Tequila

A delicious combination of creamy coconut and tangy fruits combined with a hit of spirit.

1²⁄₃oz / 5cl	tequila
²⁄₃oz / 2cl	maraschino liqueur
½oz / 1.5cl	coconut cream
½oz / 1.5cl	fresh lemon juice

Pour all ingredients into a shaker with ice. Shake. Strain into a cocktail glass. Garnish with a slice of pineapple and a slice of kiwifruit.

tequila sunrise (left) and el diablo

Cool Breeze

A Latin-inspired cocktail ideal for sipping on a summer's afternoon.

1oz / 3cl	melon liqueur
1oz / 3cl	gold tequila
1oz / 3cl	cranberry juice

Pour all ingredients into a shaker with ice. Shake. Strain into a cocktail glass. Garnish with a wedge of lime.

Dorado

A touch of honey will bring out the sweetness in you and balance the citrus ingredient.

1²⁄₃oz / 5cl	tequila
²⁄₃oz / 2cl	fresh lemon juice
2 teaspoons	honey

Pour all ingredients into a shaker with ice. Shake well to combine. Strain into a cocktail glass.

El Diablo

Translated it means "the devil." The drink doesn't originate in Mexico, but in California, during the 1940s.

1¹⁄₃oz / 4cl	silver tequila
²⁄₃oz / 2cl	crème de cassis (black-currant liqueur)
²⁄₃oz / 2cl	fresh lime juice
	ginger ale

Pour the lime juice into a highball half-filled with crushed ice. Add the tequila and crème de cassis. Top up with ginger ale. Stir. Garnish with a wedge of lime dropped in the drink. Serve with a straw.

Fine Freddie

The herbal taste in the Galliano provides a subtle flavor in this combination.

1⅓oz/4cl	gold tequila
2⅓oz/7cl	fresh orange juice
dash	Galliano

Pour all ingredients, except Galliano, into a shaker with ice. Shake. Strain into a highball filled with ice. Float the Galliano on top.

Jalisco Cocktail

An aperitif to stimulate the palate—classic flavors with a modern interpretation.

1½oz/4.5cl	aged tequila
1oz/3cl	Carpano Antica Formula (Italian vermouth)
½oz/1.5cl	Cointreau
3 dashes	homemade lime & cardamom bitters

Stir all ingredients in a mixing glass with ice. Strain into a chilled goblet glass. Garnish with a lemon zest.

Japanese Slipper

Sipped through the sugary rim, these flavors will be a treat for your palate!

1⅔oz/5cl	gold tequila
1oz/3cl	melon liqueur
⅔oz/2cl	fresh lime juice
dash	gomme syrup

Rub a wedge of lime around the rim of a cocktail glass. Dip it into a saucer of superfine (caster) sugar.

Pour all ingredients into a shaker with ice. Shake. Strain into the glass.

Juliet

A sweet cocktail with an intriguing color and the taste of pineapple.

1oz/3cl	gold tequila
⅔oz/2cl	Pisang Ambon
1oz/3cl	pineapple juice
dash	grenadine

Pour all ingredients into a shaker with ice. Shake. Strain into a cocktail glass.

La Bomba

A drink that, when you drink it, is almost as exciting as doing the dance.

1⅓oz/4cl	gold tequila
⅔oz/2cl	Cointreau
⅔oz/2cl	pineapple juice
⅔oz/2cl	fresh orange juice
2 dashes	grenadine

Rub the rim of a cocktail glass with a wedge of orange. Dip it into a saucer of superfine (caster) sugar.

Pour all ingredients into a shaker with ice. Shake. Strain into the glass. Add the grenadine. Garnish with a wedge of lime.

Marco Polo

I don't know where the name comes from—but I think Marco Polo would be happy with it!

1½oz/4.5cl	aged tequila
½oz/1.5cl	malt whiskey
½ oz/1.5cl	lime juice
2 slices	ginger
1 teaspoon	honey

Muddle the ginger in a Boston shaker. Add remaining ingredients and ice. Shake sharply. Double strain into an old-fashioned glass filled with ice cubes. Garnish with a wedge of lime.

La Conga

A slightly bitter drink, full of fruity flavor, to drink at any time of the year.

1⅔oz/5cl	silver tequila
2 teaspoons	pineapple juice
2 dashes	Angostura bitters
	club soda

Pour all ingredients, except soda, into an old-fashioned glass filled with ice. Stir. Top up with soda. Stir. Garnish with a slice of lemon.

Blackberry Margarita

What better fruit for a delicious, richly colored cocktail!

1⅔oz/5cl	silver tequila
½oz/1.5cl	blackberry liqueur
½oz/1.5cl	fresh lime juice
handful	fresh backberries

Pour all ingredients into a blender with crushed ice. Blend. Pour into a Margarita glass. Garnish with two blackberries and a sprig of mint on a cocktail stick set across the glass. Serve with a straw.

Margarita

The Margarita was, without a doubt, created after the mid-1930s. The locations of its discovery range from Mexico to California, and even New Mexico or Texas. One of the legends involves a Mrs. Margaret Sames, of Texas. In December 1948, she and her husband were entertaining friends at their villa in Acapulco. Among the guests were Nicky Hilton, of the Hilton hotel chain, and Shelton A. McHenry, owner of the Tail o' the Cock restaurant in Los Angeles. Mrs. Sames took her favorite liqueur, Cointreau, added tequila and lime juice, and added a little salt on the rim.

To celebrate the success of this drink over the period of the house party, her husband bought two glasses with the name "Margarita" etched on them— it being the Spanish equivalent of Margaret.

To others, however, the day that a young starlet named Marjorie King walked into the Rancho La Gloria restaurant, owned by Carlos "Danny" Herrera and located near Tijuana, Mexico, is the true "M" day. Herrera mixed and named this cocktail especially for her because she was allergic to every spirit but tequila. Others contenders to the claim include one Doña Bertha, proprietor of Bertita's Bar in Tasca; Pancho Morales of Tommy's Place in Juarez; and Daniel Negrete, of the Garci Crespo Hotel, in Puebla.

Songwriter Jimmy Buffet's late 1970s melody, "Margaritaville," created a demand for the cocktail throughout America and the rest of the world. Hence, a cult cocktail was born.

1oz/3cl	silver tequila
1oz/3cl	fresh lime juice
⅔oz/2cl	Cointreau

Rub a wedge of lime around the rim of a Margarita glass. Dip it into a saucer of fine salt.

Pour all ingredients into a shaker with ice. Shake. Strain into the glass. Garnish with a wedge of lime.

Cactus Pear Margarita

The delicate flavor of cactus pear is a pleasant addition to the original Margarita recipe.

1⅓oz/4cl	silver tequila
⅔oz/2cl	Cointreau
⅓oz/1cl	fresh lime juice
1	ripe cactus pear, peeled and diced

Rub a wedge of lime around the rim of a Margarita glass. Dip it into a saucer of superfine (caster) sugar.

Muddle the pear pieces in the shaker, without ice. Add a scoop of ice and the other ingredients. Shake. Strain into the glass. Mash the pulp left in the strainer to add the last drops of flavor. Garnish with a wedge of lime.

Fresh Fruit Margarita

This is the basic recipe for any fresh fruit Margarita. Always use quality fresh, soft fruit.

1 piece	fruit of your choice, diced
2oz/6cl	gold tequila
1oz/3cl	Cointreau
1oz/3cl	fresh lime juice

Rub a wedge of lime around the rim of a Margarita glass. Dip it into a saucer of superfine (caster) sugar.

Muddle the chopped fruit and other ingredients in the shaker. Add a scoop of ice. Shake. Strain into the glass. Garnish with a wedge of lime.

Golden Margarita

A completely different recipe using gold tequila as the base spirit.

1⅔oz/5cl	gold tequila
1oz/3cl	Grand Marnier
⅔oz/2cl	fresh lime juice

Rub a wedge of lime around the rim of a Margarita glass. Dip it into a saucer of fine salt.

Pour all ingredients into a shaker with ice. Shake. Strain into the glass. Garnish with a wedge of lime.

Hibiscus Margarita

Gold tequila and the aromatic flavor of hibiscus tea turn the traditional margarita on its head.

1⅓oz/4cl	gold tequila
½oz/1.5cl	Cointreau
½oz/1.5cl	fresh lime juice
1oz/3cl	strong, sweetened hibiscus tea, cooled

Rub a wedge of lime around the rim of a Margarita glass Dip it into a saucer of fine salt.

Pour all ingredients into a shaker with ice. Shake. Strain into the glass. Garnish with a whole slice of lime.

Peach Margarita

Fresh peach juice and the aroma of peach schanpps combine to create a full-flavored temptation.

1⅓oz/4cl	silver tequila
½oz/1.5cl	Cointreau
½oz/1.5cl	peach schnapps
⅓oz/1cl	fresh lime juice
1	peach, peeled and diced

Put the diced peach into the blender. Blend. Add a scoop of crushed ice. Blend again. Pour into a Margarita glass. Garnish with a wedge of peach. Serve with a straw.

Melon Margarita

Melon juice gives this version a clear and pale yellow color.

1⅓oz/4cl	tequila
½oz/1.5cl	Cointreau
½oz /1.5cl	melon liqueur
⅓oz/1cl	fresh lime juice
few slices	yellow melon, diced

Put all ingredients into a blender. Blend. Add a scoop of crushed ice. Blend again. Pour into a Margarita glass. Garnish with several small and different colored balls of melon on a cocktail stick. Serve with a straw.

Pomegranate Margarita

Pomegranate purée is a lovely, deep shade of red. Try to make your own fresh pomegranate purée.

1⅔oz/5cl	silver tequila
½oz/1.5cl	Cointreau
⅔oz/2cl	pomegranate purée
1oz/3cl	fresh lime juice

Rub a wedge of lime around the rim of a Margarita glass. Dip it into a saucer of fine salt.
Pour all ingredients into a shaker with ice. Shake. Strain into the glass.

Matador

The pineapple juice brings a touch of the Caribbean to this Mexican cocktail.

2oz/6cl	gold tequila
⅔oz/2cl	triple sec/Cointreau
⅔oz/2cl	fresh lime juice
5oz/15cl	pineapple juice

Pour all ingredients into a shaker with ice. Shake. Strain into a highball filled with ice. Garnish with a wedge of lime.

FROZEN MARGARITAS

A frozen version is made in a blender using fresh fruit, a liqueur the flavor of the fruit, and crushed ice. These are popular and require just as much attention during their preparation as does a classic Margarita.

**japanese slipper (left) and
tequila mockingbird**

Mexican Dream

A great drink to recall lazy days spent down South. Take a siesta after a few of these.

⅔oz / 2cl	silver tequila
⅔oz / 2cl	brandy
⅔oz / 2cl	fresh lemon juice
dash	grenadine

Pour all ingredients into a shaker with ice. Shake. Strain into a cocktail glass. Garnish with a twist of lemon.

Mexican Madras

This is very refreshing version of the classic Madras (which is made with vodka).

1oz / 3cl	gold tequila
3oz / 6cl	cranberry juice
½oz / 1.5cl	fresh orange juice
dash	fresh lime juice

Pour all ingredients into a shaker with ice. Shake. Strain into an old-fashioned glass filled with ice. Garnish with a slice of orange.

Mexican Mule

A great refreshing drink with a spicy finish from the ginger ale. Watch out for the kick!

1⅔oz / 5cl	gold tequila
1oz / 3cl	fresh lime juice
⅓oz / 1cl	gomme syrup
	ginger ale

Pour all ingredients into a shaker with ice. Shake. Strain into a highball filled with ice. Top up with ginger ale.

Mexican Runner

This cocktail has nothing to do with that cartoon character of my youth, Speedy Gonzales!

1oz / 3cl	gold tequila
1oz / 3cl	rum
⅔oz / 2cl	banana syrup
⅔oz / 2cl	blackberry syrup
1oz / 3cl	fresh lime juice
5	fresh strawberries

Pour all ingredients into a blender with crushed ice. Blend. Pour into a colada glass. Garnish with a strawberry.

Mexican Sal

I like the idea of the vanilla and the hint of bitterness that comes from the Campari.

2oz / 6cl	aged tequila
1oz / 3cl	Campari

Pour all ingredients into a mixing glass with ice. Stir. Strain into a cocktail glass. Garnish with a twist of lime.

Mexican Sloe Screw

Sloe gin has a sweet plum taste and is a good spirit to mix with tequila.

1²⁄₃oz / 5cl	silver tequila
½oz / 1.5cl	sloe gin
3oz / 9cl	fresh orange juice

Pour the tequila and orange juice into a highball filled with ice. Stir. Float the sloe gin on top. Serve with a stirrer.

Midsummer Night's Dream

Silver tequila to sip by the light of the moon as you dream the night away.

1²⁄₃oz / 5cl	silver tequila
½oz / 1.5cl	pineapple juice
½oz / 1.5cl	fresh lime juice
	dash grenadine

Pour all ingredients into a shaker with ice. Shake. Strain into a cocktail glass.

Multiple Orgasm

Oh, the joy of this cocktail followed by the joy of great sex. In your dreams!

1oz / 3cl	gold tequila
²⁄₃oz / 2cl	amaretto
²⁄₃oz / 2cl	coffee liqueur
²⁄₃oz / 2cl	Irish cream liqueur
1oz / 3cl	heavy (double) cream
2oz / 6cl	milk

Pour all ingredients, except tequila, into a shaker with ice. Shake. Strain into a highball filled with ice. Float the tequila on top.

Olé

An unusual pale blue color, this Mexican cocktail has a smooth banana flavor, too.

1oz / 3cl	silver tequila
1oz / 3cl	crème de bananes (banana liqueur)
2 dashes	blue curaçao

Pour all ingredients into a mixing glass with ice. Stir. Strain into an old-fashioned glass with ice. Add a twist of lemon.

Pancho Villa

An unusual tequila drink because it is created for sipping after dinner.

2oz / 6cl	tequila
½oz / 1.5cl	Cointreau
½oz / 1.5cl	Kahlua

Pour all ingredients into a shaker with ice. Shake. Strain into a cocktail glass.

Pink Caddy

This has a sharp, slightly bitter flavor balanced by the sweetness of Grand Marnier.

1oz / 3cl	gold tequila
²⁄₃oz / 2cl	Grand Marnier
1oz / 3cl	cranberry juice
²⁄₃oz / 2cl	fresh lime juice

Pour all ingredients into a shaker with ice. Shake. Strain into a cocktail glass.

Prado

A lip-smacking combination of sweet and sour flavors.

1oz/3cl	silver tequila
2 teaspoons	maraschino liqueur
⅔oz/2cl	fresh lime juice
2 dashes	grenadine
1 teaspoon	egg white powder

Pour all ingredients into a shaker with ice. Shake. Strain into an old-fashioned glass filled with ice. Garnish with a maraschino cherry and a wedge of lime.

Ridley

Golden in color from the Galliano, this has a hint of herbal flavor.

1oz/3cl	silver tequila
1oz/3cl	gin
dash	Galliano

Pour all ingredients into an old-fashioned glass filled with crushed ice. Stir. Serve with a stirrer.

Rude Cosmopolitan

A tequila-based Cosmopolitan (usually made with vodka). This is a great version.

1⅔oz/5cl	gold tequila
½oz/1.5cl	triple sec/Cointreau
1oz/3cl	cranberry juice
½oz/1.5cl	fresh lime juice

Pour all ingredients into a shaker with ice. Shake. Strain into a cocktail glass. Garnish with a twist of orange.

Ruttle & Hum

Unique combinations in this drink: the pepper works well with the tequila, giving it a long, lingering finish.

1½oz/4.5cl	silver tequila
½oz/1.5cl	Passoa liqueur
⅓oz/1cl	Van der Hum
⅓oz/1cl	honey syrup
½oz/1.5cl	lime juice
1oz/3cl	guava juice
4–5	little pieces of yellow pepper

Muddle the pepper in the bottom of a shaker. Add all remaining ingredients and ice. Shake well. Double strain into an old-fashioned filled with crushed ice. Garnish with two thin strips of yellow pepper and a sprig of mint.

Saltecca

This is the type of drink I like! It has a dry, salty finish from the capers.

2oz/6cl	gold tequila
½oz/1.5cl	dry sherry
1 teaspoon	juice of capers

Pour all ingredients into a mixing glass with ice. Stir. Strain into a cocktail glass.

Short Fuse

A long and refreshing drink with a sweet apricot flavor. Watch out for the explosions!

2oz/6cl	gold tequila
⅔oz/2cl	apricot brandy
2 teaspoons	juice maraschino cherries
1oz/3cl	fresh lime juice
3oz/9cl	fresh grapefruit juice

Pour all ingredients into a shaker with ice. Shake. Strain into a highball with ice. Garnish with a wedge of lime.

Silk Stockings

One that brings back memories of the past, with a creamy chocolate and cinnamon flavor.

1⅔oz/5cl	silver tequila
⅔oz/2cl	white crème de cacao
1oz/3cl	heavy (double) cream
dash	grenadine

Rub a wedge of lime around the rim. Dip it into a saucer full of grated cinnamon.

Pour all ingredients into a shaker with ice. Shake. Strain into a cocktail glass.

Sierra Gringo

A heady mix of tequila and bourbon brings a warmth to the texture of the amazing passion fruit juice.

1oz/3cl	silver tequila
½oz/1.5cl	bourbon
½oz/1.5cl	fresh lime juice
2oz/6cl	passion fruit juice

Pour all ingredients into a shaker with ice. Shake. Strain into an old-fashioned glass filled with ice. Garnish with a wedge of lime and a maraschino cherry.

Slow-Hand Lover

A heady mix of tequila, the depth of the dark rum, the creamy texture of the banana (gives the energy), and the rich and smooth taste of coconut cream.

1oz/3cl	silver tequila
⅔oz/2cl	dark rum
⅓oz/1cl	Tia Maria
⅔oz/2cl	coconut cream
half	fresh banana
2oz/6cl	pineapple juice

Pour all ingredients, except dark rum, into a blender with a scoop of crushed ice. Blend. Pour into a colada glass. Float the dark rum on top. Garnish with a Cape Gooseberry. Serve with a straw.

Sombrero

A classic to keep under your hat—unless you want to share the creamy flavor!

1oz/3cl	golden tequila
1oz/3cl	brown crème de cacao
1oz/3cl	heavy (double) cream

Pour all ingredients into a shaker with ice. Shake. Strain into a cocktail glass. Garnish with a sprinkling of grated nutmeg.

Tequila Breeze

The addition of soda water makes this a long and refreshing cocktail.

2oz/6cl	gold tequila
3oz/9cl	fresh grapefruit juice
	club soda

Pour all ingredients, except soda, into a highball with ice. Top up with soda. Stir. Garnish with a slice of grapefruit.

Tequila Canyon

The three juices combine to make a superbly flavored thirst quencher.

2oz/6cl	tequila
dash	triple sec/Cointreau
4oz/12cl	cranberry juice
1/3oz/1cl	pineapple juice
1/3oz/1cl	fresh orange juice

Pour the first three ingredients into a highball filled with ice. Stir. Add the pineapple and orange juices. Garnish with a slice of lime. Serve with a stirrer.

Tequila Manhattan

This is entirely different from the classic Manhattan. There's no bitters—and it has more of a sweet-and-sour flavor.

2oz/6cl	silver tequila
1oz/3cl	sweet vermouth
dash	fresh lime juice

Pour all ingredients into a shaker with ice. Shake. Strain into an old-fashioned glass filled with ice. Garnish with a maraschino cherry and a slice of orange.

Tequila-tini

Way, way back, there might be some reference to a Martini; maybe through the vermouth!

2oz/6cl	silver tequila
1/2oz/1.5cl	dry vermouth
dash	Angostura bitters

Pour all ingredients into a mixing glass with ice. Stir. Strain into a cocktail glass.

Tequila Mockingbird

A delicious drink that combines the freshness of crème de menthe and the sharpness of lime.

1 1/3oz/4cl	silver tequila
2/3oz/2cl	green crème de menthe
2/3oz/2cl	fresh lime juice

Pour all ingredients into an old-fashioned glass filled with crushed ice. Stir. Garnish with a sprig of mint and a wedge of lime. Serve with a straw.

Tequila Sunrise

A Mexican concoction created in the late 1920s, this colorful long drink has maintained a certain chic. It was a popular drink in the Prohibition era because it looked just like orange juice!

In those days, sugar was possibly added to sweeten the canned orange juice available then.

The trick for a successful two-tone drink is to add the grenadine slowly so it settles on the bottom of the glass, creating the sunrise effect.

1²⁄₃oz/5cl	tequila
5oz/15cl	fresh orange juice
2 dashes	grenadine

Pour the tequila and orange juice into the highball filled with ice. Stir. Add the grenadine slowly and watch it trickle down through the drink. Stir just before drinking to create a fabulous sunrise effect. Garnish with a slice of orange in a spiral. Serve with a straw and a stirrer.

Tequila Sour

Definitely a lip-smacking flavor in this classic sour recipe.

2oz/6cl	silver tequila
¹⁄₃oz/1cl	fresh lemon juice
1 teaspoon	superfine (caster) sugar

Pour all ingredients into a shaker with ice. Shake. Strain into a cocktail glass.

Tequila Sunset

A real sweet and sour taste, with the honey providing a smooth finish.

2oz/6cl	silver tequila
1oz/3cl	fresh lemon juice
1 teaspoon	clear honey

Pour all ingredients into a shaker with ice. Shake. Strain into a cocktail glass. Garnish with a spiral of lemon.

Texas Tea

If they "take tea" in Texas, as the English do, then this is probably what they sip!

¹⁄₂oz/1.5cl	silver tequila
¹⁄₂oz/1.5cl	white rum
¹⁄₂oz/1.5cl	gin
¹⁄₂oz/1.5cl	vodka
1oz/3cl	fresh lime juice
dash	gomme syrup
	cola

Pour all ingredients, except cola, into a shaker with ice. Shake. Strain into a highball filled with ice. Top up with cola. Stir. Garnish with a wedge of lime.

Thai Sunrise

There's a lot of fresh mango flavor in this combination of spirits and fruit.

1⅓oz/4cl	silver tequila
⅔oz/2cl	triple sec/Cointreau
⅔oz/2cl	fresh lime juice
half	mango, diced
dash	grenadine

Pour all ingredients into a blender. Blend. Add crushed ice. Blend again. Pour into a goblet.

Tijuana Mule

Named after the mules in Tijuana, Mexico, where their owners painted black stripes on them to make them look like zebras!

1½oz/4.5cl	aged tequila
⅔oz/2cl	agave syrup
2 chunks	pineapple
2 slices	fresh ginger
½oz/1.5cl	lime juice

Muddle pineapple and ginger in the bottom of a shaker. Add remaining ingredients with ice. Shake and double strain into an old-fashioned glass filled with ice. Garnish with a pineapple wedge and lime wedge.

Tijuana Taxi

A tropical flavor, with a hint of blue color, makes this an appealing cocktail.

1oz/3cl	gold tequila
½oz/1.5cl	blue curaçao
½oz/1.5cl	tropical-fruit schnapps
	club soda

Pour the tequila, curaçao, and schnapps into a highball filled with ice. Top up with soda.

Tomahawk

A colorful fruit cocktail that is not as dangerous as its namesake!

1oz/3cl	tequila
1oz/3cl	triple sec/Cointreau
2oz/6cl	cranberry juice
2oz/6cl	pineapple juice

Pour all ingredients into a shaker with ice. Shake. Strain into a highball filled with ice.

Viva La Donna!

Several of these will make you fall in love with every woman you see!

2oz/6cl	silver tequila
2oz/6cl	passion fruit juice
2oz/6cl	fresh orange juice
⅔oz/2cl	fresh lime juice

Pour all ingredients into a shaker with ice. Shake. Strain into a highball filled with ice. Garnish with a slice of star fruit.

Vampiro

This is the national drink of Mexico. It's a strange combination of orange and tomato juice, all the spices, the sweetness of the honey, and the surprise of onion.

1²⁄₃oz/5cl	silver tequila
2¹⁄₃oz/7cl	tomato juice
1oz/3cl	fresh orange juice
1 teaspoon	clear honey
¹⁄₃oz/1cl	fresh lime juice
half slice	onion, finely chopped
few slices	fresh red hot chili
few drops	Worcestershire sauce
	salt

Pour all ingredients, starting with the juices and then the tequila, into a shaker with ice. Shake well to release the flavor of the chili. Strain into a highball filled with ice. Garnish with a wedge of lime on the rim of the glass and a chili (green or red) for anyone devilish enough to dare to take a bite of it!

Voodoo Breeze

This is magical witchcraft with a fresh sidekick.

1¹⁄₃oz/4cl	silver tequila
²⁄₃oz/2cl	Midori (melon liqueur)
3oz/9cl	fresh apple juice
¹⁄₂oz/1.5cl	fresh lime juice
1	fresh kiwi fruit

Scoop out the pulp of a ripe kiwi and place in the shaker. Add remaining ingredients and fill with ice. Shake and strain over crushed ice into a highball glass, allowing the seeds of the kiwi to pass through into the drink. Garnish with two half slices of kiwi and a mint tip.

Watermelon and Basil Smash

A combination of refreshing and spicy flavors, and a hint of basil, makes this unique.

1²⁄₃oz/5cl	silver tequila
²⁄₃oz/2cl	limoncello
dash	basil syrup
¹⁄₄ slice	watermelon
	ginger beer

Pour all ingredients, except ginger beer, into a shaker with ice. Shake. Strain into a highball filled with ice. Top up with ginger beer.

White Bull

A pale and creamy version of the classic Brave Bull recipe. It's for those who like coffee.

1oz/3cl	tequila
1oz/3cl	coffee liqueur
²⁄₃oz/2cl	heavy (double) cream
²⁄₃oz/2cl	milk

Pour all ingredients into a shaker with ice. Shake. Strain into a cocktail glass.

VODKA

─── ⚭ ───

Vodka is a pure spirit, as pure as the driven snow in Russia or Poland, where most of the best vodkas are manufactured. Vodka is colorless, tasteless, and odorless.

Its mixability has made it everybody's favorite party spirit—in fact, vodka and white rum are the most popular base spirits in the world today.

Of course, the smooth and suave James Bond character in Ian Fleming's novels gave rise to the habit of taking Vodka Martinis, when situations were a little tense, shaken not stirred. Yet, we must also thank vodka for a Bloody Mary (with or without the celery), a Harvey Wallbanger, and a Screwdriver.

The name "vodka" is the diminutive of the Russian word for water, *voda*. Vodka is a good neutral spirit to use as a base for cocktails, mixing well with fruit juices and other spirits and liqueurs.

The Russian claim that vodka was first distilled in that country in the 14th century is still disputed. The Scandinavians and the Poles can also claim that vodka was made as early, or even earlier. Both use rye grain as a preferred ingredient. Vodka made in America is pure grain neutral spirit distilled from fermented corn, rye, or wheat. It is distilled in a continuous still, which produces vodka continuously, not in batches. The charcoal filtration stage ensures the resultant vodka is clear and clean-tasting.

blueberry martini (left), page 129, and **green dinosaur**, page 136

Vodka is made all over the world—in Russia, Poland, Scandinavia, Holland, France, America, and England, to name just a few countries—and when you're looking to buy a bottle, you'll not easily know how it is made. Always check the label for its proof. The higher the proof, the less flavor it will have. Here are examples of vodkas you might have already tasted: Absolut is 80 proof, Finlandia is 95 proof, and Smirnoff has both 80 and 100 proof brands.

Many new vodkas are aiming at the connoisseur market in the same way that armagnac, cognac, and whiskey have done for decades. Some are distilled up to three times, and then a trace of a separately distilled, lower-strength spirit may be added for character. These types are best drunk in a shot glass, downed in one amazing mouthful!

Flavored vodkas are also creating an interest. Lemon, lime, black currant, cherry, pineapple, orange, peach, mint, and pepper are just some of the flavors offered. These types are usually served straight from the freezer (the only place to keep vodka) as an aperitif, or mixed with tonic water.

Another recent trend is to infuse vodka with a herb such as lemongrass. The herb is placed in the vodka bottle, the cap replaced, and the bottle left for a few days. The herb is then taken out and discarded, then the bottle placed in the freezer to chill.

These flavored vodkas have also contributed to the amazing variety of "vodkatinis" being created by modern mixologists. You'll find various recipes in this section, listed alphabetically.

Always chill a cocktail glass in the freezer before use.

57 T-Bird

The drink to go with the convertible when the top's down and the sun's shining.

1oz/3cl	vodka
⅔oz/2cl	amaretto
⅔oz/2cl	melon liqueur
⅔oz/2cl	peach schnapps
1⅔oz/5cl	fresh orange juice

Pour all ingredients into a shaker with ice. Shake. Strain into an old-fashioned glass filled with ice. Garnish with two raspberries and a slice of orange on a cocktail stick.

1824 A A

Voted the best Angostura bitters cocktail in the world in 2001 at a competition held in Trinidad. Dedicated to Dr. J. G. B. Siegert, creator of the bitters. Created by Fabrizio Musarella.

⅔oz/2cl	vodka
⅔oz/2cl	Mandarine Napoléon
⅓oz/1cl	marsala
1oz/3cl	mandarin juice
2 dashes	Angostura bitters

Pour all ingredients into a shaker with ice. Shake. Strain into a cocktail glass. Garnish with a twist of mandarin, a spiral of lime, and a Cape Gooseberry set on the rim.

Absolero

A gorgeous color combined with a frothy finish makes this cocktail tempting.

1oz/3cl	black-currant vodka
1oz/3cl	lemon vodka
1oz/3cl	melon liqueur
⅔oz/2cl	fresh lime juice
⅔oz/2cl	powdered egg white
	club soda

Pour all ingredients except club soda into a shaker with ice. Shake. Strain into a highball filled with ice. Top up with soda. Stir. Garnish with a wedge of lime.

Angel Dream Special

One sip of this chocolate- and apple-flavored concoction, and you are sweet dreaming of angels.

1⅔oz/5cl	vodka
½oz/1.5cl	white crème de cacao
½oz/1.5cl	apple schnapps
⅔oz/2cl	heavy (double) cream

Pour all ingredients into a shaker with ice. Shake. Strain into a cocktail glass. Grate nutmeg over the top of the drink.

Apple Martini

This is the hottest new Martini in town. It has a stunning sour apple flavor.

2oz / 6cl   vodka
⅔oz / 2cl   apple sour liqueur
⅓oz / 1cl   Cointreau

Pour all ingredients into a shaker with ice. Shake. Strain into a cocktail glass. Garnish with apple slices.

Aquamarine

This is a great combination of apple juice with the bouquet of peach schnapps.

1oz / 3cl   vodka
⅔oz / 2cl   peach schnapps
⅓oz / 1cl   blue curaçao
⅓oz / 1cl   Cointreau
3½oz / 10cl   clear apple juice

Pour all ingredients into a shaker with ice. Shake. Strain into an old-fashioned glass filled with ice. Garnish with a slice of star fruit. Serve with a straw.

Aviation Two

This is a new version of the classic Aviation, which is made with gin.

1⅔oz / 5cl   vodka
1oz / 3cl   maraschino liqueur
⅔oz / 2cl   fresh lemon juice

Pour all ingredients into a shaker with ice. Shake. Strain into a cocktail glass. Garnish with a maraschino cherry in the drink and a twist of lemon.

Avalon

A combination of sweet and tart flavors in a long drink made refreshing by the 7UP.

1⅓oz / 4cl   vodka
⅓oz / 1cl   green banana syrup
½oz / 1½cl   fresh lemon juice
2oz / 6cl   apple juice
                     7UP

Pour all ingredients, except 7UP, into a shaker with ice. Shake. Strain into a highball filled with ice. Then, top up with 7UP. Stir. Garnish with a spiral of cucumber peel and a cherry. Serve with a straw.

Balalaika

A 1930s classic cocktail with a great combination of orange and lemon flavors.

1⅔oz / 5cl   vodka
1oz / 3cl   triple sec/Cointreau
⅔oz / 2cl   fresh lemon juice

Pour all ingredients into a shaker with ice. Shake. Strain into a cocktail glass. Garnish with a slice of orange.

Bali Trader

A sweet cocktail with the taste of Eastern pleasures and a hit from the vodka.

1⅔oz / 5cl   vodka
⅔oz / 2cl   green banana liqueur
⅔oz / 2cl   pineapple juice

Pour all ingredients into a shaker with ice. Shake. Strain into a cocktail glass.

Barbara

A classic created for a lucky woman whose identity is not known. It is full of creamy chocolaty flavors.

1oz/3cl	vodka
1oz/3cl	white crème de cacao
1oz/3cl	heavy (double) cream

Pour all ingredients into a shaker with ice. Shake. Strain into a cocktail glass. The result is a pale, creamy drink with a touch of froth. Garnish with sprinkle of ground nutmeg.

Bartender's Breakfast

A tangy flavor will start the day with a zing and this sure fits the moment.

1⅔oz/5cl	vodka
handful	cherry tomatoes
1 leaf	fresh basil
pinch	ground coriander
pinch	celery salt
sprinkling	chopped chives
pinch	cracked pepper

Pour all ingredients into a blender without ice. Blend until smooth. Strain in a highball filled with ice. Garnish with a cherry tomato and basil leaves on a cocktail stick.

Bay Breeze

A new-style cocktail, it's popular with people who like vodka and cranberry juice.

1⅓oz/4cl	vodka
⅔oz/2cl	peach schnapps
3½oz/10cl	cranberry juice
1⅔oz/5cl	pineapple juice

Pour all ingredients into a shaker with ice. Shake. Strain in to a highball filled with ice. Garnish with a wedge of lime. Serve with a straw.

Bay of Passion

I used to row around the bay at Maiori to a secluded beach for an assignation. This drink is in memory of those great moments.

1oz/3cl	vodka
1oz/3cl	Passóa
4oz/12cl	cranberry juice
2oz/6cl	fresh grapefruit juice

Pour all ingredients into a shaker with ice. Shake. Strain into a highball filled with ice. Garnish with a maraschino cherry on the rim.

Black Magic

A coffee-flavored cocktail with a hint of sharpness from the lemon juice.

1⅓oz / 4cl	vodka
⅔oz / 2cl	Kahlua
⅓oz / 1cl	fresh lemon juice
1 cup	cold coffee

Pour all ingredients into an old-fashioned glass filled with ice. Stir.

Black Russian

At the height of its popularity in the 1950s, this drink is enjoying a resurgence.

1⅓oz / 4cl	vodka
⅔oz / 2cl	Kahlua

Pour the vodka into an old-fashioned glass with ice and add the Kahlua. Stir.

Blood Orange

A more ferocious version of a regular vodka and orange cocktail.

⅔oz / 2cl	vodka
1oz / 3cl	Campari
½oz / 1.5cl	Cointreau
1⅓oz / 4cl	fresh orange juice

Pour all ingredients into a shaker with ice. Shake. Strain into a cocktail glass. Garnish with a wedge of orange.

Bloody Bull

A well-respected hangover cure with a rich flavor from the beef bouillon.

1oz / 3cl	vodka
2oz / 6cl	beef bouillon
2oz / 6cl	tomato juice
⅓oz / 1cl	fresh lemon juice
2 dashes	Worcestershire sauce
	celery salt

Pour all ingredients into a shaker with ice. Shake. Strain into a highball with ice.

Bloody Caesar

This is a restorative long drink created for crooner Tony Bennett while he was in Las Vegas. One night he felt he needed a quick reviver and the bartender at Caesar's Palace fixed him this.

1⅔oz / 5cl	vodka
5oz / 15cl	clamato juice (mix of tomato and clam juice)
⅔oz / 2cl	fresh lemon juice
pinch	celery salt
dash	Tabasco sauce
2 dashes	Worcestershire sauce
	ground black pepper

Pour the clamato and lemon juices into a highball filled with ice. Add the vodka and spices. Stir. Garnish with a wedge of lime on the rim. Serve with a stirrer.

Blue Lagoon

A 1960s creation from Andy McElhone, son of Harry of Harry's New York Bar. Designed to show off the color of a new spirit, blue curaçao, Andy served the first Blue Lagoon with fresh lemon juice instead of 7UP.

1oz / 3cl	vodka
1oz / 3cl	blue curaçao
	7UP

Pour the blue curaçao and the vodka into a highball filled with ice. Top up with 7UP. Garnish with a maraschino cherry and a slice of lemon.

Blueberry Martini

One of the new-style Martinis using fresh fruit for big flavor. It's purple-blue in color, too.

1⅔oz / 5cl	vodka
⅓oz / 1cl	blue curaçao
⅓oz / 1cl	fresh lemon juice
handful	fresh blueberries, rinsed

Cut the blueberries in half and place them in the shaker. Quickly muddle the berries. Add the remaining ingredients and fill shaker with ice. Shake vigorously to bombard the blueberries with the ice to release their flavor and color. Strain through a sieve into the cocktail glass. Place four or five blueberries on a cocktail stick across the glass.

Blueberry Muffin Martini

It really tastes like a blueberry muffin in a glass! A perfect way to start the day or night!

1oz / 3cl	vodka
⅔oz / 2cl	vanilla vodka
½oz / 1.5cl	blueberry liqueur
½oz / 1.5cl	white crème de cacao
3–4	fresh blueberries

Pour all ingredients into a shaker filled with ice. Shake hard to break down the fruit. Double strain into a chilled cocktail glass. Garnish with 3 blueberries on a cocktail stick dropped in the drink.

Bullshot

It is said that if you don't want to start lunch with soup, then start with a Bullshot. It's invigorating, with a hint of lemon.

1⅔oz / 5cl	vodka
5oz / 15cl	beef bouillon
dash	fresh lemon juice
2 dashes	Worcestershire sauce
	celery salt
	Tabasco sauce
	ground black pepper

Pour the bouillon, lemon juice, and Tabasco and Worcestershire sauces into a shaker with the vodka. Shake. Strain into a highball. Add a quick twist of black pepper. Garnish with a wedge of lime on the rim. Serve with a stirrer.

Bloody Mary

Harry's New York Bar, Paris, was the birthplace of this restorative cocktail. The year was 1921. Fernand "Pete" Petiot combined tomato juice, vodka, salt, pepper, and Worcestershire sauce. There was nothing new about the vodka and tomato combination, but the addition of spices and the name were new—his inspiration was Mary Pickford, the actress.

In 1934 Petiot moved to New York. As the name may have been offensive to some, he launched it as Red Snapper. A customer, Prince Serge Obolensky, requested his drink be "spiced up." Petiot added Tabasco sauce. From then, it became known as a Bloody Mary.

1²⁄₃oz/5cl	vodka
5oz/15cl	tomato juice
²⁄₃oz/2cl	fresh lemon juice
pinch	celery salt
2 dashes	Worcestershire sauce
2 dashes	Tabasco sauce
	ground black pepper

Fill the highball with ice cubes, then pour in the tomato and lemon juices. Add the vodka. Add the spices and stir. Add a quick twist of black pepper. Garnish with a wedge of lime on the rim and a stalk of celery if requested. Serve with a stirrer.

Caipirovska

An interpretation of the Caipirinha with a tart lime flavor.

2oz/6cl	vodka
1	whole lime, diced
¹⁄₃oz/1cl	fresh lime juice
2 teaspoons	superfine (caster) sugar

Muddle the lime and sugar in the bottom of an old-fashioned glass. Add the vodka and lime juice. Fill the glass with crushed ice. Stir. Garnish with a slice of lime. Serve with a straw.

Cape Codder

A typically American summer drink, named after the Massachusetts coastal resort.

1²⁄₃oz/5cl	vodka
5oz/15cl	cranberry juice

Pour the cranberry juice into a highball filled with ice. Add the vodka. Stir. Garnish with a wedge of lime.

Chartreuse Dragon

A cocktail that has a divine green color and an equally delicious flavor.

1²⁄₃oz/5cl	vodka
2oz/6cl	lychee juice
²⁄₃oz/2cl	green chartreuse
¹⁄₃oz/1cl	blue curaçao
¹⁄₃oz/1cl	fresh lime juice
	7UP

Pour all ingredients, except 7UP, into a shaker with ice. Shake. Strain into a highball filled with ice. Top up with 7UP. Stir. Garnish with a fresh lychee.

Chi Chi

This is for people who don't like rum, but like the style of a colada.

1²⁄₃oz / 5cl	vodka
1oz / 3cl	coconut cream
4oz / 12cl	pineapple juice

Pour all ingredients into a blender with crushed ice. Blend. Strain into a colada glass. Garnish with a small wedge of pineapple and a maraschino cherry.

Coolman Martini

Created by Jack Coleman, a bartender at the Lanesborough in London.

1²⁄₃oz / 5cl	vodka
²⁄₃oz / 2cl	apple juice
¹⁄₂oz / 1.5cl	Cointreau
¹⁄₂oz / 1.5cl	fresh lemon juice

Pour all ingredients into a shaker with ice. Shake. Strain into a cocktail glass. Garnish with an apple slice fan.

Chocolate Mint Martini

A new-style Martini with a sweet finish and a delicious chocolate mint flavor.

2oz / 6cl	vodka
1oz / 3cl	white crème de cacao
dash	white crème de menthe

To make a chocolate rim, rub a wedge of lime around the rim, then dip it in a saucer of fine chocolate powder.

Pour ingredients into a mixing glass with ice and stir. Strain into a cocktail glass.

Cosmopolitan

In the past decade, this cocktail has become a megastar as a new-style martini. The original recipe used vodka, Cointreau, and cranberry juice. But when it was first served, it had an unimpressive cold color, although the taste was fine. No one person has laid claim to inventing it—maybe it was the result of a mistake made by someone making a Kamikaze (vodka, lime juice, and Cointreau), adding cranberry juice as an extra.

What we do not know, however, is whether the original cocktail used lemon vodka or straight vodka. What we do know is that the original recipe did not use lime juice. Using lime juice binds the ingredients together and gives it a more refreshing taste.

1²⁄₃oz / 5cl	vodka
¹⁄₃oz / 1cl	Cointreau
¹⁄₃oz / 1cl	cranberry juice
¹⁄₃oz / 1cl	fresh lime juice

Pour all ingredients into a shaker with ice. Shake. Strain into a cocktail glass. Garnish with a wedge of lime.

Cliffhanger

A peppery, orange-flavored cocktail that takes you to the edge.

1²/₃oz / 5cl	pepper vodka
1oz / 3cl	Cointreau
²/₃oz / 2cl	Rose's lime cordial

Pour all ingredients into a shaker with ice. Shake. Strain into a cocktail glass. Garnish with a twist of lime.

Desirable

The winning cocktail in the United Kingdom Bartenders' Guild Competition in 1998.

1²/₃oz / 5cl	lemon vodka
½oz / 1.5cl	peach schnapps
½oz / 1.5cl	cognac
1²/₃oz / 5cl	cranberry juice
1²/₃oz / 5cl	passion fruit juice
½ teaspoon	clear honey

Pour all ingredients into a shaker with ice. Shake well to let the honey infuse. Strain into a cocktail glass. Garnish with an orange spiral on the rim.

Detroit Martini

A fresh-tasting Martini-style cocktail with a hint of mint.

2oz / 6cl	vodka
²/₃oz / 2cl	gomme syrup
6	fresh mint leaves

Place all ingredients into a shaker with ice. Shake sharply to break up the mint leaves. Strain into a cocktail glass.

Double Vision

Drink more than one of these and you will be seeing double . . . or treble!

1oz / 3cl	lemon vodka
1oz / 3cl	black-currant vodka
4 dashes	Angostura bitters
1¹/₃oz / 4cl	apple juice

Pour all ingredients into a shaker with ice. Shake. Strain into a cocktail glass.

Dragon Fly

One for those barflies who like to flit from one place to another at night.

1²/₃oz / 5cl	vodka
²/₃oz / 2cl	melon liqueur
¹/₃oz / 1cl	fresh lime juice
²/₃oz / 2cl	apple juice

Pour all ingredients into a shaker with ice. Shake. Strain into a cocktail glass. Garnish with a Cape Gooseberry.

Dyemarion

Smooth and creamy, this is a cocktail perhaps best drunk late at night.

2oz / 6cl	vanilla vodka
dash	brown crème de cacao
dash	orange bitters

Pour all ingredients into an old-fashioned glass filled with ice. Stir.

apple martini

Envy

This cocktail is fragrant and has a nutty flavor combined with a hint of lime.

⅔oz / 2cl	vodka
1oz / 3cl	melon liqueur
½oz / 1.5cl	peach schnapps
½oz / 1.5cl	hazelnut liqueur
⅓oz / 1cl	fresh lime juice

Pour all ingredients into a shaker with ice. Shake. Strain into a cocktail glass.

Evita

A touch of South American passion is hidden in this flavorful cocktail.

1oz / 3cl	vodka
1oz / 3cl	melon liqueur
2oz / 6cl	fresh orange juice
1oz / 3cl	fresh lime juice
dash	gomme syrup

Pour all ingredients into a shaker with ice. Shake. Strain into an old-fashioned glass filled with ice. Garnish with a slice of lime.

FBI

A daring, creamy cocktail for people who like coffee and ice cream in their drinks!

2oz / 6cl	vodka
1oz / 3cl	Irish cream liqueur
1oz / 3cl	coffee liqueur
3 tablespoons	ice cream

Pour all ingredients into a blender with crushed ice. Blend until smooth. Serve in a colada glass.

French Horn

You might start blowing your own trumpet after several of these!

2oz / 6cl	vodka
1oz / 3cl	Chambord liqueur
⅓oz / 1cl	fresh lemon juice

Pour all ingredients into a mixing glass with ice. Stir. Strain into a cocktail glass. Garnish with a maraschino cherry.

French Kiss

You might like to have more than one of these kisses—and the cocktail, too!

1⅔oz / 5cl	vodka
½oz / 1.5cl	crème de framboise (raspberry liqueur)
½oz / 1.5cl	white crème de cacao
⅓oz / 1cl	heavy (double) cream

Pour all ingredients into a shaker with ice. Shake. Strain into a cocktail glass.

French Martini

A sweet-style Martini with a touch of Hawaii from the pineapple flavor.

1⅓oz / 4cl	vodka
1oz / 3cl	pineapple juice
⅔oz / 2cl	Chambord liqueur

Pour all ingredients into a shaker with ice. Shake. Strain into a cocktail glass. Garnish with a twist of orange.

Fresca

An unusual cocktail, with its slightly bitter flavor balanced by addition of the sugar.

2oz/6cl — lemon vodka
4 — fresh kumquats
4 dashes — orange bitters
3 — sugar cubes

Cut the kumquats into quarters and muddle with sugar in an old-fashioned glass. Add the vodka and the orange bitters. Stir. Add crushed ice. Serve with a straw.

Fuzzy Navel

A classic cocktail with a delicious hint of peach and a definite orange flavor.

1oz/3cl — vodka
1oz/3cl — peach schnapps
5oz/15cl — fresh orange juice

Pour all ingredients into a shaker with ice. Shake. Strain into a highball filled with ice. Garnish with a slice of orange and a maraschino cherry. Serve with a straw and a stirrer.

Gensac Sour

Simply a great drink—sweet, sour, and fruity, with a long lasting finish.

1½oz/4.5cl — orange vodka
½oz/1.5cl — crème de framboise
         (wild strawberry liqueur)
½oz/1.5cl — fresh lemon juice
½ — egg white
⅓oz/1cl — gomme syrup
2 fresh — raspberries

Pour all ingredients into a shaker filled with ice. Shake sharply. Strain into a chilled champagne flute. Garnish with a raspberry placed in the middle of the drink.

Golden Cadillac II

A more subtle and creamy cocktail than a Pink Cadillac, which is without schnapps.

1⅓oz/4cl — vodka
⅔oz/2cl — peach schnapps
⅓oz/1cl — Galliano
⅔oz/2cl — heavy (double) cream

Pour all ingredients into a shaker with ice. Shake. Strain into a cocktail glass.

Golden Tang

Banana is known to give you energy, and the orange is full of vitamins.

1²/₃oz / 5cl	vodka
½oz / 1.5cl	Galliano
½oz / 1.5cl	crème de bananes (banana liqueur)
²/₃oz / 2cl	fresh orange juice

Pour all ingredients into a shaker with ice. Shake. Strain into a cocktail glass. Garnish with a spiral of orange.

Grace

This is an elegant and refreshing drink. It has a great texture for a long drink.

1½oz / 4.5cl	pear vodka
1½oz / 4.5cl	pear juice
1½oz / 4.5cl	apple juice
²/₃oz / 2cl	lemon juice
1 teaspoon	honey syrup
1 piece	of lemongrass
4 or 5	mint leaves

Cut the lemongrass into 4 or 5 pieces and muddle in the bottom of a shaker. Add remaining ingredients. Add ice. Shake vigorously for 10 seconds. Strain over crushed ice in a highball glass using a single strainer. A few particles of mint and lemongrass will pass through the filter—this is intentional. Garnish with a sprig of mint and a lemongrass straw. To make a lemongrass straw, trim a piece of lemongrass an inch shorter than a plastic straw. Insert the straw into the lemongrass and place in the drink.

Green Dinosaur

As you can tell from the list of ingredients, this is a very powerful cocktail.

²/₃oz / 2cl	vodka
²/₃oz / 2cl	gold tequila
²/₃oz / 2cl	light rum
²/₃oz / 2cl	Plymouth gin
²/₃oz / 2cl	triple sec/Cointreau
1oz / 3cl	fresh lime juice
dash	gomme syrup
dash	melon liqueur

Pour all ingredients, except melon liqueur, into a shaker with ice. Shake. Strain into a highball filled with ice. Float the melon liqueur over the top.

Green Eyes

Here's a modern version of the classic Screwdriver that's an opalescent blue.

1¹/₃oz / 4cl	vodka
²/₃oz / 2cl	blue curaçao
1oz / 3cl	fresh orange juice

Pour all ingredients into a shaker with ice. Shake. Strain into a cocktail glass.

Greyhound

This slightly bitter cocktail really moves along! It's very refreshing, with a bitter edge.

2oz/6cl   vodka
3oz/9cl   fresh grapefruit juice

Pour the vodka into a highball filled with ice. Top up with grapefruit juice. Stir. Garnish with a slice of orange.

Harvey Wallbanger

In the 1960s, a surfer named Harvey wiped out in a surf championship, then drank too much vodka and Galliano at Pancho's Bar, Manhattan Beach, California. Drunk, he banged his head against a wall until he was stopped.

1²⁄₃oz/5cl   vodka
5oz/15cl   fresh orange juice
²⁄₃oz/2cl   Galliano

Pour the vodka and orange juice into a highball filled with ice. Stir. Float the Galliano over the back of a barspoon. Garnish with a slice of orange. Serve with a straw and a stirrer.

Hawaiian Sea Breeze

This is similar to a Bay Breeze only it is a short, not long, drink.

1¹⁄₃oz/4cl   vodka
1oz/3cl   pineapple juice
1oz/3cl   cranberry juice

Pour all ingredients into a shaker with ice. Shake. Strain into a cocktail glass. Garnish with a wedge of pineapple.

Hot Passion

This cocktail has been known to stimulate more than the appetite for food.

1oz/3cl   vodka
1oz/3cl   Passóa
3oz/9cl   cranberry juice
3oz/9cl   fresh orange juice

Pour all ingredients into a shaker with ice. Shake. Strain into a highball filled with ice. Garnish with a slice of orange and a maraschino cherry.

Imagination

This has an apple-and-ginger flavor. The passion fruit pips make a great garnish.

1¹⁄₃oz/4cl   vodka
1¹⁄₃oz/4cl   clear apple juice
1   passion fruit
      ginger ale

Halve the passion fruit and scoop out the pulp and pips into a shaker with crushed ice. Add the vodka and apple juice. Shake. Pour into a highball filled with ice. Top up with ginger ale. Stir. Serve with a straw.

Intimate

Share this apricot-flavored cocktail between just the two of you on a winter's eve.

1oz/3cl	vodka
1oz/3cl	extra dry vermouth
1oz/3cl	apricot brandy
4 dashes	orange bitters

Pour all ingredients into a shaker with ice. Shake. Strain into a cocktail glass. Garnish with a lemon twist and an olive on a cocktail stick.

Italian Surfer

This cocktail presents a refreshing combination of almond and coconut flavors.

1oz/3cl	vodka
½oz/1.5cl	amaretto
½oz/1.5cl	coconut rum liqueur
⅔oz/2cl	pineapple juice
⅔oz/2cl	cranberry juice

Prepare the cocktail glass by rubbing a wedge of orange around the rim. Dip it into a saucer of shredded coconut. Pour all ingredients into a shaker with ice. Shake. Strain into the cocktail glass.

Joe Collins

Another one of the Collins family—this one has a slightly bitter, but snappy, flavor.

2oz/6cl	vodka
4 dashes	Angostura bitters
1oz/3cl	fresh lemon juice
⅔oz/2cl	Rose's lime cordial
dash	gomme syrup
	club soda

Pour all ingredients, except soda, into a shaker with ice. Shake. Strain into a highball filled with ice. Top up with soda. Stir. Garnish with a slice of lemon and a maraschino cherry.

Kamikaze

A modern version of the classic Balalaika. The change of name, and of lemon to lime juice, made it appealing.

1⅓oz/4cl	vodka
⅔oz/2cl	Cointreau
⅔oz/2cl	fresh lime juice

Pour all ingredients into a shaker with ice. Shake. Strain into an old-fashioned glass filled with ice. Drop a wedge of lime into the drink. Serve with a stirrer.

Kurrant Affair

A delicious berry flavor comes through in this cocktail, along with a hint of crisp apple.

1oz/3cl	black-currant vodka
1oz/3cl	lemon vodka
4oz/12cl	clear apple juice

Pour all ingredients into a shaker with ice. Shake. Strain into a highball filled with ice.

Limey

A mouth-watering cocktail with a bittersweet flavor, using marmalade for effect.

1oz/3cl lemon vodka
1oz/3cl orange liqueur
1oz/3cl fresh lime juice
1 barspoon lime marmalade

Pour all ingredients into a shaker with ice. Shake. Strain into a cocktail glass. Garnish with sprinkling of shredded lime peel over the drink.

Lip Smacker

The bitterness of the orange is guaranteed to get the taste buds salivating!

2oz/6cl orange vodka
1oz/3cl clear apple juice
1oz/3cl fresh orange juice
dash orange bitters
1oz/3cl passion fruit juice

Pour all ingredients into a shaker with ice. Shake. Strain into a highball filled with ice. Garnish with an orange twist.

Madras

A classic that has been usurped by the Sea Breeze in recent years. It has an interesting flavor.

1⅔oz/5cl vodka
4oz/12cl cranberry juice
1oz/3cl fresh orange juice

Pour all ingredients into a highball filled with ice. Stir. Garnish with a wedge of lime.

Madroska

A long and fruity flavored drink with a zippy tang at the finish.

2oz/6cl vodka
3oz/9cl clear apple juice
2oz/6cl cranberry juice
1oz/3cl fresh orange juice

Pour all ingredients into a highball filled with ice. Stir. Garnish with a slice of star fruit.

Medical Solution

A pale and interesting concoction disguised as lilac-colored medicine.

1⅔oz/5cl vodka
⅔oz/2cl Parfait Amour
1oz/3cl heavy (double) cream

Pour all ingredients into a shaker with ice. Shake. Strain into a cocktail glass.

Mellow Martini

The combination of banana and lychees produces a piquant flavor.

1⅓oz/4cl vodka
½oz/1.5cl lychee liqueur
½oz/1.5cl crème de bananes
   (banana liqueur)
1oz/3cl pineapple juice

Pour all ingredients into a shaker with ice. Shake. Strain into a cocktail glass.

Melon Ball

This is a classic cocktail, refreshing in the heat of a summer's day.

1oz / 3cl	vodka
⅔oz / 2cl	melon liqueur
3⅓oz / 10cl	pineapple juice

Pour all ingredients into a shaker with ice. Shake. Strain into a highball filled with ice. Garnish with a couple of tiny balls of melon, in different colors if possible, on a cocktail stick. Serve with a straw and a stirrer.

Melon Breeze

Flavored vodkas provide an intriguing base for the addition of fruit juices.

2oz / 6cl	melon vodka
3oz / 9cl	fresh grapefruit juice
3oz / 9cl	cranberry juice

Pour all ingredients into a highball filled with ice and stir. Garnish with a melon ball on a cocktail stick.

Melon Martini

A subtle, light, and fruity flavored drink that's also an attractive color.

1⅔oz / 5cl	vodka
quarter slice	watermelon
dash	fresh lemon juice

Put the melon in the bottom of the shaker. Muddle to release the flavor and color. Add ice cubes and vodka. Shake. Strain into a cocktail glass.

Merry Widow

A wine- and fruit-flavored cocktail with an orange bitters finish.

1oz / 3cl	vodka
1oz / 3cl	Dubonnet
1oz / 3cl	dry vermouth
dash	orange bitters

Pour all ingredients into a mixing glass with ice. Stir. Strain into a cocktail glass. Garnish with a twist of lemon.

Metropolitan

A variation on the popular Cosmopolitan using black-currant vodka.

1⅔oz / 5cl	black-currant vodka
⅔oz / 2cl	Cointreau
1oz / 3cl	cranberry juice
⅓oz / 1cl	fresh lime juice

Pour all ingredients into a shaker with ice. Shake. Strain into a cocktail glass. Garnish with an orange twist.

Monza

This is a bittersweet cocktail for those who like black currants and vodka.

⅔oz / 2cl	vodka
⅔oz / 2cl	crème de cassis (black-currant liqueur)
2⅔oz / 8cl	fresh grapefruit juice

Pour all ingredients in an old-fashioned glass filled with crushed ice. Stir to create the color. Serve with a straw.

Monte Rosa

A refreshing short aperitif with a hint of bitter orange at the finish.

1⅓oz/4cl	vodka
⅔oz/2cl	triple sec/Cointreau
⅔oz/2cl	Campari
⅔oz/2cl	fresh orange juice

Pour all ingredients in a shaker with ice. Shake. Strain into a cocktail glass. Garnish with a twist of orange.

Naked New York

Someone's imagination went wild here! Drink as you watch reruns of the television series Naked City.

3oz/9cl	vodka
⅓oz/1cl	dry vermouth
few	green pitted olives
	slice of blue cheese

Pour all ingredients, except olives and blue cheese, into a mixing glass. Stir. Pour into a cocktail glass. Stuff the olives with blue cheese and drop in the drink.

New England Iced Tea

A modern version of the classic Long Island Iced Tea and just as drinkable.

⅔oz/2cl	vodka
⅔oz/2cl	triple sec/Cointreau
⅔oz/2cl	gold tequila
⅔oz/2cl	light rum
⅔oz/2cl	gin
1oz/3cl	fresh lime juice
⅔oz/2cl	gomme syrup
	cranberry juice

Pour all ingredients, except cranberry juice, into a shaker with ice. Shake. Strain into a highball filled with ice. Top up with cranberry juice. Stir. Garnish with a wedge of lime. Serve with straws.

Niagara Falls

The perfect honeymoon cocktail that will spice up your married life.

1oz/3cl	vodka
1oz/3cl	orange liqueur
⅔oz/2cl	fresh lemon juice
⅓oz/1cl	gomme syrup
	ginger ale

Pour all ingredients, except ginger ale, into a shaker with ice. Shake. Strain into a champagne flute. Top up with ginger ale. Stir. Garnish with a slice of orange.

Moscow Mule

This 1940s cocktail was the marketing idea of John G. Martin, who worked for Heublein & Co., a spirits distributor. In the 1930s, vodka was unknown in America, and in 1934 Martin bought the American rights to a Russian vodka, Smirnoff. The decision became known as "Martin's folly" so he set out to sell the "new" spirit around the West Coast. In Hollywood, he dined at the Cock 'n' Bull, owned by Jack Morgan, who had a glut of ginger beer stock. Morgan had a friend who had to offload some copper mugs. The three of them sat down and concocted the Moscow Mule, which was to be sold in a copper mug stamped with a kicking mule to warn of its kick.

Adding a dash of Angostura bitters is optional these days.

1²⁄₃oz / 5cl	vodka
¹⁄₃oz / 1cl	fresh lime juice
	ginger beer

Pour the vodka and the lime juice into a highball filled with ice. Top up with ginger beer. Stir. Garnish with a wedge of lime in the drink. Serve with a stirrer.

Nureyev

A sensual cocktail dedicated to the brilliant dancer Rudolph Nureyev.

1²⁄₃oz / 5cl	vodka
1²⁄₃oz / 5cl	white crème de cacao

Pour both ingredients into a shaker with ice. Shake. Strain into an old-fashioned glass filled with ice.

Nutty Russian

The addition of the liqueur Frangelico makes this different from a classic Black Russian.

1oz / 3cl	vodka
1oz / 3cl	Frangelico (hazelnut liqueur)
1oz / 3cl	coffee liqueur

Pour all ingredients into a shaker with ice. Shake. Strain into an old- fashioned glass filled with ice.

Off the Rails

A sweet cocktail using the unique taste of lychee liqueur and a hint of pineapple.

1³⁄₄oz / 5cl	vodka
²⁄₃oz / 2cl	pineapple juice
²⁄₃oz / 2cl	lychee liqueur

Pour all ingredients into a shaker filled with ice. Shake. Strain into a cocktail glass. Garnish with a lychee and mint.

desirable (left) and **strawberry basil martini**

Orang-a-tang

Patience and a steady hand are required for floating the rum over the top of the drink.

1²⁄₃oz/5cl	vodka
²⁄₃oz/2cl	triple sec/Cointreau
3oz/9cl	fresh orange juice
1oz/3cl	fresh lime juice
½ teaspoon	grenadine
dash	golden rum

Pour all ingredients, except rum, into a shaker with ice. Shake. Strain into a highball filled with ice. Carefully float the rum over the top. Garnish with a wedge of lime.

Orange Caipirovska

A sweet, orange-flavored cocktail perfect to drink on hot summer nights.

2oz/6cl	orange vodka
²⁄₃oz/2cl	fresh lime juice
²⁄₃oz/2cl	fresh lemon juice
half	orange, diced
1 teaspoon	superfine (caster) sugar

Muddle the orange and the sugar in an old-fashioned glass. Add the remaining ingredients and fill with crushed ice.

Orange Passion

A colorful cocktail with a taste of the exotic from the Passóa ingredient.

1oz/3cl	vodka
1²⁄₃oz/5cl	Passóa
5oz/15cl	fresh orange juice

Pour all ingredients into a shaker with ice. Shake. Strain into a highball filled with ice. Garnish with a slice of orange.

Passover

Too many of these and people may pass over you as you lay on the couch.

1oz/3cl	vodka
1²⁄₃oz/5cl	Passóa
5oz/15cl	fresh grapefruit juice

Pour all ingredients into a shaker with ice. Shake. Strain into a highball filled with ice. Garnish with a slice of orange in the glass.

Peach Blossom

All the flavors of fresh peach and the spiciness of cardamom appear in this amazing cocktail.

1½oz/4.5cl	Stolichnaya vodka
⅓oz/1cl	Peche de Vigne
²⁄₃oz/2cl	peach purée
⅓oz/1cl	fresh lemon juice
2	cardamom pods

Muddle the cardamom pods in the bottom of a shaker. Add remaining ingredients and ice. Shake. Strain into a chilled cocktail glass.

Pearl Harbor

An enticing combination of pineapple and melon flavors with the strength of vodka.

1⅓oz/4cl	vodka
⅔oz/2cl	melon liqueur
1oz/3cl	pineapple juice

Pour all ingredients into a shaker with ice. Shake. Strain into a cocktail glass.

Polish Martini

This is a smooth combination of flavored vodkas with the crispness of apple juice.

1oz/3cl	Polish vodka
1oz/3cl	honey vodka
1oz/3cl	clear apple juice

Pour all ingredients into a mixing glass with ice and stir. Strain into a cocktail glass.

Pure Fetish

If you have a penchant for kinkiness in any form, then this is your cocktail.

1oz/3cl	vodka
1oz/3cl	peach schnapps
2oz/6cl	cranberry juice
2oz/6cl	fresh orange juice

Pour all ingredients into a shaker with ice. Shake. Strain into an old-fashioned glass filled with ice. Garnish with a wedge of lime.

Purple Flirt

Licorice and berry flavors are provided by sambuca and cranberry juice.

1oz/3cl	vodka
½oz/1.5cl	black sambuca
2oz/6cl	cranberry juice

Pour all ingredients into a shaker with ice. Shake. Strain into a cocktail glass.

Quiet Storm

A mixture of tropical juices creates a refreshing cocktail. The quiet before the storm?

1⅔oz/5cl	vodka
2oz/6cl	guava juice
2⅓oz/7cl	pineapple juice
4	fresh lychees
1oz/3cl	coconut cream
dash	grenadine

Pour all ingredients into a blender with crushed ice. Blend. Pour into a highball glass. Garnish with a Cape Gooseberry.

Raspberry Martini

The tartness of raspberries combines well with the liqueur and fresh fruit.

1⅔oz/5cl	vodka
⅓oz/1cl	crème de framboise (raspberry liqueur)
10	fresh raspberries

Put the raspberries in the bottom of a shaker. Muddle. Add the vodka and crème de framboise. Shake. Strain into a cocktail glass. Garnish with raspberries.

Rosemary Cooler

This is the ultimate cooler . . . refreshing and full of Mediterranean flavors.

1½oz/4.5cl	vodka
½oz/1.5cl	mango syrup
½oz/1.5cl	fresh lime juice
2½oz/7.5cl	orange juice (when in season, use blood oranges)
1 dash	grenadine
1 stalk	fresh rosemary

Muddle the rosemary in the bottom of a shaker. Add remaining ingredients, and shake. Double strain into a highball glass filled with ice. Garnish with a stalk of rosemary and a wedge of orange.

Salty Dog

I am bemused by the variety of recipes for this classic. Some say gin; others say vodka. I prefer the salt and grapefruit combination, which produces a slightly bitter flavor.

1⅓oz/4cl	vodka
1⅓oz/4cl	fresh grapefruit juice

Rub the rim of a cocktail glass with a wedge of lemon. Dip it into a saucer of fine salt. Pour the vodka and the grapefruit juice into a shaker with ice. Shake. Strain into the cocktail glass.

San Francisco

A long drink with the kick of vodka subtly hidden beneath layers of fruit flavors.

2oz/6cl	vodka
½oz/1.5cl	triple sec/Cointreau
½oz/1.5cl	crème de bananes (banana liqueur)
2⅔oz/8cl	fresh orange juice
2⅔oz/8cl	pineapple juice
⅓oz/1cl	grenadine

Pour all ingredients into a shaker with ice. Shake. Strain into a highball filled with ice. Garnish with a wedge of lime.

Screwdriver

Created in the 1950s when an American oil man based in Iran allegedly stirred this mix with a screwdriver.

1⅔oz/5cl	vodka
5oz/15cl	fresh orange juice

Pour the vodka into a highball filled with ice. Add the orange juice. Stir. Garnish with a slice of orange. Serve with a stirrer.

Sea Breeze

There have been different versions of the Sea Breeze since the 1930s. This is the classic recipe.

1²/₃oz / 5cl	vodka
3¹/₃oz / 10cl	cranberry juice
1²/₃oz / 5cl	fresh grapefruit juice

Pour the ingredients into a highball filled with ice. Stir. Garnish with a wedge of lime. Serve with a stirrer.

Sex on the Beach

There are many versions of this drink around today. The popular version is below.

1oz / 3cl	vodka
½oz / 1.5cl	peach schnapps
½oz / 1.5cl	Chambord liqueur
1²/₃oz / 5cl	fresh orange juice
1²/₃oz / 5cl	cranberry juice

Pour all ingredients in a shaker with ice. Shake. Strain into a highball filled with ice. Garnish with a slice of lime.

Silver Sunset

This drink's been in existence for awhile and retains its popularity. The egg white powder helps to combine the ingredients and gives the drink a little head.

1oz / 3cl	vodka
½oz / 1.5cl	apricot brandy
½oz / 1.5cl	Campari
3oz / 9cl	fresh orange juice
½oz / 1.5cl	fresh lemon juice
1 teaspoon	egg white powder

Pour all ingredients into a shaker with ice. Shake. Strain into a highball with ice. Garnish with a slice of orange and a maraschino cherry. Serve with a straw.

St. James Cobbler

A magical concoction—the more you let it rest, the nicer it gets! The Guinness helps to obtain a fascinating texture.

1½oz / 4.5cl	vodka
½oz / 1.5cl	orange curacao
½oz / 1.5cl	Dubonnet
	Guinness
4	fresh blackberries
1 teaspoon	demerara sugar
4	fresh mint leaves

Gently muddle the blackberries in the bottom of a shaker. Add all remaining ingredients, except the Guinness. Add ice. Shake. Double strain into a goblet glass. Top up with the Guinness and stir. Garnish with a twist of orange, fresh blackberry, and a sprig of mint.

Strawberry and Basil Martini

The basil herb provides the concentration needed after a few of these cocktails. This is a great-tasting cocktail!

2oz / 6cl	vodka
3 to 4	fresh strawberries
1 to 2	fresh basil leaves

Pour all ingredients into a shaker with ice. Shake. Strain into a cocktail glass. Garnish with a strawberry and a small sprig of basil leaves.

Sweetie

This is an aperitif with hints of bitter flavors balanced by the sweet limoncello.

1oz / 3cl	vodka
⅔oz / 2cl	Campari
⅔oz / 2cl	limoncello
⅔oz / 2cl	fresh lemon juice
3oz / 9cl	cranberry juice

Pour all ingredients into a shaker with ice. Shake. Strain into a highball filled with ice. Garnish with red currants.

Testarossa

Get ready for a Ferrari-like ride of a lifetime when you sip this classic cocktail.

1⅔oz / 5cl	vodka
1⅔oz / 5cl	Campari
dash	club soda

Pour ingredients into an old-fashioned glass filled with ice. Stir. Top up with soda. Garnish with a slice of orange.

Tropical Breeze

A delicious long drink with a combination of fruity flavors that enliven the taste buds.

1oz / 3cl	vodka
1⅔oz / 5cl	Passóa
4oz / 12cl	cranberry juice
2oz / 6cl	fresh grapefruit juice

Pour all ingredients into a shaker with ice. Shake. Strain into a highball filled with ice. Garnish with a maraschino cherry on a cocktail stick.

Vanity

An aperitif with a subtle, dry flavor combined with a hint of spicy cinnamon.

1⅔oz / 5cl	vodka
⅔oz / 2cl	cinnamon liqueur
⅔oz / 2cl	dry vermouth
dash	champagne

Pour all ingredients, except champagne, into a mixing glass with ice. Stir. Strain into a cocktail glass. Add champagne.

Vodka Gimlet

This 1930s classic aperitif was originally made with gin. Now, it is made with vodka.

1⅔oz / 5cl	vodka
⅔oz / 2cl	Rose's lime cordial

Pour the vodka into an old-fashioned glass with ice. Add the lime cordial. Stir. Garnish with a wedge of lime.

Vodka Sour

This contemporary classic differs from a whiskey sour, which has an earthy taste, in that it is lighter. It is also known as a Lemon Drop.

2oz / 6cl	vodka
⅔oz / 2cl	fresh lemon juice
dash	gomme syrup
1 teaspoon	egg white powder

Pour all ingredients into a shaker with ice. Shake. Strain into a cocktail glass. Garnish with a maraschino cherry dropped into the drink.

Vodka Stinger

A popular vodka digestif with a fantastic peppermint finish. Try it and make your digestive system happy!

1⅓oz / 4cl	vodka
⅔oz / 2cl	white crème de menthe

Pour the vodka into an old-fashioned glass filled with ice. Add the crème de menthe. Stir. Serve with a stirrer.

Vodkatini

This is the most requested Martini, with vodka replacing gin. A good bartender will refuse to shake it!

3oz / 9cl	chilled vodka
2 dashes	extra dry vermouth in a small bitters bottle

Place a cocktail glass in the freezer before using. Pour the vodka into the glass. Splash the vermouth on top of the vodka. Garnish with a twist of lemon or an olive.

Wasabi Bliss

This is a sweet and sour oriental delight.

1½oz / 4.5cl	Stolichnaya Vodka
½oz / 1.5cl	saké
½oz / 1.5cl	fresh lime juice
½oz / 1.5cl	gomme syrup
1	pea-sized wasabi paste

Pour all ingredients into a shaker filled with ice. Shake. Strain into a chilled cocktail glass. Garnish with a strip of toasted seaweed floating on drink.

White Russian

The only difference between this and a Black Russian is the addition of cream.

1⅓oz / 4cl	vodka
⅔oz / 2cl	Kahlua
⅔oz / 2cl	lightly whipped cream

Pour the vodka and the Kahlua into an old-fashioned glass filled with ice. Stir. Float the whipped cream over the top of the drink. Serve with a stirrer.

White Out

A creamy chocolate-flavored cocktail with a hit from the vodka base.

1⅔oz / 5cl	vodka
⅔oz / 2cl	white crème de cacao
⅔oz / 2cl	heavy (double) cream

Pour all ingredients into a shaker with ice. Shake. Strain into a cocktail glass. Garnish with a few flakes of grated white chocolate.

Woo Woo

Formerly known as a Teeny-Weeny Woo-Woo. Really, it's true-woo!

1oz / 3cl	vodka
⅔oz / 2cl	peach schnapps
1⅔oz / 5cl	cranberry juice

Pour all ingredients into a shaker with ice. Shake. Strain into an old-fashioned glass filled with ice. Garnish with a wedge of lime dropped in the drink.

Yellow Fever

A great combination of herbal Galliano, tart lime, and sweet pineapple flavors.

1⅔oz / 5cl	vodka
⅓oz / 1cl	Galliano
⅓oz / 1cl	fresh lime juice
1oz / 3cl	pineapple juice

Pour all ingredients into a shaker with ice. Shake. Strain into a cocktail glass. Garnish with a spiral of orange trailing over the edge of the glass.

white russian

WHISKEY & BOURBON

—⚬⚬⚬—

There is bourbon, and there is Irish whiskey, Scotch whisky, rye, and Tennessee whiskey. Each type has a unique flavor. It is worth noting, the first whiskey was, in fact, Irish.

Scotland's whisky came to the fore when the phylloxera crisis in the late 1870s devastated Cognac's vineyards. Scotch whisky distributors quickly established their product in all world territories.

Bourbon is America's spirit, born in Kentucky more than 200 years ago. The limestone spring waters are credited with making the whiskey as sweet and as smooth as honey.

Distilled from grain with not less than 50 percent corn and balanced with either barley and wheat or rye, bourbon is matured in white oak barrels and burnt to bring out the sugars in the oak. Bourbon must be aged for a minimum of two years; however, most are aged for between four and 12 years. It cannot be distilled above 160 proof and is bottled at 80 proof.

Scotch whisky (aways spelled without an "e" to differentiate it from Irish!) is produced only in Scotland and is of two types: blended and single malt (the original Scotch).

Blended Scotch whiskies are made of both malt and grain whisky; one blend may contain up to 40 diferent malts. Its age is determined by the age of the youngest whiskey in the blend. Most are a minimum of four years old and are 80 proof. Malts are aged for at least eight years and

bourbon pick-me-up (left), page 157, and **raspberry lynchburg**, page 168

are defined by the natural characteristics of the region where they are produced. Malts with more peaty flavor are from Islay, where the water seeps from the peat areas.

Highland malts are distinguished as dry, smooth, and smoky, whereas Island malts bear the flavor of the Atlantic Ocean atmosphere. For those who enjoy the flavors of barley malt, the mild Lowland malts might be the answer. Speyside whiskies are produced in distilleries located on the banks of the River Spey, which is fed by the soft waters from granite mountains.

The taste of Western Highland malts is deemed to be a balance of the Island malts and those of the Highlands.

Irish whiskey distillers produce both blended and malt styles, made from malted and unmalted barley as well as grains, but the malts are distilled in sealed kilns to prevent any taste of peat. Some malts are triple distilled to produce a smoother texture. Legally, whiskies must be matured for a minimum of three years; premium brands are aged for at least 12 years.

Canadian whisky is made from a variety of grains, including rye, barley, wheat, and corn. The overall style of a blended Canadian whisky is light, smooth, soft, and slightly sweet. Continuous still distillation is laid down by law, as is a three-year minimum ageing in oak period, although most brands are matured for longer.

A typical blend will contain up to 20 whiskies, which might have been aged in old brandy, bourbon, or sherry casks, in a new cask, or in a charred cask.

Japan has been producing blended whisky since the start of the 20th century, when Masataka Taketsuru traveled to Scotland to see how whisky was made. Taketsuru, heir to a saké brewery, produced his first whisky in 1929. He set up a chain of whisky bars to promote its success.

SERVING WHISKEY & SCOTCH

When serving a malt straight up (without ice), plain water, in a small pitcher, is served on the side. Bottled mineral and sparkling water are not recommended because they change the taste of a malt.

Always chill a cocktail glass in the freezer before use.

Adam and Eve

There is a bit of a fizzy finish to this herbal-based, slightly bitter cocktail.

2oz / 6cl	bourbon
⅓oz / 1cl	Galliano
4 dashes	Angostura bitters
dash	gomme syrup
	club soda

Half-fill an old-fashioned glass with ice. Add the gomme syrup, bitters, bourbon, and Galliano. Stir. Top up with soda. Stir.

Affinity

An aperitif fashionable in the 1920s and now considered one for the purists.

1oz / 3cl	Scotch
1oz / 3cl	sweet vermouth
1oz / 3cl	dry vermouth
dash	Angostura bitters

Pour both vermouths into a mixing glass with ice. Add the Scotch and Angostura bitters. Stir. Strain into a cocktail glass. Add a twist of lemon.

Algonquin

A favorite of the literary set who drank at this famed Manhattan hotel bar.

2oz / 6cl	rye whiskey
1⅓oz / 4cl	extra dry vermouth
1⅓oz / 4cl	pineapple juice
4 dashes	Peychaud bitters

Pour all ingredients into a shaker with ice. Shake. Strain into an old-fashioned glass filled with ice.

Black Shadow

A popular combination—a rich and earthy flavor fills every mouthful of this cocktail.

1⅔oz / 5cl	bourbon
⅔oz / 2cl	Chambord liqueur
4 to 5	fresh blackberries
⅓oz / 1cl	fresh lemon juice
dash	gomme syrup

Pour all ingredients into a shaker with ice. Shake. Strain into an old-fashioned glass filled with crushed ice.

Blood & Sand

A classic cocktail created for the premiere of the Rudolph Valentino movie.

1oz / 3cl	J & B Rare Scotch
⅔oz / 2cl	cherry brandy
⅔oz / 2cl	sweet vermouth
⅔oz / 2cl	fresh orange juice

Pour all ingredients into a shaker with ice. Shake. Strain into a cocktail glass.

Bobby Burns

Invented at the famous pre-Prohibition bar in New York City, the Big Brass Rail, and named for the Scottish poet Robert Burns, it was traditionally served on Robert Burns Day. Harry Craddock also acclaimed it as "one of the best whisky cocktails a very fast mover on St. Andrew's Day" in The Savoy Cocktail Book.

2oz/6cl	Scotch whisky
1oz/3cl	Martini Rosso
⅓oz/1cl	Benedictine liqueur

Stir all ingredients in a mixing glass with ice. Strain in a chilled cocktail glass. Garnish with a twist of lemon, and for an extra Scottish touch serve with a shortbread biscuit.

Boomerang

So named because when you think the flavor has disappeared, it comes back!

1⅔oz/5cl	rye whiskey
1oz/3cl	vermouth
⅔oz/2cl	fresh lemon juice
4 dashes	Angostura bitters
4 dashes	maraschino liqueur

Pour all ingredients into a shaker with ice. Shake. Strain into a cocktail glass. Garnish with a slice of lemon.

Boston Flip

The flip was traditionally made by the old method of flipping the combination between two containers to obtain a smooth consistency. In the 17th century, a flip featured beaten eggs, sugar, spices, rum, and a hot ale. The innkeeper would mull the mixture with a hot iron "loggerhead" before serving it.

The cocktail has changed dramatically since then. It is now a short drink, served cold with a finish of sprinkled nutmeg. It can be made with any spirit, and egg yolks.

2oz/6cl	bourbon
2oz/6cl	Madeira
1	free-range egg yolk
dash	gomme syrup

Pour all ingredients into a shaker with ice. Shake well. Strain into a goblet. Garnish with a sprinkling of grated nutmeg.

Bourbon Pick-Me-Up

This cocktail provides an energy from the bourbon and the Branca Menthe.

1²⁄₃oz / 5cl	bourbon
²⁄₃oz / 2cl	Branca Menthe
²⁄₃oz / 2cl	fresh lemon juice
sprig	fresh mint

Pour all ingredients into a shaker with ice. Shake. Strain into an old-fashioned glass filled with ice. Garnish with a sprig of fresh mint.

Bourbon Pressure

A tangy, orange flavor comes to the fore in this combination.

1²⁄₃oz / 5cl	bourbon
1 teaspoon	orange marmalade
dash	Peychaud bitters

Pour all ingredients into a shaker with ice. Shake. Strain into an old-fashioned glass filled with ice.

Bourbon Smash

The strength of bourbon, the freshness of raspberries, and the tartness of cranberries are all wrapped into one flavor.

1²⁄₃oz / 5cl	bourbon
handful	fresh raspberries
2¹⁄₃oz / 7cl	cranberry juice
²⁄₃oz / 2cl	fresh lime juice
½ teaspoon	superfine (caster) sugar
dash	Angostura bitters

Place the lime juice and raspberries in the bottom of a highball, then add the sugar and bitters. Muddle until the sugar is dissolved. Add the bourbon and stir. Add crushed ice. Top up with cranberry juice. Garnish with a stem of red currants on the rim of the glass. Serve with a straw.

Boston Sour

A good combination of bitter and sour flavors, with a smooth bourbon finish. Good any time of the day.

1²⁄₃oz / 5cl	bourbon
²⁄₃oz / 2cl	fresh lemon juice
2 dashes	Angostura bitters
dash	egg white powder
dash	gomme syrup

Pour all ingredients into a shaker with ice. Shake. Strain into a cocktail glass. Garnish with a slice of lemon and a maraschino cherry.

Brooklyn Cocktail

Lesser known than the Manhattan, this drink also takes its name from a New York borough, but in my opinion is just as exceptional thanks to its stunning taste.

1½oz/4.5cl	rye whiskey
⅔oz/2cl	dry vermouth
1 teaspoon	Amer Picon
1	Maraschino cherry

Stir ingredients in a mixing glass filled with ice. Strain into a chilled cocktail glass. Garnish with a cherry.

Daisy

A tart berry flavor is balanced by a crisp apple flavor in this refreshing cocktail.

1⅔oz/5cl	whiskey
⅔oz/2cl	fresh lemon juice
⅔oz/2cl	clear apple juice
⅔oz/2cl	crème de framboise (raspberry liqueur)
⅓oz/1cl	gomme syrup

Pour all ingredients into an old-fashioned glass with ice. Stir. Garnish with a slice of apple.

Derby Smash

One for celebrating Derby Day—wherever you might be and whatever you might be doing.

1⅓oz/4cl	bourbon
⅔oz/2cl	Pimm's No. 1 Cup
⅓oz/1cl	crème de framboise (raspberry liqueur)
1oz/3cl	watermelon juice
	ginger ale

Pour all ingredients, except ginger ale, into a shaker with ice. Shake. Strain into a highball filled with ice. Top up with ginger ale. Garnish with two raspberries and a sprig of mint.

Diva

An unusual ingredient like lychee liqueur adds a piquancy to this cocktail.

1⅓oz/4cl	whiskey
½oz/1.5cl	lychee liqueur
1oz/3cl	fresh lemon juice
1⅔oz/5cl	cranberry juice
⅓oz/1cl	gomme syrup
	ginger ale

Pour all ingredients, except ginger ale, into a shaker with ice. Shake. Strain into a highball filled with ice. Top up with ginger ale.

Flamingo

There's not a hint of pink in this earthy flavored cocktail, but there is a touch of froth.

1oz/3cl	bourbon
1oz/3cl	crème de bananes (banana liqueur)
2oz/6cl	fresh orange juice
1oz/3cl	fresh lemon juice
2 teaspoons	egg white powder

Pour all ingredients into a shaker with ice. Shake. Strain into an old-fashioned glass filled with ice.

Fourth of July

Something to drink while you celebrate Independence Day.

²⁄₃oz/2cl	bourbon
²⁄₃oz/2cl	Galliano
²⁄₃oz/2cl	coffee liqueur
²⁄₃oz/2cl	fresh orange juice
²⁄₃oz/2cl	heavy (double) cream
	ground cinnamon

Pour the bourbon and Galliano into a warm cocktail glass. Ignite, and sprinkle with cinnamon. Pour the remaining ingredients into a shaker with ice. Shake. Strain into the glass.

Georgia Julep

The classic Mint Julep has been reinterpreted with the addition of peach flavor.

1²⁄₃oz/5cl	bourbon
1²⁄₃oz/5cl	fresh peach purée
sprig	fresh mint

Pour all ingredients into a shaker with ice. Shake well to infuse the flavor of the mint. Strain into an old-fashioned glass filled with ice. Garnish with a sprig of fresh mint.

Godfather

A classic after-dinner drink with only two ingredients! But they are full of flavor.

2oz/6cl	Scotch
1oz/3cl	amaretto

Pour both ingredients into a shaker with ice. Shake. Strain into an old-fashioned glass filled with ice. Garnish with a maraschino cherry.

Highland Fling

A great drink to see in Hogmonay and, of course, to sip on Robert Burns Night.

1²⁄₃oz/5cl	Scotch
²⁄₃oz/2cl	dry vermouth
6 dashes	orange bitters

Pour all ingredients into a mixing glass filled with ice. Stir. Strain into a cocktail glass. Garnish with a twist of orange.

High Voltage

This is a refreshing Scotch whisky cocktail with a hint of orange from the triple sec.

1⅔oz / 5cl	Scotch
1oz / 3cl	triple sec/Cointreau
1oz / 3cl	fresh lime juice
	club soda

Pour all ingredients, except soda, into a shaker with ice. Shake. Strain into an old-fashioned glass filled with ice. Top up with soda. Stir.

Honey Barrel

The medicinal qualities of the manuka honey gives you a good excuse to enjoy this one!

2oz / 6cl	bourbon
4	fresh strawberries
1 teaspoon	vanilla sugar
1 teaspoon	manuka honey
	Freshly ground black pepper

Gently muddle the strawberries in the bottom of a shaker. Add all remaining ingredients and ice. Shake. Double strain into a honey- and sugar-rimmed cocktail glass. Garnish with two twists of black pepper on top of the drink.

Howling Monkey

An exciting and vibrant concoction for a whisky cocktail, combining earthiness with sweetness and strength.

1½oz / 4.5cl	Monkey Shoulder (malt whisky)
⅓oz / 1cl	absinthe
⅓oz / 1cl	amaretto
1	lump of sugar
4–5 drops	Peychaud bitters
4–5 drops	orange juice
5	mint leaves

Soak the lump of sugar with bitters and orange juice, then muddle it with the mint leaves in an old-fashioned glass. Add ice and stir in whisky. Garnished with a twist of orange.

Hunter

This drink has a smoky flavor combined with a cherry finish. A mellow drink for the end of an evening.

| 2oz / 6cl | bourbon |
| 1oz / 3cl | cherry brandy |

Pour the bourbon into an old-fashioned glass filled with ice. Add the cherry brandy. Stir.

International Cocktail

A dark and rusty color, this is a cocktail with an intriguing taste of wine and whiskey.

2oz/6cl   bourbon
1oz/3cl   dry sherry
2 dashes   Angostura bitters

Pour all ingredients into a mixing glass with ice. Stir well. Strain into an old-fashioned glass filled with ice. Garnish with a twist of orange.

Julep Martini

A powerful, refreshing cocktail with a real flavor of mint over the bourbon.

2oz/6cl   bourbon
sprig   fresh mint
⅓oz/1cl   gomme syrup

Muddle the mint with bourbon in a shaker. Add ice and shake. Strain into a cocktail glass. Garnish with a sprig of fresh mint.

Just Peachy

When everything's going well, have one or two of these. Or more.

1½oz/4.5cl   bourbon
½oz/1.5cl   peach schnapps
4oz/12cl   fresh orange juice

Pour the bourbon and orange juice into a highball filled with ice. Float the peach schnapps over the top of the drink. Garnish with a wedge of fresh peach.

Kentucky Colonel

Not for the faint at heart, this cocktail from the heart of America has a rich, earthy flavor.

2oz/6cl   bourbon
⅓oz/1cl   Bénédictine

Pour ingredients into a mixing glass with ice. Stir. Strain into an old-fashioned glass filled with ice.

Kentucky Kiss

An ideal cocktail to sip on a chilly day at the horse races to (perhaps) celebrate success! And warm you up.

2oz/6cl   bourbon
⅓oz/1cl   Southern Comfort

Pour ingredients into a mixing glass with ice. Stir. Strain into an old-fashioned glass filled with ice.

Kentucky Mac

Here's a spicy, smooth cocktail to warm both body and soul.

1⅔oz/5cl   bourbon
1oz/3cl   ginger wine
2 slices   fresh gingerroot
2   large mint leaves
          clear apple juice

Pour all ingredients into a shaker with ice. Shake. Strain into an old-fashioned glass filled with crushed ice. Top up with apple juice. Stir. Garnish with a sprig of fresh mint.

Kiss on the Lips

An easy-to-mix cocktail with a hint of peach flavor on top of the taste of bourbon.

2oz/6cl	bourbon
5oz/15cl	apricot nectar

Pour the bourbon and apricot nectar into a highball filled with ice. Stir. Serve with a straw.

Leatherneck

This combination offers a touch of sky blue to the rusty bourbon.

2oz/6cl	bourbon
½oz/1.5cl	blue curaçao
½oz/1.5cl	fresh lime juice

Pour all ingredients into a shaker with ice. Shake. Strain into a cocktail glass. Garnish with a twist of lime.

Leila

A smoky sensation from a vibrant concoction.

1½oz/4.5cl	smoky malt whisky
½oz/1.5cl	peach liqueur
½oz/1.5c	cranberry juice
	pulp of a quarter of a pomegranate
2 barspoons	vanilla sugar

Muddle the pomegranate in the bottom of a shaker. Add remaining ingredients and ice. Shake. Strain into a chilled cocktail glass. Garnish with a twist of orange flame in the drink.

L and G

Not only is this a delicious color, it has a great flavor to enchant your guests!

1⅔oz/5cl	bourbon
⅔oz/2cl	crème de framboise (raspberry liqueur)
⅔oz/2cl	Grand Marnier

Pour all ingredients into a mixing glass with ice. Stir. Strain into a cocktail glass.

Loch Almond

A great combination of flavors from the home of Scotch whisky.

1oz/3cl	Scotch
1oz/3cl	amaretto
	ginger ale

Pour the amaretto into a highball filled with ice. Add the Scotch. Top up with ginger ale. Stir. Garnish with a spiral of orange in the drink.

Louisville Lady

This combination offers a touch of Southern elegance in a satisfying drink.

1oz/3cl	bourbon
½oz/1.5cl	white crème de cacao
½oz/1.5cl	heavy (double) cream

Pour the bourbon and crème de cacao into a shaker with ice. Shake. Strain into a liqueur glass. Using a barspoon, gently float the cream on top.

Lucky Summer

A refreshing drink of orange and other citrus flavors, with a whiskey finish.

1oz/3cl	whiskey
1oz/3cl	triple sec/Cointreau
1⅓oz/4cl	fresh orange juice
½oz/1.5cl	fresh lemon juice
dash	grenadine

Pour all ingredients into a shaker with ice. Shake. Strain into an old-fashioned glass filled with ice.

Lynchburg Lemonade

A classic from Jack Daniel's distillery in the town of Lynchburg, in Tennessee.

2oz/6cl	Jack Daniel's whiskey
1oz/3cl	triple sec/Cointreau
1oz/3cl	fresh lemon juice
	7UP

Pour all ingredients, except 7UP, into a shaker with ice. Shake. Strain into a highball filled with ice. Top up with 7UP.

Mad Hatter

Not the drink for a tea party! It's a refreshing combination of sweet and citrus flavors.

2oz/6cl	rye whiskey
½oz/1.5cl	fresh lemon juice
½oz/1.5cl	fresh lime juice
dash	Pernod
dash	gomme syrup

Pour all ingredients into a mixing glass with ice. Stir. Strain into a cocktail glass.

Manhattan

A recipe for this cocktail was first published in bartenders' guides of the 1880s. The origins of the name are unclear—some say it was created in 1874 at the Manhattan Club, New York, for Lady Randolph Churchill.

2oz/6cl	rye whiskey
1oz/3cl	sweet vermouth
dash	Angostura bitters

Pour all ingredients into a mixing glass. Stir. Strain into a cocktail glass. Garnish with a maraschino cherry.

Dry Manhattan

2oz/6cl	Canadian Club whisky
1oz/3cl	dry vermouth
dash	Angostura bitters

Garnish with a twist of lemon.

Perfect Manhattan

2oz/6cl	Canadian Club whisky
½oz/1.5cl	dry vermouth
½oz/1.5cl	sweet vermouth
dash	Angostura bitters

Garnish with a maraschino cherry and a twist of lemon dropped in the drink.

Mantini

A good combination of the strength of whiskey with the tart flavor of the juices.

1oz/3cl	bourbon
1oz/3cl	triple sec/Cointreau
½oz/1.5cl	fresh lime juice
2oz/6cl	cranberry juice

Pour all ingredients into a shaker with ice. Shake. Strain into a highball filled with ice.

Maple Leaf

A combination of sweet and sour with an earthy finish from the bourbon.

2oz/6cl	bourbon
1oz/3cl	fresh lemon juice
2 dashes	maple syrup

Pour all ingredients into a shaker with ice. Shake. Strain into a cocktail glass. Garnish with a spiral of lemon.

Millionaire No. 2

A classic rye whiskey cocktail drunk as an aperitif. This has a frothy head and a hint of orange and aniseed flavors.

2oz/6cl	rye whiskey
½oz/1.5cl	triple sec/Cointreau
dash	pastis
1 teaspoon	egg white powder

Pour all ingredients into a shaker with ice. Shake. Strain into a cocktail glass. Garnish with a maraschino cherry.

Mint Julep

The drink's name is derived from an Arabic word translated as "julab," meaning "rose water." The bourbon-based cocktail possibly originates from Virginia.

Other states lay claim to its origin, although a 1975 treatise, by Richard B. Harwell, states: "Clearly the Mint Julep originated in the northern Virginia tidewater, spread soon to Maryland, and eventually all along the seaboard and even to Kentucky."

By 1800 it had become Americanized, made with brandy until after the Civil War, when bourbon became more available.

1⅔oz/5cl	bourbon
bunch	fresh mint leaves
1 teaspoon	superfine (caster) sugar
1 tablespoon	cold water
	club soda

Place the mint in an old-fashioned glass. Add the sugar and water. Muddle until the sugar is dissolved. Add the bourbon. Fill the glass with crushed ice. Stir. Garnish with a sprig of mint. Serve with a straw and a stirrer.

New Orleans Bourbon Fizz

A whiskey version of the classic cocktail that was originally created at the Sloppy Joe Bar, in Havana, with gin as the base spirit.

2oz / 6cl	bourbon
1 teaspoon	superfine (caster) sugar
1 teaspoon	powdered egg white
2 dashes	kirsch
1oz / 3cl	heavy (double) cream
	club soda

Pour all ingredients, except soda, into a shaker with ice. Shake. Strain into a highball filled with ice. Top up with soda. Stir. Garnish with two maraschino cherries.

New Yorker

A wonderful combination of sweet and sour, much like a true New Yorker!

2oz / 6cl	bourbon
1oz / 3cl	fresh lemon juice
dash	grenadine

Pour all ingredients into a shaker filled with ice. Shake. Strain into a cocktail glass. Garnish with a twist of orange.

Old Pal

One for the Canadians who appreciate dry and bitter flavors in their cocktails.

1oz / 3cl	Canadian Club rye whisky
1oz / 3cl	dry vermouth
1oz / 3cl	Campari

Pour all ingredients into a mixing glass filled with ice. Stir. Strain into a cocktail glass. Garnish with a twist of orange.

Oriental

Smooth and chocolately flavored, this cocktail also has a hint of citrus at the finish.

1⅓oz / 4cl	rye whiskey
⅔oz / 2cl	dry vermouth
⅔oz / 2cl	white crème de cacao
⅔oz / 2cl	fresh lime juice

Pour all ingredients into a shaker with ice. Shake. Strain into a cocktail glass.

Pappy's Mango Cooler

An interesting combination of exotic fruit flavors comes up in this cooler.

2oz / 6cl	rye whiskey
1	peach, diced
dash	peach schnapps
⅔oz / 2cl	fresh lime juice
dash	grenadine

Pour all ingredients into a blender. Blend. Add crushed ice. Blend for again. Pour into a goblet.

Old-Fashioned

Colonel James E. Pepper, a Kentucky-based bourbon distiller, and the bartender of the Pendennis Club in Louisville, were jointly responsible for the creation of this cocktail around 1900. Once called a "palate-paralyzer," this cocktail has a song in its honor, "Make It Another Old-Fashioned, Please," written by the ubiquitous lyricist Cole Porter.

6cl/2oz	bourbon
1	white sugar cube
	Angostura bitters
	club soda

Place the sugar cube in the base of an old-fashioned glass. Soak with the bitters and a dash of soda water. Crush the sugar with the back of a barspoon. Add one third of the bourbon and two ice cubes. Stir. Add more ice and another third of the bourbon. Stir. Add more ice and the final third of the bourbon. Stir. Decorate with half a slice of orange and a cherry. Serve with a stirrer. The Old-Fashioned should never be rushed; it takes time and care to achieve the perfect result.

Passionate Bourbon

A mixture of toffee-apple and ginger flavors. The lychee flavor gives it an exotic taste.

2oz/6cl	bourbon
1oz/3cl	lychee juice
1oz/3cl	passion fruit juice
⅔oz/2cl	apple schnapps
	ginger ale

Pour all ingredients, except ginger ale, into a shaker with ice. Shake. Strain into a highball filled with ice. Top up with ginger ale. Stir. Garnish with a wedge of apple. Serve with a straw.

Peach Crush

Peaches have a fantastic subtle flavor when made into a purée.

2oz/6cl	rye whiskey
1	peach, diced
dash	peach schnapps
⅔oz/2cl	fresh lime juice
dash	grenadine

Pour all ingredients into a blender. Blend. Add crushed ice. Blend again. Pour into a goblet.

whiskey sour

Pineapple Julep

A tropical fruit flavor dominates in this modern version of a classic julep.

2oz/6cl	bourbon
1oz/3cl	pineapple juice
few sprigs	fresh mint
⅓oz/1cl	maraschino liqueur

Pour all ingredients into a shaker with ice. Shake. Strain into an old-fashioned glass filled with crushed ice. Garnish with a sprig of mint. Serve with a straw.

Purple Emperor

A powerful cocktail with a slightly bitter flavor and a hint of citrus to balance the drink.

2oz/6cl	bourbon
2oz/6cl	cranberry juice
½oz/1.5cl	fresh lime juice
1 to 2 dashes	Angostura bitters

Pour all ingredients into a shaker with ice. Shake. Strain into an old-fashioned glass filled with ice.

Pussycat

Here is a sensual, citrus-flavored cocktail to get your hips wiggling.

1⅔oz/5cl	bourbon
1oz/3cl	fresh lime juice
2oz/6cl	fresh orange juice
⅓oz/1cl	grenadine
⅔oz/2cl	gomme syrup

Pour all ingredients into a shaker with ice. Shake. Strain into an old-fashioned glass filled with ice.

Raspberry Lynchburg

A fruity version of the Tennessee classic cocktail. It is a superb combination, with a dominance of tart raspberries at the finish.

2oz/6cl	Tennessee whiskey
⅔oz/2cl	crème de framboise (raspberry liqueur)
⅔oz/2cl	fresh lime juice
⅓oz/1cl	gomme syrup
	7UP

Pour all ingredients, except 7UP, into a shaker with ice. Shake. Strain into a highball filled with ice. Top up with 7UP. Stir gently.

Remember the Maine

A rusty red cocktail with a bittersweet taste and an aniseed-flavored overlay.

1²⁄₃oz / 5cl	bourbon
²⁄₃oz / 2cl	sweet vermouth
²⁄₃oz / 2cl	cherry brandy
²⁄₃oz / 2cl	Pernod
dash	orange bitters

Pour all ingredients into a mixing glass with ice. Stir. Strain into an old-fashioned glass filled with ice. Garnish with a maraschino cherry.

Ritz Old-Fashioned

A modern version of the classic Old-Fashioned with a hint of orange and cherry flavors, with a citrus finish.

2oz / 6cl	bourbon
²⁄₃oz / 2cl	Grand Marnier
¹⁄₃oz / 1cl	maraschino liqueur
²⁄₃oz / 2cl	fresh lemon juice
1	sugar cube
dash	Angostura bitters
	club soda (optional)

Rub a wedge of lemon around the rim of an old-fashioned glass. Dip it in a saucer of superfine (caster) sugar.

Place the sugar cube in the glass and add the bitters. Shake other ingredients, except soda, in a shaker with ice. Strain into the glass, filled with ice. Top up with soda if you like. Stir. Garnish with a maraschino cherry and a slice of lemon on a cocktail stick.

Sazerac

This cocktail made its film debut in the James Bond movie *Live and Let Die*. Its story, however, begins in New Orleans. In the early 1800s, Antoine Peychaud created it in the French Quarter and named it for his favorite cognac, Sazerac-de-Forge et fils. In 1870, the cocktail was changed when American rye whiskey was substituted for the cognac. A dash of absinthe was also added by Leon Lamothe, a bartender. Today, he is regarded as the originator of the drink we now sip. Although legal now, in 1912, absinthe was banned, so Pernod is used instead.

2oz / 6cl	rye whiskey
2 dash	absinthe or Pernod
3 dash	peychaud bitters
1	sugar cube
	club soda

Take two rock glasses, one large and one small. In the small one, add crushed ice and the absinthe and stir. Place the sugar cube in the large glass and soak it with the bitters. Add a dash of soda and crush the sugar with the back of a barspoon. Add the whiskey and stir to dissolve the sugar. Add ice and stir. Empty the small glass—this will now be chilled and flavored with absinthe—and strain the prepared drink into it. Garnish with a twist of lemon.

Rob Roy

The only cocktail for a Scotsman to imbibe on St. Andrew's Day! It takes its name from the Scottish rebel leader Rob Roy.

1⅓oz/4cl	Scotch
1⅓oz/4cl	sweet vermouth
1 to 2 dashes	Angostura bitters

Pour all ingredients into a mixing glass with ice. Stir. Strain into a cocktail glass. Garnish with a twist of orange for extra zest! Or use a maraschino cherry.

Rockwell Iced Tea

A herbal-based cocktail with a fresh spicy flavor to wake up your taste buds.

1⅔oz/5cl	bourbon
3⅓oz/10cl	hibiscus tea
1 to 2 slices	fresh gingerroot
	cinnamon
	cloves

Infuse tea with cinnamon, cloves, and ginger. Place it on the stovetop to warm. When the tea is hot, strain it in a shaker. Add bourbon and ice. Shake. Strain into a highball filled with ice. Garnish with a wedge of lime.

Rusty Nail

A classic cocktail with orange and honey flavors. It hits the nail on the head after dinner.

| 2oz/6cl | Scotch |
| 1oz/3cl | Drambuie |

Pour the Scotch into an old-fashioned glass with ice. Add the Drambuie and stir. Garnish with a twist of lemon.

Saint Patrick's Day

A good cocktail to celebrate St. Patrick's Day, with mint and bitter herbal flavors.

1oz/3cl	Irish whiskey
1oz/3cl	green crème de menthe
1oz/3cl	green Chartreuse
4 drops	Angostura bitters

Pour all ingredients into a shaker with ice. Shake. Strain into a cocktail glass.

Stiletto

You could definitely make a strong point with this earthy cocktail!

1⅔oz/5cl	bourbon
⅔oz/2cl	amaretto
⅔oz/2cl	fresh lime juice

Pour all ingredients into a shaker with ice. Shake. Strain into an old-fashioned glass filled with ice. Garnish with a wedge of lime.

Tennessee Squirrel

Simply a great interpretation of a sour.

1½oz / 4.5cl	Jack Daniel's
⅔oz / 2cl	Amaretto di Saronno
1	fresh passionfruit pulp
1oz / 3cl	lemon juice
⅓oz / 1cl	passion fruit syrup

Place all ingredients into a shaker filled with ice. Shake. Strain over ice into an old-fashioned glass. Garnish with a wedge of passion fruit and a spring of mint.

Thriller

A more accessible version of a Whisky Mac, this is an aperitif with orange to soothe and lengthen the taste.

1⅔oz / 5cl	Scotch
½oz / 1.5cl	Stone's ginger wine
½oz / 1.5cl	fresh orange juice

Pour all ingredients into a shaker. Shake. Strain into cocktail glass.

Ward Eight

Named after an old Irish area in New York known for its corruption. This is also the drink of the Scottish Guards.

2oz / 6cl	bourbon
½oz / 1.5cl	fresh lemon juice
½oz / 1.5cl	fresh orange juice
dash	grenadine
dash	gomme syrup

Pour all ingredients into a shaker with ice. Shake. Strain into a cocktail glass.

What's the Rush?

Exactly. Take your time to drink this refreshing and sparkling cocktail.

1oz / 3cl	Irish whiskey
dash	clear apple juice
3oz / 9cl	7UP

Pour all ingredients into a highball filled with ice. Stir. Top up with 7UP. Stir. Garnish with a slice of orange.

Whiskey Sour

The original sour of the 1850s was made with brandy sour. Now it is made with whiskey.

1⅔oz / 5cl	rye whiskey
⅔oz / 2cl	fresh lemon juice
1 teaspoon	egg white powder
dash	gomme syrup

Pour all ingredients into a shaker with ice. Shake. Strain into a cocktail glass. Garnish with a maraschino cherry and a slice of orange if you like.

White Knight

A creamy texture with a hint of coffee and orange coming through the whisky.

⅔oz / 2cl	Scotch
⅔oz / 2cl	coffee liqueur
⅔oz / 2cl	Drambuie
⅔oz / 2cl	heavy (double) cream
⅔oz / 2cl	milk

Pour all ingredients into a shaker with ice. Shake. Strain into a cocktail glass.

CHAMPAGNE & WINE

⊸⊶

This section presents a collection of recipes using champagne, wine, and fortified wine. The light golden color and effervescence of a champagne cocktail, such as Bellini, classic Champagne Cocktail, and Kir Royale, are as popular as ever. Other types of Bellini, using purées other than peach, are now being served. They rely on the familiarity of the Bellini so people know what to expect: a fresh fruit purée with champagne.

CHAMPAGNE

A blended wine made primarily from black pinot noir and gold chardonnay grapes, it is produced in an *appellation controllée* region of France and only wine from this region can be labeled "Champagne." Wine labeled "Methode Champenoise" is made in a similar way, possibly with the same grape stock, but it is not from the Champagne region.

STYLES OF CHAMPAGNE

Brut: only a tiny amount of sweetening is added to remove the dryness

Extra Sec: dry champagne

Sec: medium-sweet champagne

Demi-sec: sweet champagne

Rosé: made by blending some of the still red wine of the Champagne region with the white wine.

Vintage: when weather conditions have been good, a "vintage year" is declared by

bellini (left), page 176, and **rosewood fizz**, page 183

the Champagne authorities. Non-vintage champagne is the regular type and can be dry, sweeter, or full-bodied.

WINE

A bar must stock a variety of styles of white wine to please most people: sauvignon blanc, chablis, chardonnay, and a light wine will satisfy both dry and medium-dry palates.

A selection of red wines ought to include robust and full-bodied clarets, as well as a less ebullient wine that can be drunk on its own, without a meal. Burgundy, Pinot Noir, Rioja, Cabernet Sauvignon, Merlot, and Zinfandel are a few of the types of red wine to try.

The fascinating aspect of wine is that each type has its own character. It is fun learning about aroma and bouquet, and the more you taste, the more you will learn about the type of wine most suitable for your palate.

However, an individual's taste buds appreciate different aspects of a wine. There are numerous books on wine appreciation to give you advice.

SERVING WINE

As an aperitif, serve wine-based Dubonnet, or dry vermouth on the rocks or with a mixer. Or a lighter wine. Serve red wines at room temperature; white wines and rosés are best when served chilled. Champagne is always served very cold and in a chilled champagne flute.

For a dinner party, set the table with a selection of both red and white glasses if you are serving more than one wine.

GLOSSARY

ACIDITY the presence of tartness from fruit acids

AROMA the fragrance released by the wine process

BALANCE describes the harmony of complex flavors in the wine

BODY describes the fullness of wine bouquet aromas released when the wine is opened

DRY a wine with no sweetness in its complexity

FERMENTATION the act of converting natural grape sugar to alcohol when yeast is added

NOSE a mix of aroma and bouquet

TANNIN astringent ingredient that leaves a slightly bitter aftertaste

CHAMPAGNE COCKTAILS

Alcazar

A great predinner cocktail after a day hunting around the bazaar in some exotic Middle Eastern city.

²⁄₃oz / 2cl   apricot purée
²⁄₃oz / 2cl   vodka
dash   apricot liqueur
          champagne

Pour all ingredients, except champagne, into a shaker with ice. Shake. Strain into a champagne flute. Top up with champagne. Stir. Garnish with a wedge of fresh apricot.

Alfonso

A champagne cocktail named after the deposed Spanish king, Alfonso XIII (1886–1941), who first had the pleasure of tasting this combination while in exile in France from 1931 until his death.

1oz / 3cl   Dubonnet
1   sugar cube
2 dashes   Angostura bitters
          champagne

Place the sugar cube in the champagne flute and soak with Angostura bitters. Add the Dubonnet. Top up with champagne. Stir. Add a twist of lemon.

American Fizz

A full banana flavor hits the taste buds at about the same time as a hint of rum and pineapple juice.

²⁄₃oz / 2cl   banana purée
²⁄₃oz / 2cl   pineapple juice
²⁄₃oz / 2cl   dark rum
          champagne

Pour all ingredients, except champagne, into a shaker with ice. Shake. Strain into a champagne flute. Top up with champagne. Stir. Garnish with a slice of banana.

Apple Blow Fizz

Crisp and fruity, with lots of fizz from the champagne, this is a refreshing cocktail.

¹⁄₃oz / 1cl   apple schnapps
¹⁄₃oz / 1cl   cranberry juice
          champagne

Pour the schnapps and juice into a champagne flute. Stir. Top up with champagne. Stir. Garnish with a small wedge of green apple.

Bastile

A very French cocktail—it would be a crime to use anything but real champagne!

3	blackberries
⅓oz / 1cl	crème de mûre (blackberry liqueur)
1oz / 3cl	white rum
½ slice	orange
dash	gomme syrup
	champagne

Muddle the berries with the gomme syrup and crème de mûre in the shaker. Add the rum. Squeeze a half slice of orange over the mixture. Add ice cubes. Shake. Strain into a highball filled with crushed ice. Top up with champagne. Stir. Garnish with a blackberry and a slice of orange.

Black Velvet

A velvet-smooth champagne cocktail created by the bartender at Brooks' Club, in London, in 1861. England was in mourning for Prince Albert and the bartender felt that champagne also should to be in mourning, so he combined it with dark Guiness stout. The tipple was the favorite of Prince Otto von Bismarck of Germany.

draught or bottle	Guiness stout
	champagne

Half-fill a champagne flute with Guinness and top up with champagne. Stir.

Bellini

The delicate pink hues of paintings by the Venetian painter Giovanni Bellini inspired Giuseppi Cipriani, bartender at Harry's Bar in Venice, to create this drink. It is an old Italian tradition to marinade a fresh peach in wine, and Cipriani took it one step further using champagne with puréed peach flesh. It was a favorite of Noel Coward and Ernest Hemingway whenever they visited the bar.

I recommend you use fresh white peach purée. When this delicate peach is in season, buy a whole lot and prepare them: blanch to remove the skins, remove the pits, and place the flesh in a blender with a dash of fresh lemon juice. Blend for a few seconds and then freeze. As an alternative, you can squeeze the peach using a manual squeezer and put the flesh and liquid through a strainer.

white peach purée
champagne

Quarter-fill a champagne flute with the peach purée and top up with the champagne. Stir. Garnish with a peach slice on the rim if you like.

Buck's Fizz

Mr. McGarry, of Buck's Club, in London, created this in 1921. The ratio is two-thirds champagne/one-third juice.

fresh orange juice
brut champagne

Fill a quarter of a champagne flute with fresh orange juice. Top up with champagne. Stir gently.

Casanova

A sharp-tasting cocktail designed for men who like to seduce women.

1oz/3cl	raspberry purée
1oz/3cl	clear apple juice
2⅓oz/7cl	champagne

Pour the raspberry purée into a chilled flute. Add the apple juice and stir. Top up with champagne. Stir. Garnish with two fresh raspberries in the drink.

Casa Rosa

Strawberries are so perfect with champagne, whether it be summer or winter.

1oz/3cl	strawberry purée
⅔oz/2cl	cognac
dash	Grand Marnier
	champagne

Pour all ingredients, except champagne, into a shaker with ice. Shake. Strain into a champagne flute. Top up with champagne. Stir. Garnish with a fresh strawberry dropped in the drink.

Champagne Pick-Me-Up

The addition of the seemingly miraculous qualities of brandy give this cocktail a kick!

1oz/3cl	brandy
⅔oz/2cl	fresh orange juice
⅔oz/2cl	fresh lemon juice
	champagne

Pour first three ingredients into a shaker with ice. Shake. Strain into a champagne flute. Stir. Top up with champagne. Stir.

Dark Gray Goose

A new cocktail from Monte's, in London. A French vodka inspired this combination.

⅔oz/2cl	vodka
1oz/3cl	black cherry purée
dash	cherry liqueur
	champagne

Pour the vodka, cherry purée, and cherry liqueur into a champagne flute. Stir. Top up with champagne. Stir.

Dream Cocktail

Dubonnet's a classic spirit that, when combined with other flavors, comes to life!

1oz/3cl	Dubonnet
½oz/1.5cl	triple sec/Cointreau
½oz/1.5cl	grapefruit juice
	champagne

Pour all ingredients, except champagne, into a mixing glass filled with ice. Stir. Strain into a champagne flute and top up with champagne. Stir.

Classic Champagne Cocktail

The origin of this cocktail is shrouded in mystery. However, its journey into cocktail history is interesting.

In 1889, a New York journalist organized a competition among New York bartenders to create a cocktail. The prize was a gold medal, which was won by a John Doughty, with a drink he named Business Brace. The original recipe included a dash of spring water. And it is this drink that's thought to be the origin of the Champagne Cocktail.

⅔oz / 2cl	cognac
2 dashes	Angostura bitters
1	sugar cube
	champagne

Place the sugar cube in a champagne flute and soak with Angostura. Add the cognac and top up with champagne. Stir. Garnish with a slice of orange and a maraschino cherry.

Father Christmas Fizz

Created for Santa as an alternative to a glass of milk. Red and white, this has cognac to keep him warm and champagne.

⅔oz / 2cl	Aperol
⅓oz / 1cl	cherry liqueur
⅔oz / 2cl	fresh orange juice
½oz / 1.5cl	cognac
½oz / 1.5cl	heavy (double) cream
	pink champagne

Pour the Aperol, cherry liqueur, and orange juice into a shaker with ice. Shake. Strain into a flute. Top up with champagne until three-quarters full. Stir gently. Pour the cognac and cream into a shaker. Shake. Strain into a small pitcher. Gently float the mix over the cocktail. Light a twist of orange peel and hold over the drink, dropping it in to extinguish the flame. Garnish with a sprig of red currants and a holly leaf speared by a cocktail stick.

Fifty Fizz

A simply delicious combination of herb and berry flavors with a fizzy finish.

1oz / 3cl	raspberry puree
½oz / 1.5cl	Bénédictine
	champagne

Shake puree and Bénédictine together. Strain into an art deco coupe or a champagne flute. Top up with champagne and garnish with two raspberries and a mint leaf on a cocktail stick.

French 74

A different version of the classic French 75 cocktail, this contains vodka instead of gin.

⅔oz / 2cl   vodka
⅔oz / 2cl   fresh orange juice
⅓oz / 1cl   gomme syrup
           champagne

Pour all ingredients, except champagne, into a shaker with ice. Shake. Strain into a champagne flute. Top up with champagne. Gently stir.

French 75

A creation from Henry of Henry's Bar in Paris to celebrate the fire power of the famous French 75 light field gun used in the First World War. Originally called the "75 Cocktail," the combination was added to by Harry of Harry's New York Bar in Paris after the war and became known as the French 75. He added champagne to a short drink.

⅔oz / 2cl   gin
⅔oz / 2cl   fresh lemon juice
dash   gomme syrup
           champagne

Pour all the ingredients, except champagne, into a shaker. Shake. Strain into a champagne flute. Top up with champagne. Stir.

French Kiss

A double fizz and a burst of berries come together in this romantic combination.

⅔oz / 2cl   raspberry purée
1oz / 3cl   ginger beer
dash   apricot brandy
           champagne

Pour the raspberry purée, apricot brandy, and ginger beer into a champagne flute. Stir gently. Top up with champagne. Garnish with a fresh raspberry dropped in the drink.

Fru Fru

A bit of frothy nonsense with a tart flavor from the grapefruit juice balanced by the strawberry liqueur.

1oz / 3cl   Passoá
1oz / 3cl   crème de fraises
           (strawberry liqueur)
1oz / 3cl   grapefruit juice
           champagne

Pour all ingredients, except champagne, into a shaker with ice. Shake. Strain into a champagne flute. Top up with champagne. Stir. Garnish with a small strawberry set on the rim.

Ginger Fizz

Fresh ginger and bourbon provide a spicy flavor, which is balanced by the sweet pineapple.

1oz / 3cl	bourbon
1oz / 3cl	pineapple juice
2 to 3 slices	fresh gingerroot
	champagne

Muddle the fresh ginger in the shaker. Add the bourbon and pineapple juice and ice. Shake. Strain into a champagne flute. Top up with champagne. Stir. Garnish with a wedge of pineapple.

Jacuzzi

A delicious combination of peach and orange flavors, with a hint of juniper from the gin.

1oz / 3cl	gin
²⁄₃oz / 2cl	peach schnapps
1oz / 3cl	fresh orange juice
	champagne

Pour all ingredients, except champagne, into a shaker with ice. Shake. Strain into a champagne flute. Stir gently. Top up with champagne. Stir.

Ja-mora

A light and refreshing fruity cocktail with a sweet note from the raspberry liqueur and an alcoholic hit from the vodka.

1oz / 3cl	vodka
1oz / 3cl	fresh orange juice
1oz / 3cl	clear apple juice
1oz / 3cl	crème de framboise (raspberry liqueur)
	champagne

Pour all ingredients, except champagne, into a shaker with ice. Shake. Strain into a champagne flute. Then carefully float the champagne over a barspoon to create a two-layered drink.

Juniper Royale

The taste of juniper and the tart flavors of cranberry and orange are a great mix.

1oz / 3cl	gin
½oz / 1.5cl	fresh orange juice
½oz / 1.5cl	cranberry juice
dash	grenadine
	champagne

Pour all ingredients, except champagne, into a shaker with ice. Shake. Strain into a champagne flute. Stir gently. Top up with champagne. Stir.

Kir Imperial

A version of Kir Royale, using raspberry instead of black-currant liqueur.

⅔oz / 2cl   crème de framboise
             (raspberry liqueur)
             champagne

Pour the raspberry liqueur into a champagne flute. Top up with champagne. Stir gently.

Kir Royale

The mayor of Dijon, Canon Félix Kir, is the hero of the original Kir combination. With champagne, it became a Kir Royale.

⅔oz / 2cl   crème de cassis
             (black-currant liqueur)
             champagne

Pour the cassis into a champagne flute. Top up with champagne. Stir gently.

La Dolce Vita

Literally translated, this means "the good life!" After a taste of this, you will be in heaven.

1oz / 3cl   vodka
4   seedless white grapes
1 barspoon   clear honey
               prosecco

Muddle the grapes in a shaker. Add the vodka and honey. Shake. Strain into a champagne flute. Top up with prosecco. Stir gently. Add a twist of lemon.

Lush

So named because it is full of sensual flavor, strong from the addition of vodka.

1oz / 3cl   vodka
⅔oz / 2cl   Chambord liqueur
               champagne

Pour the vodka and Chambord liqueur into a champagne flute. Stir gently. Top up with champagne. Stir.

Mayfair Fizz

An elegant taste sensation with a sweet orange flavor combined with the floral notes of the cognac.

1oz / 3cl   cognac
⅔oz / 2cl   fresh lemon juice
1 dash   orange bitters
1 dash   egg white
3 barspoons   honey syrup
               champagne

Place all ingredients, except the champagne, into a cocktail shaker filled with ice. Shake. Strain into a chilled champagne flute and top up with champagne. Place a fresh mint leaf on top of the drink.

Mimosa

A classic cocktail from 1925, created at the Ritz Hotel in Paris, it is named after the tropical flowering shrub.

2oz/6cl	fresh orange juice
2 dashes	Grand Marnier
	champagne

Fill a champagne flute to one quarter with orange juice. Add the Grand Marnier. Top up with champagne. Stir.

Perini

A balanced combination of cranberry juice and pear, with champagne adding the sparkle.

⅔oz/2.5cl	cranberry juice
⅔oz/2.5cl	fresh pear purée
⅓oz/1cl	pear schnapps
dash	white wine
dash	champagne

To make the purée, peel the pear and remove the core. Put in a blender with a dash of white wine and blend until smooth. Add equal proportions of pear purée and cranberry juice to a champagne flute. Add a dash of pear schnapps and top up with champagne. Stir. Garnish with a slice of pear and a few cranberries on a stem.

Pimm's Royale

A sparkling version of the Pimm's No.1 cocktail with a refined, dry flavor at the finish from the champagne.

1⅔oz/5cl	Pimm's No.1 Cup
	champagne
slices	lemon and orange
	cucumber peel
sprig	fresh mint

Pour the Pimm's into a highball filled with ice. Top up with champagne. Stir. Garnish with the orange and lemon slices, cucumber peel, and the mint dropped in the drink. Do not use too much fruit because it will detract from the taste of the Pimm's and the champagne.

Raspini

It has a real fruity flavor, with the raspberry providing a major role in the taste.

1oz/3cl	fresh raspberry juice
½oz/1.5cl	Cointreau
½oz/1.5cl	crème de bananes
	(banana liqueur)
	champagne

Pour all ingredients, except champagne, into a shaker with ice. Strain the mixture into a champagne flute. Top up with champagne. Stir. Garnish with two raspberries and a small sprig of mint.

Rosewood Fizz

Created for the Rosewood Hotel & Resort Group for a special occasion.

²⁄₃oz / 2cl   fresh raspberry juice
²⁄₃oz / 2cl   fresh orange juice
²⁄₃oz / 2cl   Bénédictine
              champagne

Pour all ingredients into a shaker with ice. Shake. Strain into a champagne flute and top up with champagne. Stir. Garnish with a blackberry, a raspberry, and a blueberry on a cocktail stick set across the rim if you like.

Saronno Imperial

A version of Kir Royale, using amaretto instead of black-currant liqueur.

1oz / 3cl   amaretto
             champagne

Pour the amaretto into a champagne flute. Top up with champagne. Stir gently. Garnish with a twist of lemon.

Sherry Cobbler

If someone would have waved a list under the nose of the average drinking man of 1863 and made him choose one drink that would stand the test of time, odds are heavy he would have gone for the Sherry Cobbler.

2 barspoons   Demerara sugar
2–3 slices   fresh orange
2oz / 6cl   medium dry sherry

Muddle orange and sugar into a wine glass. Add crushed ice and sherry and stir well until diluted. Top up with more crushed ice. Garnish with berries, a slice of orange, and a mint tip.

Sleepy Joe

A superb mix of mint and vanilla flavors. This is a shimmery, soft lilac color.

²⁄₃oz / 2cl   white rum
¹⁄₃oz / 1cl   white crème de menthe
²⁄₃oz / 2cl   Parfait Amour
              champagne

Pour all ingredients, except champagne, into a mixing glass with ice. Stir. Strain into a champagne flute. Top up with champagne. Stir gently.

Slow Seduction

A cocktail you don't want to rush. Its effect unfolds slowly throughout the drink.

½oz / 1.5cl	crème de framboise (raspberry liqueur)
½oz / 1.5cl	Cointreau
1oz / 3cl	pink grapefruit juice
	champagne

Pour all ingredients, except champagne, into a shaker with ice. Shake. Strain into a champagne flute. Top up with champagne. Stir gently.

Strawberry and Basil Fizz

You might think an herb and a fruit would not mix with the effervescent champagne—yet they do! Brilliantly.

5	fresh strawberries
2	fresh basil leaves
dash	gomme syrup
	prosecco or champagne

Put the strawberries in a blender with the basil leaves, gomme syrup, and a drop of prosecco. Blend for 10 seconds. Mash through a strainer and then chill for an hour. Pour enough mix to fill one quarter of a champagne flute. Top up prosecco. Stir gently. Garnish with a strawberry and a basil leaf.

Wimbledon Cocktail

Inspired by the strawberries and cream served during the Wimbledon tennis season.

⅔oz / 2cl	crème de framboise (raspberry liqueur)
5 to 6	strawberries, cut in half
⅔oz / 2cl	heavy (double) cream
⅔oz / 2cl	white rum
	champagne

Blend the strawberries and crème de framboise and place in the refrigerator for a couple of hours. Pour the berry mixture to a quarter of a champagne flute. Top up with champagne to three-quarters full. Stir. Mix the cream and rum in a mixing glass and float it over the back of a barspoon on top of the champagne. Garnish with a strawberry and a small sprig of mint.

Verticoli

A nice and refreshing combination of flavors.

1	chunk fresh pineapple
½oz / 1.5cl	orange vodka
½oz / 1.5cl	Chambord liqueur
⅓oz 1cl	Dubonnet
½tsp	strawberry puree
	champagne

Muddle pineapple in a shaker. Add remaining ingredients, except for the champagne. Shake. Strain into a chilled champagne flute. Top up with champagne. Garnish with a half strawberry.

WINE

Adonis

An aperitif, this was mixed in 1886 to celebrate the success of a Broadway musical.

1²⁄₃oz / 5cl	dry sherry
1oz / 3cl	sweet vermouth
dash	orange bitters

Pour the dry sherry into a mixing glass. Add the vermouth. Stir. Strain into a cocktail glass. Garnish with a twist of orange.

Alfonso II

Although its name refers to the classic champagne cocktail Alfonso, there is little similarity betwen the two. It's a good combination.

| 1²⁄₃oz / 5cl | Dubonnet |
| 1²⁄₃oz / 5cl | medium sherry |

Pour all ingredients into a mixing glass with ice. Stir. Strain into a cocktail glass.

Apocrapher

A combination of dry and bitter flavors with a minty finish. A good digestif.

1oz / 3cl	dry vermouth
1oz / 3cl	Campari
1oz / 3cl	white crème de menthe

Pour all ingredients into a mixing glass with ice. Stir. Strain into a cocktail glass.

Bamboo

An aperitif with a dry, wine flavor and a hint of bitter orange lingers.

2oz / 6cl	dry sherry
²⁄₃oz / 2cl	dry vermouth
4 drops	orange bitters

Pour all ingredients into a mixing glass with ice. Stir. Strain into a cocktail glass. Garnish with a spiral of orange.

Bartender

An excellent classic with the fragrance of a fortified wine and the spicy aroma of gin.

²⁄₃oz / 2cl	gin
²⁄₃oz / 2cl	dry sherry
²⁄₃oz / 2cl	Dubonnet
²⁄₃oz / 2cl	dry vermouth
dash	Grand Marnier

Pour all ingredients into a mixing glass with ice. Stir. Strain into a cocktail glass. Garnish with a maraschino cherry.

Bittersweet II

Well-named! A fine combination of sweet and dry with a hint of bitterness. An excellent aperitif.

1oz/3cl	dry vermouth
1oz/3cl	sweet vermouth
dash	Angostura bitters

Pour all ingredients into a mixing glass with ice. Stir. Strain into a small wine glass. Garnish with a twist of orange.

Brazil

A great aperitif, dry with a hint of bitterness and a sublime licorice finish.

1²/₃oz/5cl	dry sherry
1²/₃oz/5cl	dry vermouth
2 dashes	Angostura biters
2 dashes	pastis

Pour all ingredients into a mixing glass with ice. Stir. Strain into a small wine glass. Garnish with a twist of lemon.

Diplomat

A classic, smooth-talking cocktail guaranteed not to ruffle any feathers.

2oz/6cl	dry vermouth
1oz/3cl	sweet vermouth
dash	maraschino liqueur

Pour all ingredients into a mixing glass with ice. Stir. Strain into a cocktail glass. Garnish with a maraschino cherry dropped into the drink.

Dubonnet Cocktail

This is a classic predinner cocktail. At the height of its popularity during the late 1920s, it survives because of its flavor and color.

1¹/₃oz/4cl	Dubonnet
1¹/₃oz/4cl	gin

Pour both ingredients into a mixing glass with ice. Stir. Strain into a cocktail glass. Garnish with a twist of lemon.

Lovely Butterfly

An elegant taste sensation with a sweet orange flavor. A wonderful aperitif.

1oz/3cl	dry vermouth
1oz/3cl	sweet vermouth
¹/₂oz/1.5cl	Dubonnet
¹/₂oz/1.5cl	fresh orange juice

Pour all ingredients into a shaker with ice. Shake. Strain into a cocktail glass. Garnish with a twist of orange.

Port Flip

A classic cocktail to give you the strength to party all night long.

2oz / 6cl   ruby port
1oz / 3cl   brandy
1   free-range egg yolk

Pour all ingredients into a shaker with ice. Shake. Strain into a small wine glass. Garnish with a dusting of fresh grated nutmeg.

Spritzer

Many people put a slice of lemon in this drink, but you need only the essence of the twist before you drop it in the drink, not the full citrus flavor.

½ glass   dry white wine
½ glass   club soda

Pour the wine into a wine glass with ice. Add the club soda. Stir. Garnish with a twist of lemon in the drink.

Kir

In the early 1850s, the mayor of Dijon, France, was Canon Félix Kir, a colorful politician. At his official receptions, held in the Duke's Palace, he used to serve an aperitif made with crème de cassis (black-currant liqueur) from Dijon and a white wine called Bourgogne Aligoté. This was a purely economic practice whose goal was to promote this white wine and take the place of the usual aperitifs. Very quickly the "black-currant white wine" became known as "Canon Kir's aperitif," then "Father Kir's aperitif" and finally throughout the region as the "Kir" aperitif.

⅔oz / 2cl   crème de cassis
                 (black-currant
                 liqueur)
                 dry white wine, chilled

Pour the crème de cassis into a champagne flute. Top up with wine.

BITTERS &
OTHER SPIRITS

This section includes types of herbal bitters made by the ancient apothecaries, as well as other spirits such as akvavit (aquavit), aniseed-based spirits such as Pernod, ouzo, saké, schnapps, and pastis.

Bitters are made from herbs, roots, and other botanicals and contain less sugar and less fruit pulp than regular liqueurs. They are either drunk as a cure for a hangover, or to soothe indigestion. Angostura is the most well known bar bitters. The result of studies by a Prussian army surgeon, Dr. J. G. B. Siegert, to develop a medicine to fight off malaria and named after the city of Angostura in Venezuela, it has a rum base mixed with angostura bark and aromatic plants. Peychaud is an orange-flavored bitters produced in New Orleans.

Known for their soothing effect on the digestive system, Fernet Branca and Underberg are made from secret recipes with a herbal base. Jägermeister is a German digestif produced since 1895.

Bitters are also drunk as an aperitif. There are many brands, of which the Italian-made Campari, an orange-based bitters, brilliant red in color, is the most familiar. Punt e Mes, Aperol, and Cynar are bitters produced in Italy. Suze is a French bitters also drunk as an aperitif.

Aniseed-based spirits are made by distillation of the fermented aniseeds plus other botanicals, or these are macerated in spirit. Anis (Pernod) is distilled and has a complex aroma and flavor. (Anis is the French description for both the plant and

campari lady (left), page 192, and **negroni**, page 195

the drink; anise is used in English.) Pastis (Ricard) is a French aniseed-flavored spirit, made by maceration.

The Pernod family had been producing absinthe, with extract from wormwood, since 1805. It contained absinthe and other botanicals. When it was banned in 1915 in France and Switzerland, the Pernods closed the business. In 1920, the production of aniseed drinks was again legalized, but wormwood remained outlawed. Pernod, introduced in 1928, is flavored with extract from the star anise plant and fennel.

Absinthe is again being produced in Europe, and sipping absinthe is once again fashionable in London bars.

SAMBUCA

Sambuca is a distillate with a high sugar level. A liqueur, not an aperitif, it is made with the essential oil of fennel (green anise), which retains a natural fragrance.

GREEK OUZO

This is a clear distillate, with a dryish taste, made with anise or fennel. Good

quality ouzo needs to be at least 46 percent abv. It is a café drink taken with a little water.

SAKÉ

Saké is simply saké. Often mistakenly called rice wine, saké is brewed like beer, yet it is noncarbonated, and with an alcohol level similar to wine (13.5 to 15 percent abv). Serve saké chilled, not hot—its subtle aromas would be lost if heated.

AKVAVIT (AQUAVIT)

A Scandinavian specialty, made from potatoes or grain that are distilled and blended. It is served ice cold, usually with a beer chaser.

SCHNAPPS

This is a term for the range of white and flavored spirits produced in Germany, Holland, and Scandinavia. Schnapps may be made from grain, potato, or molasses. It is usually drunk in one swift swallow.

Americano

This is a refreshing aperitif said to have first been served in 1861 at Gaspare Campari's bar, a chic meeting place frequented by the composer Verdi, Edward VII, and in later years, the writer Ernest Hemingway. Yet it wasn't until Italy became popular with American tourists that it became known as the Americano. The tourists took the cocktail recipe back home and legally sipped it throughout Prohibition—Campari was classified as a medicinal product!

1oz/3cl	Campari
1oz/3cl	sweet vermouth
	club soda

Pour the sweet vermouth, then the Campari into a highball filled with ice. Garnish with lemon and orange twists. Club soda is optional—but for summer, it gives the drink its freshness.

Apothecary Cocktail

This is a wonderful digestif to serve after a heavy dinner. Fernet Branca and white crème de menthe easily settle the digestive system.

1oz/3cl	Fernet Branca
1oz/3cl	white crème de menthe
1oz/3cl	Punt e Mes

Pour all ingredients in a mixing glass filled with ice. Stir. Strain into a cocktail glass.

Baracas Cocktail

A cocktail to revive the spirits; this is a combination of bitter and sweet, like the memories of the night before.

2oz/6cl	sweet red vermouth
1oz/3cl	Fernet Branca

Pour all ingredients into a shaker with ice. Shake. Strain into a cocktail glass.

Bloodhound

One whiff of this and you'll be off into the night—again.

2oz/6cl	Campari
1oz/3cl	vodka
	fresh grapefruit juice

Pour the Campari and vodka into a highball filled with ice. Top up with grapefruit juice. Stir. Garnish with half a slice of grapefruit dropped in the drink.

Body & Soul Reviver

Guaranteed to soothe the soul when you awaken from the night before.

1oz/3cl	Branca Menthe
1oz/3cl	cognac
dash	orange bitters

Pour all ingredients into a shaker with ice. Shake. Strain into a shot glass.

Campari Classic

One of the Italians' favorite aperitifs, usually sipped sitting in a street café watching life walk by.

2oz/6cl	Campari
dash	sparkling mineral water

Pour the Campari into an old-fashioned glass filled with ice. Add a splash of sparkling mineral water. Stir.

Campari Cooler

The name reflects the drink—cool and refreshing on a summer's day.

1oz/3cl	Campari
1oz/3cl	peach schnapps
2oz/6cl	cranberry juice
2oz/6cl	fresh orange juice
⅔oz/2cl	fresh lime juice
dash	gomme syrup
	7UP

Pour the first six ingredients into a shaker filled with ice. Shake. Strain into a highball. Top up with 7UP. Stir. Garnish with a slice of orange.

Campari Lady

An elegant drink with a bit of a kick for men who like their ladies like that!

1oz/3cl	Campari
½oz/1.5cl	gin
3oz/9cl	fresh orange juice
3oz/9cl	fresh grapefruit juice
dash	gomme syrup

Pour all ingredients into a highball filled with ice. Stir. Garnish with a slice of orange.

Campari Laguna

A strong-flavored tonic full of goodness from the brandy, Campari, and Fernet Branca.

1oz/3cl	brandy
½oz/1.5cl	vodka
½oz/1.5cl	dry vermouth
½oz/1.5cl	Campari
dash	Fernet Branca

Pour all ingredients into a shaker with ice. Shake. Strain into a cocktail glass. Garnish with a red maraschino cherry.

Campari Sky

Created to match the color of the sky at sunset. Many people will know this as a Negrosci.

1oz/3cl	Campari
1oz/3cl	sweet red vermouth
1oz/3cl	vodka

Pour all ingredients into an old-fashioned glass filled with ice. Stir.

Campari Testarossa

Literally translated, it means "red-head" but really, this is a cocktail for Ferrari fans.

1oz/3cl	Campari
1oz/3cl	vodka
dash	tonic water

Pour the Campari and vodka into an old-fashioned glass filled with ice. Stir. Top up with tonic water. Stir. Garnish with a slice of orange.

Camparinha

An Italian version of the Caipirinha—a balanced aperitif with a hint of lime over the Campari.

2oz/6cl	Campari
1	lime, cut into eight pieces
3	sugar cubes

Place the lime pieces and sugar cubes into an old-fashioned glass. Muddle firmly to release the juices. Add the Campari and a scoop of crushed ice. Stir.

Camparosa

Although its ingredients have bitter flavors, they combine well, creating a delicate and refreshing cocktail

| 2oz/6cl | Campari |
| 4oz/12cl | pink grapefruit juice |

Pour the Campari into a highball filled with ice. Add the grapefruit juice. Stir. Garnish with a slice of orange.

Citrus Cooler

A refreshing, long drink with an effervescent finish—ideal for summer days.

2oz/6cl	Campari
1oz/3cl	fresh lime juice
	sparkling orange

Pour all ingredients into a highball filled with ice. Stir. Top up with sparkling orange. Stir. Add a slice of orange.

Cynar Cola

Cynar is a bitters made from artichokes. The cola sweetens the slightly bitter taste of this long drink.

| 2oz/6cl | Cynar |
| | cola |

Pour the Cynar into a highball filled with ice. Top up with cola. Stir. Garnish with a slice of lemon.

Dobbs

This is the butler's recommendation for an excellent digestif, especially good after a heavy meal late in the evening.

| 1⅔oz/5cl | white crème de menthe |
| ⅔oz/2cl | Fernet Branca |

Fill an old-fashioned glass with crushed ice and pour in the crème de menthe. Gently float the Fernet Branca on top. Serve with a straw.

Drugstore

A great restorative with a kick from the herbal Fernet Branca, a hint of sweetness from the vermouth, and mint to soothe.

1oz/3cl	Fernet Branca
½oz/1.5cl	sweet vermouth
½oz/1.5cl	white crème de menthe

Pour all ingredients into a mixing glass with ice. Stir well. Strain into a liqueur glass.

Friends

Aperol is made from rhubarb essence and has a unique flavor.

1oz/3cl	Aperol
1oz/3cl	gin
1oz/3cl	dry vermouth

Pour all ingredients into a mixing glass with ice. Stir well. Strain into a cocktail glass. Squeeze a twist of lemon over the drink and drop it in.

Garibaldi

This drink is named after General Garibaldi, the great 19th-century hero who liberated Italy. It is a classic, with a wonderful citrus flavor.

1⅔oz/5cl	Campari
3½oz/10cl	fresh orange juice

Pour the Campari, then the orange juice, into an old-fashioned glass filled with ice. Stir. Garnish with half a slice of orange.

Gilia

A tasty aperitif with the peaty flavor of whisky balanced by Aperol's flavor.

2oz/6cl	Aperol
1oz/3cl	Scotch whisky

Place all ingredients in a mixing glass with ice. Stir. Strain into a cocktail glass. Garnish with a twist of orange.

I. B. F. Pick-Me-Up

A good combination of earthy flavors, with a bubbly finish.

1oz/3cl	Fernet Branca
1oz/3cl	triple sec/Cointreau
1oz/3cl	brandy
	champagne

Place one ice cube in a white wine glass. Add all ingredients, except champagne. Stir. Top up with champagne. Stir. Add a twist of lemon.

Ignorance Is Bliss

This can become a long drink by serving in a highball and using more apple juice.

1oz/3cl	Campari
1oz/3cl	vodka
⅔oz/2cl	passion fruit syrup
⅔oz/2cl	apple juice

Pour all the ingredients into a shaker with ice. Shake. Strain into a cocktail glass. Squeeze a wedge of lime over the drink and drop it in.

Negroni

The name originates from a Florentine, Count Camillo Negroni, who regularly visited the Casoni Bar in Florence. The story goes that he ordered his usual Americano with a little gin and the resulting drink became known as the Negroni! This has the right balance of sweet to bitter and stimulates the appetite. To make it a long drink, add soda.

The very important trick to this cocktail is to ensure you measure the ingredients exactly. That way, you can guarantee the flavor.

1oz / 3cl	Campari
1oz / 3cl	gin
1oz / 3cl	sweet vermouth
	club soda (optional)

Pour ingredients into an old-fashioned glass filled with ice. Stir. Add soda if required. Stir. Garnish with a slice of orange dropped into the drink. Serve with a stirrer.

Pink Pussy

A delightful long drink, with a peach flavor, to make you purr all night long.

2oz / 6cl	Campari
1oz / 3cl	peach brandy
	bitter lemon

Pour the first two ingredients into a shaker filled with ice. Shake. Strain into a highball filled with ice. Top up with bitter lemon. Stir.

Red Sky

A warm red-colored aperitif with a slightly bitter taste combined with zesty vodka.

1oz / 3cl	Campari
1oz / 3cl	vodka
1oz / 3cl	fresh orange juice

Pour all ingredients into an old-fashioned glass filled with ice. Stir. Garnish with a twist of orange dropped in the drink.

Serenissima

Don't worry—be happy! That's the meaning of this drink's name. Sip to chill out after a day at the office.

1oz / 3cl	Campari
1oz / 3cl	vodka
1oz / 3cl	fresh grapefruit juice

Pour all ingredients into a shaker with ice. Shake. Strain into a cocktail glass. Garnish with a twist of orange.

Shaft

A dry and effervescent aperitif to stimulate your appetite.

1oz / 3cl	Aperol
1oz / 3cl	gin
	prosecco

Pour the gin and Aperol into a mixing glass with ice. Stir. Strain into a highball filled with ice. Top up with prosecco. Drop a slice of orange into the drink.

Shakerato

Popular in Italy as an aperitif, this has a fresh taste of citrus with the bitter.

2oz / 6cl	Campari
⅔oz / 2cl	fresh lemon juice

Pour all ingredients into a shaker with ice. Shake. Strain into a cocktail glass. Drop a twist of lemon into the drink.

Special Americano

A version of the classic Americano—the orange juice provides a citrus finish.

1oz / 3cl	Campari
1oz / 3cl	sweet red vermouth
1oz / 3cl	gin
1oz / 3cl	fresh orange juice
	club soda

Pour the Campari, vermouth, gin, and orange juice to a highball filled with ice. Stir. Top up with soda. Stir. Garnish with a spiral of orange and lemon peels.

Stomach Reviver

Just the thing when you are not feeling well after a heavy meal partaken with a variety of alcohols.

1oz / 3cl	Fernet Branca
1oz / 3cl	brandy
3 dashes	Angostura bitters

Pour all ingredients into a shaker with ice. Shake. Strain into a shot glass. Knock it back. Breathe a sigh of relief.

Titian's Temptation

Named after the painter's penchant for using red pigments in his paintings.

1oz / 3cl	sambuca
1oz / 3cl	Campari
1oz / 3cl	fresh lemon juice

Pour all ingredients into a shaker with ice. Strain into a cocktail glass. Garnish with a slice of lemon.

Velvet and Silk

A tangy aperitif, with a spicy flavor from the gin.

2oz / 6cl	Cynar
1oz / 3cl	gin

Pour both ingredients into an old-fashioned glass filled with ice. Stir. Drop a slice of lemon in the drink.

SAKÉ COCKTAILS

Black Sea

Here's an unusual flavor experience. Personally, I prefer the ink with spaghetti.

1²⁄₃oz / 5cl	saké
½oz / 1.5cl	gin
½oz / 1.5cl	fresh lemon juice
½oz / 1.5cl	squid ink
dash	gomme syrup
pinch	fresh ground coriander root

Pour all ingredients into a shaker with ice. Shake. Strain into a cocktail glass.

Ginger Saké

A combination of spice and citrus flavors is balanced here by the saké flavor.

2oz / 6cl	saké
few slices	gingerroot
²⁄₃oz / 2cl	fresh lime juice

Pour all ingredients into a shaker with ice. Shake. Strain into a cocktail glass. Garnish with a wedge of lime.

Passion Tsuzis

A great balance of sweet and sour with an an intense finish of delicate pear flavor.

1²⁄₃oz / 5cl	pear saké
²⁄₃oz / 2cl	Poire William
½oz / 1.5cl	fresh lemon juice
½oz / 1.5cl	passion fruit syrup

Pour all ingredients into a shaker with ice. Shake. Strain into a cocktail glass.

Rising Sun

A restorative cocktail with spicy elements to wake up your body's energy center.

1oz / 3cl	saké
dash	wasabi
dash	soy sauce
dash	Tabasco sauce
	tomato juice

Pour all ingredients, except tomato juice, into a shaker with ice. Shake. Strain into a highball filled with ice. Top up with tomato juice. Stir. Garnish with a sprig of parsley.

Saké Cosmopolitan

A Japanese version of the modern classic Cosmopolitan, replacing the vodka with lemon-flavored saké.

1oz / 3cl	lemon saké
½oz / 1.5cl	Cointreau
1oz / 3cl	cranberry juice
½oz / 1.5cl	fresh lime juice
⅓oz / 1cl	gomme syrup

Pour all the ingredients into a shaker with ice. Shake. Strain into a cocktail glass. Garnish with an orange twist.

Saké Margarita

This has got a long way to go before it has the style of the original Margarita.

1oz / 3cl	saké
1oz / 3cl	orange curaçao
1oz / 3cl	fresh lime juice

Rub a wedge of lemon around the rim of a cocktail glass. Dip it into a saucer of fine salt. Pour all ingredients into a shaker with ice. Shake. Strain into the glass. Garnish with a wedge of lime.

Silver Surfer

This has a sweet-and-sour flavor combination with a floral finish. It's a delicate pale lilac color.

1²⁄₃oz / 5cl	saké
¹⁄₃oz / 1cl	vodka
½oz / 1.5cl	Parfait Amour
½oz / 1.5cl	fresh lemon juice
¹⁄₃oz / 1cl	passion fruit syrup

Pour all ingredients into a shaker with ice. Shake. Strain into a cocktail glass. Garnish with a slice of star fruit.

Tokyo Bloody Mary

Just as interesting to sip as the original Bloody Mary, with a bit more oomph of flavor from the saké ingredient.

2oz / 6cl	saké
4oz / 12cl	tomato juice
²⁄₃oz / 2cl	fresh lemon juice
8 dashes	Tabasco sauce
4 dashes	Worcestershire sauce
4 dashes	medium sherry
1 pinch	celery salt
1 pinch	black pepper

Pour all ingredients into shaker with ice. Shake. Strain into a highball filled with ice. Garnish with a stick of celery.

ANISEED-BASED COCKTAILS

Anisette Cocktail

A sweet-and-creamy anisette flavor dominates in this after-dinner drink.

1²⁄₃oz / 5cl	anisette liqueur
²⁄₃oz / 2cl	gin
²⁄₃oz / 2cl	heavy (double) cream

Pour all ingredients into a shaker with ice. Shake. Strain into a cocktail glass. Grate fresh nutmeg over the top.

Black Orchid

In 1979 a Major Henri Dubied bought the recipe for Pernod from a Madame Henriot, who had been bequeathed it by its creator, Dr. Ordinaire.

1oz/3cl	Pernod
1/2oz/1.5cl	Cointreau
1/2oz/1.5cl	blackberry brandy
	tonic water
	7UP

Pour the first three ingredients into a highball filled with ice. Stir. Add a splash of tonic water, then top up with 7UP. Stir. Garnish with a pink slipper orchid.

Blondie

A drink for a blonde or blonde pretenders! The Galliano lends it a golden air.

| 1oz/3cl | anisette liqueur |
| 1oz/3cl | Galliano |

Pour all ingredients into a mixing glass with ice. Stir. Strain into a cocktail glass.

Blue Negligee

Created by Frank Clarke, this was winner of the National Cocktail Competition, in Australia, in 1975.

1oz/3cl	ouzo
1oz/3cl	Parfait Amour
1oz/3cl	green Chartreuse

Pour all ingredients into a mixing glass with ice. Stir. Strain into a cocktail glass. Garnish with a maraschino cherry dropped in the drink.

Fancy Angel

A great combination of aniseed and berry flavors with a wonderful citrus finish. Vodka adds strength.

1oz/3cl	anisette liqueur
1oz/3cl	vodka
1/2oz/1.5cl	crème de mûre
	(blackberry liqueur)
1/2oz/1.5cl	fresh lemon juice
1 teaspoon	egg white powder

Pour all ingredients into a shaker with ice. Shake. Strain into a highball filled with crushed ice. Serve with a straw.

Glad Eye

An elegant and tangy cocktail designed to soothe the digestive system after dinner.

| 1²/₃oz/5cl | pastis |
| 1oz/3cl | green crème de menthe |

Pour all ingredients into a mixing glass with ice. Stir. Strain into a cocktail glass. Garnish with a sprig of mint.

Greek Doctor

A great combination of aniseed flavor and sharp citrus flavors.

1oz/3cl	ouzo
1oz/3cl	vodka
1oz/3cl	fresh orange juice
⅔oz/2cl	fresh lemon juice

Pour all ingredients into a shaker with ice. Strain into an old-fashioned glass filled with ice. Garnish with a slice of orange.

Naked Waiter

It's hard to say which waiter, of all the waiters, would work naked!

1oz/3cl	Pernod
1oz/3cl	Mandarine Napoléon
2oz/6cl	pineapple juice
	bitter lemon

Pour all ingredients, except bitter lemon, into a highball filled with ice. Stir. Top up with bitter lemon. Stir.

Ouzo and Water

This is the traditional Greek café drink taken with chilled water and no ice.

1⅔oz/5cl	ouzo
1⅔oz/5cl	water

Pour the ouzo into an old-fashioned glass filled with ice. Add the water to create an opaque, milky mixture. How much water you add depends upon how much aniseed flavor you prefer.

Tour de France

This recipe uses two of the most popular spirits in France. It has an aniseed-berry flavor.

1⅔oz/5cl	Pernod
½oz/1.5cl	crème de cassis (blackcurrant liqueur)
1 teaspoon	superfine (caster) sugar 7UP

Place the sugar in an old-fashioned glass. Add the spirits. Stir until the sugar is dissolved. Add a scoop of crushed ice. Top up with 7UP. Stir. Garnish with two blackberries and a sprig of mint.

Waldorf

A hint of bitter flavor invades this aperitif. A great mix of Irish and French influences.

1oz/3cl	Pernod
1oz/3cl	Irish whiskey
2 dashes	Angostura bitters

Pour all ingredients into a shaker with ice. Shake. Strain into a cocktail glass.

Yellow Parrot

Created in 1935 by Albert Coleman at the Stork Club, in New York, using absinthe.

1oz/3cl	Pernod
1oz/3cl	yellow Chartreuse
1oz/3cl	apricot brandy

Pour all ingredients into a mixing glass with ice. Stir. Strain into a cocktail glass. Garnish with a twist of orange.

SCHNAPPS-BASED COCKTAILS

Danish Mary

A Danish interpretation of the classic Bloody Mary, but with akvavit as the base spirit.

1oz/3cl	akvavit
3oz/9cl	tomato juice
2 dashes	fresh lemon juice
2 dashes	Worcestershire sauce
pinch	celery salt

Pour all ingredients into a shaker with ice. Shake. Strain into a highball filled with ice. Garnish with a slice of lemon.

Kelvin 66

A good combination of orange and wine flavors, with the basic strength of akvavit.

⅔oz/2cl	akvavit
⅔oz/2cl	Grand Marnier
⅔oz/2cl	Dubonnet
⅔oz/2cl	fresh orange juice

Pour all ingredients into a shaker with ice. Shake. Strain into a cocktail glass. Garnish with a maraschino cherry.

Jumping Jack

An aperitif, with the taste of strawberries and orange and a hit of powerful schnapps.

1⅔oz/5cl	korn schnapps
3oz/9cl	fresh orange juice
½oz/1.5cl	strawberry syrup
½oz/1.5cl	fresh lemon juice

Pour all ingredients into a shaker with ice. Shake. Strain into a highball filled with ice. Garnish with a slice of orange and a maraschino cherry.

Rose Cocktail

An aromatic aperitif with the lovely taste of cherries mixed with the taste of vermouth.

1⅔oz/5cl	kirsch
1oz/3cl	dry vermouth
dash	grenadine

Pour all ingredients into a mixing glass with ice. Stir. Strain into a cocktail glass.

Strawberry Fetish

The taste of strawberries and cream wrapped up in one creamy cocktail.

1⅔oz/5cl	strawberry schnapps
⅔oz/2cl	Frangelico
dash	grenadine
1oz/3cl	heavy (double) cream
	club soda

Pour all ingredients, except soda, into a shaker with ice. Shake. Strain into a highball filled with ice. Top up with soda. Stir. Garnish with a strawberry.

PUNCHES, CUPS & EGGNOGS

Traditionally, a punch was made of rum and water (hot or chilled), with sugar added to taste, plus lemon and orange juices, or fresh lime juice.

The British were introduced to this drink in the mid-17th century when they took Jamaica from the Spanish. A century later, it was being mixed at the table in a Punch House, in a bowl (hence the term "punch bowl") by the host or hostess. Rum was the main spirit. Nutmeg and other spices, as well as orange and lemon slices, were added as a decoration. Older punch recipes use a dark spirit, such as brandy or dark rum, as a base. Red and white wine-based punches are now popular because they are lighter and less alcoholic. If a drink is too strong, add 7UP or ginger ale to taste.

Use a large block of ice, rather than ice cubes, in a punch bowl. This will not dilute the drink as quickly.

CUPS

A cup is also made in bulk and is a British traditional offering to hunt-riders before they set off across the fields. They contain wine or a low-alcohol spirit like sloe gin.

EGGNOGS

Traditionally, eggnogs contained a combination of warm spiced ale with sugar, spirit, and eggs. They can be made as a single drink, or in bulk, as long as the proportions are maintained.

planter's punch for one, and in a pitcher, page 207

PUNCHES

Bombay Punch

Serves 6
Using fruit of the season
gives it a fresher flavor.

6oz / 18cl	brandy
6oz / 18cl	dry sherry
1oz / 3cl	maraschino liqueur
1oz / 3cl	orange curaçao
1 bottle	champagne
	diced fruit of the season
18oz / 54cl	club soda

Pour all ingredients, except champagne, fruit, and soda, into a punch bowl. Stir. Just before guests arrive, add ice and the fruit of the season, such as oranges, strawberries, kiwifruit slices, and so on. Add soda. Fill with champagne. Stir. Serve in wine glasses.

Brandy Punch

Serves 6
This is a perfect drink to
share with your friends at a
party. It looks great in the
punch bowl.

6oz / 18cl	brandy
4oz / 12cl	orange curaçao
3oz / 12cl	fresh lemon juice
2oz / 6cl	fresh orange juice
1oz / 3cl	grenadine
2 teaspoons	superfine (caster) sugar
half	orange, sliced
half	lemon, sliced
1 quart / liter	club soda

Pour all ingredients into a punch bowl. Stir. Just before guests arrive, add a block of ice, then the slices of fruit. Add soda. Stir. Serve in a wine glass.

Champagne Punch

Serves 8
This is a traditional punch
served especially at family
celebrations.

4oz / 12cl	brandy
4oz / 12cl	orange curaçao
4oz / 12cl	maraschino liqueur
3 tablespoons	superfine (caster) sugar
handful	strawberries, sliced
handful	raspberries
half	orange, sliced
2 bottles	champagne

Pour all ingredients, except champagne, into a punch bowl. Add the fruit. Just before guests arrive, add ice. Fill with champagne. Stir. Serve in wine glasses, making sure one or two pieces of fruit slip in each as well.

Cranberry Punch

Serves 12
This is the perfect punch to
share with friends at a party.

15oz / 45cl	vodka
1 quart / liter	cranberry juice
1 quart / liter	clear apple juice
1 quart / liter	pineapple juice
	7UP

Pour all ingredients, except 7UP, into a punch bowl. Add the garnishes—wedges of pineapple, a stem of cranberries, and slices of apple. Place a small sprig of fresh mint in the middle of the bowl. Add ice and 7UP when the first guests arrive so the latter doesn't lose its fizz. Stir. Serve in small wine glasses or punch glasses.

Fish House Punch

A true classic punch, it was first concocted in 1732 at the State in Schuylkill Fishing Club, in Philadelphia, where it was alleged to have been sipped at the start of every meeting. It is also purported to have been responsible for several blank pages in George Washington's diary. It's a superb pick-me-up for stormy weather, retaining its tropical taste while maintaining an air of respectability.

Described by Fannie Merritt Farmer in her 1896 edition of *The Boston Cooking-School Book* as a "much-esteemed and highly potent punch," it smacks of quaint good manners in a time of chaos.

Serves 10
6oz/18cl	peach brandy
12oz/36cl	cognac
6oz/18cl	dark rum
6oz/18cl	fresh lemon juice
3oz/9cl	gomme syrup
1 quart/liter	sparkling water

Pour all ingredients, except sparkling water, into a large punch bowl. Top up with sparkling water. Add wedges of peach and slices of lemon into the punch bowl. Before guests arrive, add a large block of ice. Serve in wine glasses.

Italian Punch

Serves 6
This punch is refreshing, dry, slightly bitter taste. It looks good and is simple to make.

1 bottle	dry white wine
1²⁄₃oz/5cl	fresh lemon juice
3¹⁄₃oz/10cl	Campari
3¹⁄₃oz/10cl	Aperol
1 quart/liter	club soda
1	orange, thinly sliced
1	lemon, thinly sliced

Pour all ingredients, except soda, into a punch bowl. Add ice and then the soda. Add the orange and lemon slices to the bowl. Serve in wine goblets.

Japanese Spring Punch

To make in bulk, multiply the ingredients by the number of guests.
Just the drink for when spring is bursting out all over. It's tart, with a raspberry finish.

1²⁄₃oz/5cl	raspberry saké
²⁄₃oz/2cl	crème de framboise (raspberry liqueur)
1oz/3cl	fresh lemon juice
1oz/3cl	raspberry purée
¹⁄₃oz/1cl	gomme syrup
	champagne

Pour all ingredients, except champagne, into a shaker with ice. Shake. Strain into a highball. Top up with champagne and a tiny layer of crushed ice. Garnish with two straws, two slices of lemon, and three raspberries.

Melon Punch

Serves 6

If you prepare the punch before guests arrive, don't add the ice because it will dilute the ingredients.

8oz/24cl	vodka
3⅓oz/10cl	melon liqueur
1⅓oz/4cl	peach schnapps
1⅔oz/5cl	fresh lemon juice
17oz/50cl	ginger beer
1	kiwifruit
6	strawberries, diced

Pour all ingredients, except ginger beer, into a pitcher. Stir. Add ice to a punch bowl. Add the mixture and fill with ginger beer. Add the diced fruit. Stir. Serve in wine glasses.

Paradise Punch

To make in bulk, multiply the ingredients by the number of guests.

If Paradise is half as nice as the state of mind that this cocktail brings on, then lead me to it!

1oz/3cl	Southern Comfort
⅔oz/2cl	vodka
½oz/1.5cl	amaretto
1⅔oz/5cl	fresh orange juice
1⅔oz/5cl	pineapple juice
⅔oz/2cl	Rose's lime cordial
2 dashes	grenadine

Pour all ingredients into a shaker with ice. Shake. Strain into a highball filled with ice. Garnish with a slice of lime and a maraschino cherry.

Parisiana Punch

Serves 11

A warming brandy and wine-flavored punch.

10oz/30cl	madeira
4oz/12cl	cognac
4oz/100g	superfine (caster) sugar
2	lemons, cut in half
1 bottle	champagne

Pour all ingredients, except champagne, into a large pitcher and stir until the sugar dissolves. Place in the refrigerator for two to three hours. When guests arrive, fill with champagne. Serve in wine glasses.

Patriot Punch

Serves 20

"Professor" Jerry Thomas wrote in his 1887 edition of How to Mix Drinks: *"This is sufficient for a mixed company of 20, not 20 of the Light Guards." It packs a strong and spirited kick!*

1 bottle	cognac
4	oranges, sliced
1	pineapple, sliced
1 bottle	champagne

Place the orange and pineapple slices in a punch bowl. Pour the cognac over them. Let them steep for a couple of hours. Add the champagne, stir, and serve immediately in wine glasses. According to the Professor, you must add "ice direct from the Rocky Mountains."

CLASSIC COCKTAIL

Planter's Punch

This drink was created in 1879 to celebrate the opening of Myers's Rum Distillery in Jamaica. Gossip about the mixture created in Fred L. Myers's honor spread across the island, and was tasted by just about everybody at Kelly's Bar on Sugar Wharf. Visitors to the island took the recipe away with them.

By 1934 it had reached *Esquire* magazine's best drinks listing and was established as a refreshingly mellow drink. Now, it has more texture and has also become sweeter. The key to its success is to use well-aged rum.

To make in bulk, multiply the ingredients by the number of guests.

1²⁄₃oz / 5cl	Myers's dark rum
1 dash	Angostura bitters
½oz / 1.5cl	fresh lemon juice
2 dashes	gomme syrup

Pour all ingredients into a shaker with ice. Shake. Strain into a wine glass with ice. Garnish with a slice of orange and a maraschino cherry and a sprig of fresh mint. Serve with a straw.

Planter's Punch No. 2

This is a more interesting drink, longer and fruitier, full of texture and more flavors. It includes white as well as dark rum and lime, instead of lemon, juice.

²⁄₃oz / 2cl	Myers's dark rum
¹⁄₃oz / 1cl	white rum
¹⁄₃oz / 1cl	Cointreau
1²⁄₃oz / 5cl	pineapple juice
1²⁄₃oz / 5cl	fresh orange juice
¹⁄₃oz / 1cl	fresh lime juice
2 dashes	grenadine

Pour all ingredients, except the dark rum, into a shaker with ice. Shake. Strain into a highball with ice. Carefully float the dark rum on top. Garnish with a slice of orange and a maraschino cherry. Serve with a straw.

If you want to make this in a punch bowl, add small wedges of pineapple without its skin and slices of lime, orange, and lemon. Add a few sprigs of mint on top of the bowl.

Pineapple Pisco Punch

Serves 10
Guaranteed to get the party going!!

1 bottle	pisco brandy
10oz/30cl	fresh lemon juice
5oz/15cl	pineapple syrup
12 dashes	aromatic bitters
2oz/6cl	cane syrup

Pour all ingredients directly into a large punch bowl over one large block of ice or ice cubes. Stir well and garnish with macerated pineapple chunks. Serve in a wine glass or goblet.

Plantation Punch

This was an entry at a competition where the challenge was to create a pairing with an exotic duck dish. I was so impressed that I had to include it in my book!

1½oz/4.5cl	aged rum
2oz/6cl	pineapple juice
1½oz/4.5cl	passion fruit juice
⅔oz/2cl	gomme syrup
3 dash	angostura bitters
small piece	celery

Muddle the celery in a Boston shaker. Add remaining ingredients and ice. Shake. Double strain into a highball glass filled with crushed ice. Garnish by placing a few leaves of curly endive on top of the drink and finish with 3 raspberries soaked in hoisin sauce on a cocktail stick. Serve with a straw.

Russian Spring Punch

To make in bulk, multiply the ingredients by the number of guests.

2oz/6cl	vodka
⅔oz/2cl	fresh lemon juice
⅔oz/2cl	crème de cassis (black-currant liqueur)
⅔oz/2cl	gomme syrup
	champagne

Pour all ingredients into a shaker with ice. Shake. Strain into a highball filled with ice. Top up with champagne. Garnish with two raspberries and a slice of lemon on a cocktail stick set across the glass.

Thanksgiving Punch

Serves 6

1 bottle	dry sparkling white wine
3⅓oz/10cl	brandy
3⅓oz/10cl	crème de framboise (raspberry liqueur)
18oz/54cl	cranberry juice
8⅓oz/25cl	fresh orange juice
handful	fresh raspberries
handful	cranberries
sprig	fresh mint
2	oranges, sliced

Pour all ingredients into a punch bowl. Stir. Just before guests arrive, add ice cubes, the slices of orange, the mint, and the berries.

Tropical Love Punch

Serves 12
This is simple to make and has all the tropical essences that you desire in a drink without being too sweet. When you have a party, you want your friends to enjoy a cool, refreshing drink.

11½oz/35cl	golden rum
8¾oz/25cl	apricot brandy
8¾oz/25cl	Passóa
25oz/75cl	pineapple juice
25oz/75cl	pink grapefruit juice
1oz/3cl	fresh lemon juice
4 teaspoons	superfine (caster) sugar
1	orange
8	strawberries, sliced top to bottom
half	lemon, sliced

Sprinkle the sugar in the punch bowl. Add each liquid ingredient one by one, starting with the juices and ending with the spirits. Stir the mixture well to ensure the sugar is dissolved. Place the bowl in the refrigerator for a couple of hours before the guests arrive. Take it out, add the orange, strawberries, and lemon pieces, and a sprig of fresh mint. Add ice as guests arrive. Serve in goblets.

CLASSIC COCKTAIL

Sangria

There are many versions of Sangria, a classic Spanish party drink. Sangria is the Spanish word for bleeding and comes from *sangre*, meaning the color of blood. It is drunk at many festivals with much theatricality—it is poured directly into the mouth from a long-spouted jug. The art lies in being able to drink it from varying heights without spilling any!

Serves 4	
1 bottle	Spanish red wine
4oz/12cl	Spanish brandy
1oz/3cl	triple sec/Cointreau
2 teaspoons	superfine (caster) sugar
½oz/1.5cl	fresh lemon juice
½oz/1.5cl	fresh orange juice
half	each: apple, orange, lemon, and lime, sliced
	club soda (optional)

Pour all ingredients, except soda, into a pitcher or punch bowl, starting with the sugar. Stir to dissolve sugar. Leave to marinate in the refrigerator for a few hours before serving. When guests arrive, add the slices of lemon, orange, lime, and apple. Add large ice cubes and soda. Serve in goblets.

CUPS

Amarelle Cherry Cup

Serves 10
If you cannot find amarelle
cherries, use morello cherries,
which are darker and have a
colored juice.

2 jars	pitted amarelle cherries
3oz/9cl	apricot brandy
2 bottles	red wine
2	fresh apricots
3 bottles	sparkling wine
	or champagne

Drain the cherries and place in a punch bowl. Drizzle the apricot brandy over them. Place the bowl in the refrigerator for half an hour. Take it out and add the red wine. Stir. When guests are due, add ice and a few slices of apricot. Fill with champagne. Stir. Serve in wine glasses.

Pimm's No. 1 Cup

Created in 1840 as a digestive tonic by James Pimm and served at his Oyster Bar in London's financial district, this concoction of herbs and quinine caught on. By the 1920s, Pimm's No. 1 was distributed throughout England and exported to the Colonies. After the Second World War, the Pimm's company introduced Pimm's No. 2 with Scotch as a base, No. 3 with brandy, No. 4 with rum, and No. 5 with rye whiskey as a base. No. 6 had a vodka base.

Pimm's No. 1 Cup has a recipe that, as legend has it, is known to only six people.

To make in bulk, multiply the ingredients by the number of guests.

1⅔oz/5cl	Pimm's No. 1 Cup
	7UP or ginger ale
few slices	lemon
few slices	orange
few strips	cucumber peel
sprig	fresh mint

Pour the Pimm's into a highball filled with ice. Top up with 7UP or ginger ale. Add the fruit and stir. Garnish with a slice of lemon and orange, the peel of a cucumber, and a sprig of fresh mint in the glass. Serve with a straw.

Cider Cup No. 2

Serves 4

A refreshing cup full of apple flavor and a hint of citrus.

2oz/6cl	calvados
2oz/6cl	brandy
2oz/6cl	orange curaçao
1 bottle	cider
half	apple, thinly sliced
half	orange, thinly sliced
half	lemon, thinly sliced
small bottle	club soda

Pour all ingredients into a large pitcher. Stir. Add slices of apple, lemon, and orange. Just before guests arrive, add ice. Serve in an old-fashioned glass and garnish with a sprig of mint.

Strawberry Cup

Serves 4

This is a traditional fruit cup made with an extremely popular fruit—the strawberry.

1½lb/680g	hulled, diced strawberries
3½oz/10cl	crème de fraises (strawberry liqueur)
2 bottles	white wine
2 bottles	sparkling wine or champagne
2 tablespoons	superfine (caster) sugar

Pour the liqueur over the strawberries in a punch bowl. Place in the refrigerator to infuse for half an hour. Then, add the white wine. Stir. When guests are due, add ice and fill with sparkling wine. Stir. Serve in wine glasses.

Peach Wine Cup

Serves 4

A delicious, simple fruit cup. Peach is one of my favorite fruits, and I love to sip this cup at the beach in the summer when I am on vacation on the Amalfi Coast.

1 bottle	chilled dry white wine
2	skinned peaches, diced

Pour both ingredients into a large pitcher. Stir. Leave in the refrigerator for at least half an hour to let the fruit soak up the wine. Serve in wine glasses, making sure everyone gets a piece of peach in his or her glass.

EGGNOGS

Baltimore Eggnog

In Baltimore, it was traditional for young men to call upon their friends on New Year's Day. At each of the many homes they were offered a cup of eggnog and thus they became more and more inebriated!

1oz/3cl	brandy
1oz/3cl	madeira
⅔oz/2cl	dark rum
1⅓oz/4cl	gomme syrup
1	free-range egg, beaten
⅔oz/2cl	heavy (double) cream
3oz/9cl	milk

Pour all ingredients into a shaker filled with ice. Shake. Strain into a highball filled with ice. Grate fresh nutmeg over the top.

Serves 10 to 12

5oz/15cl	brandy
5oz/15cl	madeira
5oz/15cl	dark rum
13⅓oz/40cl	gomme syrup
10	free-range eggs, beaten
12oz/42cl	heavy (double) cream
12oz/42cl	milk

Separate the eggs. Beat the egg yolks until light. In a separate bowl, beat the egg whites until stiff. Slowly pour the brandy, madeira, and dark rum into a punch bowl. Add the beaten yolks and egg whites. Add the gomme syrup. Whip the cream and fold it into the mixture. Repeated folding and standing helps ripen an eggnog.

Eggnog

This is the traditional, simple eggnog recipe.

1	free-range egg
1oz/3cl	brandy
1oz/3cl	dark rum
3oz/9cl	milk
1 tablespoon	gomme syrup

Pour all ingredients, except milk, into a shaker. Shake. Strain into a goblet. Stir in the milk. Grate fresh nutmeg on top.

Vacation Eggnog

Serves 10
A double hit of spirit comes with using both rum and bourbon.

6oz/18cl	dark rum
6oz/18cl	bourbon
6	free-range eggs, beaten
6oz/175g	superfine (caster) sugar
½ teaspoon	salt
15oz/45cl	heavy (double) cream
15oz/45cl	milk

Pour all ingredients into a punch bowl and stir until the sugar dissolves. Place in the refrigerator for four hours. Take out of refrigerator and stir again. Serve in wine glasses. Grate fresh nutmeg over the top of each glass.

eggnog

LIQUEURS

Aaah, liqueurs! Liqueurs are an essential part of modern cocktails. They bring sweetness, color, and flavor to a recipe, as you will discover when you make some of the cocktails in this chapter.

A liqueur is not a cordial, and I hope this explains the true distilled liqueur clearly. The word "liqueur" comes from the Latin word *liquefacere*, meaning to melt or dissolve. Therefore, a liqueur is the result of the liquefying of its ingredients. Many liqueurs were originally distilled from a recipe kept in the family vaults, handed down from one distiller to the next, its secret never revealed. These sweet mysteries of life can trace their origins back to the Middle Ages and the religious monks and apothecaries who created potions and medicines to cure various ailments. Many of these cures were unpleasant to taste, so herb and fruit essences were added to mask the bitter flavors.

According to historians, the first liqueur was a preparation made from caraway (called kummel), and distilled in 1575 by Lucas Bols in Holland. Bols knew that caraway was good for the digestive system, and he hoped it would be popular when combined with the anesthetic effect of alcohol.

In the rest of Europe, most of the research into the medicinal properties of herbs and berries was carried out by monks. One of the famous liqueurs with religious origins is Bénédictine, made since 1510.

perfect love (left), page 225, and **green dragon**, page 222

Chartreuse was made for the brothers at an abbey in northern France before it became widely available in 1848. It is a favorite digestif as well as a great mixer. Today, liqueurs are used in recipes for both pre- and after-dinner cocktails.

Brandy, cognac, whiskey, rum, and other spirits are used as the base for many liqueurs. Fruits, plants, seeds, fruit skins, or roots are placed in alcohol in a still, heated, and the vapors are condensed. When cool, this becomes the aromatic spirit.

The other process used to create liqueurs is known as maceration. It is used only for fruit with pulp—raspberries, black currants, and strong aromatic plants, such as tea. When picked, the fruits are put into vats with alcohol and they remain there for weeks. The result is called an infusion.

A crème is a very sweet and thick liqueur with 28-percent sugar content. It adds smooth texture as well as sweetness to a cocktail. A cream means it is a combination of alcohol and dairy cream—for example, Baileys Irish Cream. A cream and a crème are not the same.

EAUX-DE-VIE FRUIT BRANDIES

These are the spirits of other distilled fruits such as pears, apricots, plums, raspberries, and apples and are classified under the term eaux-de-vie.

Calvados is a fruit brandy made from the mash of cider apples. Only apple brandy produced in the defined areas of the French provinces of Brittany, Normandy, and the state of Maine in America can be called calvados. The fermented mixture is double-distilled in a pot still and matured in oak casks for up to 25 years.

Applejack is an apple brandy made in New England. The liquid is double-distilled in pot stills and is aged for a minimum of two years.

Poire William is distilled from the Bartlett or Williams pear. The Germans call this Birnenwasser.

Prunelle is a sloe brandy. Kirsch is a genuine cherry brandy, since it is made from fermented cherries and brandy. Framboise is made from fermented raspberries, and slivovich is made from fermented plums.

SERVING LIQUEURS

Always serve a liqueur at room temperature and in a small liqueur glass. A liqueur is to be sipped, not gulped, since each has a specific flavor and aroma of its own that are best savored slowly.

Serve applejack and calvados at room temperature in a balloon or tulip-shaped glass after dinner.

Serve kirsch, slivovich, and framboise in a chilled shot or liqueur glass. Pour 1⅔oz (5cl) into the glass—do not fill it up.

Preferably drink a liqueur after dinner. The current fashion for serving some liqueurs—like Cointreau, Baileys Irish Cream, and Drambuie—over ice in an old-fashioned glass does no real harm to the flavor, but it does dilute the liqueur's strength.

POPULAR LIQUEURS AND THEIR FLAVORS

ADVOCAAT Dutch liqueur made from egg yolks and grape brandy

AMARETTO almond and apricot liqueur created by the widow who modeled for the Madonna in the *Adoration of the Magi* fresco in the Santa Maria delle Grazie sanctuary in Saronno. She used plants from her garden to create it.

ANISETTE French brand Marie Brizard anisette is the original aniseed-flavored liqueur

APRICOT BRANDY brandy with an apricot flavor

BAILEYS IRISH CREAM Irish cream liqueur consisting of a mixture of Irish whiskey and dairy cream

BÉNÉDICTINE D.O.M. herbal liqueur from Fécamp, in France

CHARTREUSE herbal liqueur from Grenoble, France. There are several styles, including green chartreuse (the original) and yellow, which is lighter and sweeter.

CHERRY BRANDY brandy with a cherry flavor

COINTREAU triple sec curaçao created in the 1850s by Edouard Cointreau, after experimentation with both bitter and sweet dried orange peels

CRÈME DE BANANES banana liqueur (white and brown types)

CRÈME DE CACAO cocoa and vanilla liqueur (white and brown types)

CRÈME DE CAFÉ coffee liqueur

POPULAR LIQUEURS AND THEIR FLAVORS *CONTINUED*

CRÈME DE CASSIS black-currant liqueur from Djion, France

CRÈME DE FRAISES strawberry liqueur

CRÈME DE FRAMBOISE raspberry liqueur

CRÈME DE MENTHE peppermint liqueur (white and green types)

CRÈME DE MŰRE blackberry liqueur originally made in France

CRÈME DE NOYAU almond-flavored liqueur made from oils of peach and apricot kernels.

CRÈME DE VIOLETTE violet liqueur (In Europe, this is Crème Yvette.)

CURAÇAO term for orange-based liqueurs made from dried bitter orange peels

DRAMBUIE made from a mixture of Scottish herbs and Scotch. Honey and herbs are added to a syrup, which is then added to a blend of malt and grain Scotch.

GRAND MARNIER cognac-based orange liqueur from France

GALLIANO created in 1896 by Armando Vaccari as a tribute to the Italian hero Giuseppe Galliano. It is a mixture of 40 herbs and other botanicals, including vanilla and anise.

KAHLUA coffee liqueur made in Mexico from cane spirit, coffee, and vanilla

KUMMEL popular digestif made from a neutral spirit flavored with caraway seeds. Created in 1575 by the Dutch distiller Lucas Bols.

LIMONCELLO Italian lemon-flavored liqueur that dates back many centuries. It is an infusion made from lemon peel, sugar, and water, combined with a neutral spirit.

MANDARINE NAPOLÉON launched in 1892, this is a Belgian tangerine- and cognac-flavored liqueur

PASTIS licorice-based liqueur from Marseilles, in France

PARFAIT AMOUR sweet pink or violet liqueur with a citrus base containing spices and extract of flower petals

ROYAL MINT CHOCOLATE French drink composed to taste like the flavor of an after-dinner mint

SAMBUCA aniseed-flavored liqueur made in Italy. Usually served with three coffee beans on the surface, which has coined the phrase *con mosca*—with flies. Black and white types available.

SOUTHERN COMFORT peach-flavored American liqueur with a whiskey spirit base and more than 100 ingredients. It was created in the 1890s by a New Orleans bartender who was trying to improve the whiskey he served.

STREGA (Italian for "witch") herbal liqueur from Benevento in southern Italy.

TIA MARIA Jamaican coffee liqueur with a chocolate finish that was first made in the 1600s.

Amaretto Sour

A classic. The egg white powder creates a luscious foam on top of the drink.

1⅔oz/5cl	amaretto
⅔oz/2cl	fresh lemon juice
1 teaspoon	egg white powder

Pour all ingredients into a shaker with ice. Shake. Strain into an old-fashioned glass filled with ice.

Angel's Tit

A quick and easy classic drink that leaves you with a sweet and smooth aftertaste.

1⅓oz/4cl	maraschino liqueur
⅔oz/2cl	heavy (double) cream

Pour the maraschino into a liqueur glass and float the cream on top. Garnish with a maraschino cherry in the middle of the creamy top.

Angel's Wing

A 1930s classic with the ability to take you higher and higher.

1oz/3cl	white crème de cacao
1oz/3cl	prunelle brandy
dash	heavy (double) cream

Pour the white crème de cacao over a barspoon into a liqueur glass, followed by the prunelle brandy. Float the cream over the top to finish.

Avalanche I

One sip and you'll feel yourself free-falling down a powdery snow slope.

1oz/3cl	crème de bananes (banana liqueur)
½oz/1.5cl	white crème de cacao
½oz/1.5cl	amaretto
1oz/3cl	heavy (double) cream
half	banana, peeled

Pour all ingredients into a blender with crushed ice. Blend. Pour into an old-fashioned glass. Garnish with a maraschino cherry and a slice of banana.

Baldy

An intriguing and exotic combination of fresh fruit and citrus flavors.

1oz/3cl	green Chartreuse
⅔oz/2cl	fresh lychee juice
⅔oz/2cl	passion fruit juice
⅓oz/1cl	fresh lemon juice
1 teaspoon	brown sugar
1oz/3cl	clear apple juice
1oz/3cl	pineapple juice

Pour all ingredients into shaker with ice. Shake. Strain into an old-fashioned glass filled with crushed ice. Garnish with a wedge of pineapple.

Blackjack

For anyone who likes to while away the hours at a casino table. Drink before you play, not during!

1oz/3cl	kirsch
1oz/3cl	iced coffee
½oz/1.5cl	brandy

Pour all ingredients into a shaker with ice. Shake. Strain into an old-fashioned glass filled with ice.

Blanche Cocktail

A classic dating from the 1920s, creating a pale and interesting vision.

1oz/3cl	anisette
1oz/3cl	Cointreau
1oz/3cl	white curaçao

Pour all ingredients in a shaker with ice. Shake. Strain into a cocktail glass.

Brown Squirrel

A blended, cold, and creamy drink that's a bit like a sorbet to cleanse the palate.

1oz/3cl	amaretto
1oz/3cl	dark crème de cacao
1oz/3cl	heavy (double) cream
2 scoops	vanilla ice cream

Place all ingredients in a blender with crushed ice. Blend. Pour into a colada glass. Garnish with a maraschino cherry.

China Blue

A divine shade of blue, with the exotic flavor of lychees and a hint of bitterness.

1oz/3cl	blue curaçao
1oz/3cl	lychee liqueur
1oz/3cl	grapefruit juice

Pour all ingredients into a shaker with ice. Shake. Strain into a cocktail glass. Garnish with a wedge of lime.

Colorado

Strength, vitality, and sweetness are just three little words to describe this drink's qualities.

1oz/3cl   kirsch
1oz/3cl   cherry brandy
1oz/3cl   heavy (double) cream

Pour all ingredients into shaker with ice. Shake. Strain into a cocktail glass. Garnish with a maraschino cherry.

Crème de Menthe Frappé

This is simply a good digestif since it gives you a superb, refreshing feeling.

2oz/6cl   green crème de menthe
           crushed ice

Pour the crème de menthe into an old-fashioned glass filled with crushed ice. Serve with a straw.

Diana Cocktail

A 1920s classic immortalized in Harry Craddock's The Savoy Cocktail Book *for a Diana from another era. This is a fine digestif.*

1²⁄₃oz/5cl   white crème de menthe
²⁄₃oz/2cl   brandy

Fill an old-fashioned glass with crushed ice and pour in the crème de menthe. Gently float the brandy on top. Serve with a short straw.

Ferrari

Named after my favorite racing car. Speedsters like me will get a buzz from the flavors in this drink.

1oz/3cl   amaretto
1²⁄₃oz/5cl   dry vermouth

Pour the amaretto into an old-fashioned glass filled with ice, then add the vermouth. Stir.

Fifth Avenue

A 1930s favorite with those who enjoy the taste of apricot and the smoothness of creamy chocolate.

1oz/3cl   brown crème de cacao
1oz/3cl   apricot brandy
1oz/3cl   heavy (double) cream

Pour the brown crème de cacao into a liqueur glass. Float the apricot brandy over a barspoon on top. Finally, float the cream over the drink.

Give Me a Dime

For those who love the taste of toffee and chocolate after dinner. Plus, it's real creamy.

1oz/3cl   white crème de cacao
1oz/3cl   butterscotch schnapps
1oz/3cl   heavy (double) cream

Pour all ingredients into shaker with ice. Shake. Strain into a cocktail glass. Garnish with grated chocolate.

Golden Cadillac

One of the most popular drinks. One of these and you may be tempted to say "Baby, you can drive my car . . ."

1oz / 3cl	Galliano
1oz / 3cl	white crème de cacao
1oz / 3cl	heavy (double) cream

Pour all ingredients into a shaker with ice. Shake. Strain into a cocktail glass.

Golden Dream

A classic with a superb orange flavor and a hint of vanilla from the Galliano. It looks impressive in the glass and tastes like a dream.

1oz / 3cl	Galliano
½oz / 1.5cl	Cointreau
½oz / 1.5cl	fresh orange juice
½oz / 1.5cl	heavy (double) cream

Pour all ingredients into a shaker with ice. Shake. Strain into a cocktail glass.

Golden Slipper

The original 1920s recipe contained Eau-de-vie de Danzig. This is how the drink is served today.

1oz / 3cl	yellow Chartreuse
1oz / 3cl	apricot brandy
1	egg yolk

Pour all ingredients into a shaker with ice. Shake. Strain into a cocktail glass.

Grasshopper

A classic drink that, along with Brandy Alexander, is often requested.

1oz / 3cl	green crème de menthe
1oz / 3cl	white crème de cacao
1oz / 3cl	heavy (double) cream

Pour all ingredients into a shaker with ice. Shake. Strain into a cocktail glass.

Green Dragon

A fiery 1920s concoction made with kummel. A good digestif that can chase away any lingering demons.

1oz / 3cl	gin
⅔oz / 2cl	kummel
⅔oz / 2cl	green crème de menthe
⅔oz / 2cl	fresh lemon juice
4 dashes	peach bitters

Pour all ingredients into a shaker with ice. Shake. Strain into a cocktail glass.

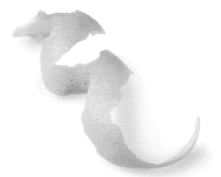

Honolulu Juicer

Freshness personified, with the peach-flavored Southern Comfort providing the sweetness.

1 oz / 3 cl	Southern Comfort
²⁄₃ oz / 2 cl	golden rum
²⁄₃ oz / 2 cl	Rose's lime cordial
¹⁄₃ oz / 1 cl	fresh lime juice
3¹⁄₃ oz / 10 cl	pineapple juice

Pour all ingredients into a shaker with ice. Shake. Strain into a colada glass filled with crushed ice. Garnish with a slice of pineapple and a maraschino cherry. Serve with a straw.

Illusion

There's a touch of magic in this cocktail, and it's a lovely shade of green.

1 oz / 3 cl	melon liqueur
½ oz / 1.5 cl	vodka
½ oz / 1.5 cl	triple sec/Cointreau
2 oz / 6 cl	pineapple juice
1 oz / 3 cl	fresh lemon juice

Pour all ingredients into a shaker with ice. Shake. Pour into a highball filled with ice. Garnish with two melon balls.

Intrigue

It's all in the name!

1 oz / 3 cl	grappa moscato
²⁄₃ oz / 2 cl	Mandarin Napoleon liqueur
½ oz / 1.5 cl	maraschino liqueur
1½ teaspoons	aged balsamic vinegar

Place all the ingredients into a shaker filled with ice. Shake. Strain into a chilled cocktail glass.

Italian Stallion

Every sip will bring out the stallion in every Italian male! Guarantees satisfaction.

1²⁄₃ oz / 5 cl	amaretto
²⁄₃ oz / 2 cl	white crème de cacao
²⁄₃ oz / 2 cl	crème de noyau
1 oz / 3 cl	heavy (double) cream

Pour all ingredients into shaker with ice. Shake. Strain into an old-fashioned glass filled with ice.

Lady Love Cocktail

A wonderful combination: a hint of mint and blackberry with an overlay of orange, held together by the port.

1 oz / 3 cl	orange curaçao
1 oz / 3 cl	ruby port
½ oz / 1.5 cl	white crème de menthe
½ oz / 1.5 cl	crème de mûre (blackberry liqueur)

Pour all ingredients into a shaker with ice. Shake. Strain into a cocktail glass.

Limoncello Sour

This is one of my favorite sours made with a liqueur. It's incredibly refreshing.

1⅓oz / 4cl	limoncello
⅓oz / 1cl	vodka
1oz / 3cl	fresh lemon juice
1 teaspoon	egg white powder

Pour all ingredients into a shaker with ice. Shake. Strain into an old-fashioned glass filled with ice. Garnish with a slice of lemon and a cherry on a cocktail stick.

London Fog

Not quite the color of a modern London fog but definitely as misty.

1oz / 3cl	white crème de menthe
1oz / 3cl	anisette
few dashes	Angostura bitters

Pour all ingredients into a shaker with ice. Shake. Strain into a cocktail glass. Serve immediately for the misty effect.

Lover's Kiss

Lingering flavors of almond, cherry, and chocolate will make the kiss last and last.

1oz / 3cl	amaretto
½oz / 1.5cl	cherry brandy
½oz / 1.5cl	brown crème de cacao
1oz / 3cl	heavy (double) cream

Pour all ingredients, except cream, into a shaker with ice. Shake. Strain into a cocktail glass. Float the cream over the top. Garnish with grated chocolate.

Melon Sour

A lightly flavored sour. It's very refreshing with a hint of sweetness.

1oz / 3cl	melon liqueur
1oz / 3cl	fresh orange juice
1oz / 3cl	fresh lime juice
1oz / 3cl	pasteurized egg white

Pour all ingredients into shaker with ice. Shake. Strain into an old-fashioned glass filled with ice.

Nutty Irishman

All the nutty flavors together in one. It's creamy, with the whimsy of whiskey.

1oz / 3cl	Irish cream liqueur
1oz / 3cl	hazelnut liqueur
1oz / 3cl	Irish whiskey

Pour all ingredients into a shaker with ice. Shake. Strain into an old-fashioned glass filled with ice.

Orgasm

I discovered this years ago when a lady walked into my bar and asked for one! Much to my bemusement, I knew exactly what she meant.

1oz / 3cl	Irish cream liqueur
1oz / 3cl	Cointreau
1oz / 3cl	heavy (double) cream

Pour all ingredients into shaker with ice. Shake. Strain into a cocktail glass. Serve at the right moment.

Perfect Love

There can be no half-measures with a rich and fruity taste sensation such as this.

2oz / 6cl	red-currant vodka
½ oz / 1.5 cl	crème de cassis
½ oz / 1.5 cl	fresh lemon juice
1 dash	gomme syrup
garnish	orange twist

Shake all ingredients with ice. Strain into a chilled cocktail glass. Add the garnish on the rim of the glass.

Quarterback Cocktail

Here's a fun after-dinner cocktail for all American football fans.

1oz / 3cl	yellow Chartreuse
1oz / 3cl	Cointreau
1oz / 3cl	heavy (double) cream

Pour all ingredients into a shaker with ice. Shake. Strain into a cocktail glass. Serve with an oval-shaped chocolate egg on the side!

Pousse-Café

This is always served after-dinner, and each liqueur has a different density, allowing one to sit on top of another. Syrups are heavier than liqueurs, and spirits are even lighter. Pour the heaviest ingredient first, usually the first one listed.

You can use any combination to make a pousse-café. This is the classic recipe.

⅓oz / 1cl	grenadine
⅓oz / 1cl	green crème de menthe
⅓oz / 1cl	Galliano
⅓oz / 1cl	kummel
⅓oz / 1cl	brandy

Pour the grenadine into a shot glass as a base. Over the back of a barspoon, gently add the crème de menthe. Pause, add the Galliano the same way. Pause, add the kummel and, finally, the brandy. Serve carefully. If you move the glass quickly, you will upset the perfect dividing lines!

Road Runner

A classic after-dinner digestif with an almond and coconut finish.

1⅓oz/4cl	vodka
⅔oz/2cl	amaretto
⅔oz/2cl	coconut cream

Pour all ingredients into a shaker with ice. Shake. Strain into a cocktail glass.

Rose

Cherries, pomegranates, and wine flavors all combine to create a taste sensation.

1oz/3cl	kirsch
1oz/3cl	dry vermouth
dash	grenadine

Pour all ingredients into a mixing glass with ice. Stir. Strain into a cocktail glass. Garnish with a rose petal dropped into the drink.

Tootie-Fruity Lifesaver

A cutie-cutie cocktail full of fresh fruit flavors and a herbal hint from the Galliano.

1⅔oz/5cl	crème de bananes
⅔oz/2cl	Galliano
2oz/6cl	cranberry juice
2oz/6cl	pineapple juice
2oz/6cl	fresh orange juice

Pour all ingredients into shaker with ice. Shake. Strain into a highball filled with ice. Garnish with a stem of red currants.

Velvet Hammer

This is the classic recipe. A recipe using vodka, Tia Maria, and cream in the same proportion is also known as a Velvet Hammer!

1oz/3cl	Tia Maria
1oz/3cl	Cointreau
1oz/3cl	heavy (double) cream

Pour all ingredients into a shaker with ice. Shake. Strain into a cocktail glass.

Wet Dream

What a drink! Tart raspberry and creamy banana flavors shaken into one delicious hit.

⅔oz/2cl	crème de framboise (raspberry liqueur)
⅔oz/2cl	crème de bananes
1oz/3cl	heavy (double) cream
2oz/6cl	fresh orange juice

Pour all ingredients into a shaker with ice. Shake. Strain into a cocktail glass.

White Cadillac

A distinctly elegant, creamy cocktail perfect for sipping late at night by the ocean.

1oz/3cl	Cointreau
2⁄3oz/2cl	Galliano
1oz/3cl	heavy (double) cream

Place all ingredients in a blender with crushed ice. Blend. Pour into a cocktail glass.

Yellow Parrot

A 1930s classic drink with an apricot flavor and a spicy anise finish.

1oz/3cl	yellow Chartreuse
1oz/3cl	apricot brandy
2⁄3oz/2cl	anisette

Pour all ingredients into a shaker with ice. Shake. Strain into a cocktail glass.

Yum

This is indeed "yum" because it has such a superb selection of flavors to enjoy.

1²⁄3oz/5cl	Grand Marnier
2⁄3oz/2cl	peach schnapps
1⁄3oz/1cl	crème de framboise (raspberry liqueur)
1oz/3cl	fresh lemon juice
3oz/9cl	clear apple juice
dash	gomme syrup

Pour all ingredients into a shaker with ice. Shake. Strain into a highball filled with ice. Garnish with two raspberries and a leaf of mint on a cocktail stick.

SHOOTERS

———⚬⚬⚬———

Shooters have such great names, like Fallen Angel, Kamikaze, Sex on the Beach, and Tony's Screaming Weenie—what is that? It's no wonder that these are popular throughout the world.

Originally, these were spirits served in a shot glass and downed in one single gulp. This had the fantastic effect of making one as drunk as could be in a short time.

Traditionally, shots were of straight whiskey; however, now they can have any number of ingredients, it seems to me, as long as these are alcoholic . . . juice is allowed in dashes only.

Modern shooters and slammers are a combination of a spirit, lower-proof liqueurs, and juices or mixers. The size of the glass, holding only 2oz to 3oz/6cl to 9cl, limits the amount of pure spirit in one shot, so while it looks as though you're downing a lot of alcohol, you're really not, unless you're swallowing them one after the other after the other!

Some shooters look magnificent. Multilayers of colorful liqueurs, skillfully and patiently created and presented, only for guests to decimate in seconds. And what fun those seconds are! Taste sensations squeezed into nanoseconds. And don't bother to serve with a straw. The rituals associated with shooters and slammers are weird and wonderful. The most famous, of course, being a lick of salt, followed by a gulp of straight tequila, a quick suck on a wedge of lime, and the involuntary grimace as your taste buds come to terms with this sour assault. Other slammers lay seige to its position

flatliner (left) and irish flag, both on page 234

as Number One Lethal Cocktail, but so far they are all in second place. There is a recipe that takes the Tequila Slammer a step further—it's tequila with champagne—but it's messy to drink (the champagne fizzes up and over onto your hands as you slam it down on the table top), so I didn't include it! But you might like to try it anyway.

Shooters and slammers are great fun. In recent years, bars have realized the potential of these drinks to bring in customers, and they have responded with theme evenings, presenting the shots in entertaining ways.

On the following pages you will find classic recipes like Slippery Nipple, Rattlesnake, and B-52 presented among modern concoctions. You can be as creative as you like once you follow the subtle rules of flavor. Do not use too much of one ingredient, and balance the others. Patience is definitely required for some of the pousse-café–style shooters, perfect for making an impression after dinner (and these are good for the digestion, too!).

Look out for interesting glass shapes to add even more style to presentation.

Traditional shot glasses are really no more than miniature versions of a beer glass, but you can find some fabulous designs in stores that specialize in glassware. Not everything has to come in a set, especially shot glasses.

Who's looking closely, anyway, after one or two?

After Six

A dreamy coffee and cream after-dinner cocktail.

⅔oz / 2cl	coffee liqueur
⅔oz / 2cl	white crème de menthe
⅔oz / 2cl	Irish cream liqueur

Pour each ingredient, in the order listed, over the back of a barspoon directly into a shot glass.

American Flag

This is perfect for celebrating the Fourth of July, or any great American occasion.

⅔oz / 2cl	crème de fraises (strawberry liqueur)
⅔oz / 2cl	Cointreau
⅔oz / 2cl	vodka
dash	blue curaçao

Pour the crème de fraises into a shot glass. Float the Cointreau over the back of a barspoon. Then pour the vodka and the curaçao in a mixing glass. Stir to make it blue. Float it over the Cointreau.

All Fall Down

This is a very alcoholic after-dinner cocktail with a coffee flavor.

½oz / 1.5cl	coffee liqueur
½oz / 1.5cl	gold tequila
½oz / 1.5cl	dark rum

Pour each ingredient, in the order listed, over the back of a barspoon directly into a shot glass.

Atomic Dog

Melon and coconut produce a piquant flavor.

⅔oz / 2cl	melon liqueur
⅔oz / 2cl	coconut rum
⅔oz / 2cl	white rum

Pour melon and coconut liqueurs into a shot glass. Stir. Then carefully float the rum over the top.

Avalanche II

Here's a drop of whiskey with a creamy coffee flavor.

⅔oz / 2cl	coffee liqueur
⅔oz / 2cl	white crème de cacao
⅔oz / 2cl	whiskey liqueur

Pour each ingredient, in the order listed, over a barspoon into a shot glass.

B-52

One way to drink this is to light the top of the drink with a match, put a straw in the bottom of the glass, and suck the liquid up quickly in one long, but quick, movement.

⅔oz / 2cl	Kahlua
⅔oz / 2cl	Baileys Irish Cream
⅔oz / 2cl	Grand Marnier

Pour the Kahlua into a shot glass. Over the back of a barspoon, gently pour the Baileys, then the Grand Marnier to finish. Serve with a stirrer on the side.

B-53

A version of the 1980s classic with vodka instead of Grand Marnier liqueur.

⅔oz/2cl	Kahlua
⅔oz/2cl	Baileys Irish Cream
⅔oz/2cl	vodka

Pour each ingredient, in the order listed, over the back of a barspoon into a shot glass.

B-54

A version of the 1980s classic with amaretto instead of Grand Marnier liqueur.

⅔oz/2cl	Kahlua
⅔oz/2cl	Irish cream liqueur
⅔oz/2cl	amaretto

Pour each ingredient, in the order listed, over the back of a barspoon into a shot glass.

Baby Woo Woo

A balanced version based on the classic Teeny Weeny Woo-Woo of the 1980s.

⅔oz/2cl	vodka
⅔oz/2cl	peach schnapps
⅔oz/2cl	cranberry juice

Pour all ingredients into a shaker with ice. Shake. Strain into a shot glass.

Beam-Me-Up Scotty

All Trekkies will be familiar with the creamy banana flavor of this cocktail.

⅔oz/2cl	coffee liqueur
⅔oz/2cl	crème de bananes (banana liqueur)
⅔oz/2cl	Baileys Irish Cream

Pour each ingredient, in the order listed, over the back of a barspoon into a shot glass.

Bit-O-Honey

A delicious toffee-flavor combined with a creamy texture is tempting.

1oz/3cl	butterscotch schnapps
1oz/3cl	Irish cream liqueur

Pour each ingredient, in the order listed, over the back of a barspoon into a shot glass.

Bittersweet Pill

A hint of bitters and the delicacy of passion fruit make this an enticing gulp.

⅔oz/2cl	vodka
⅔oz/2cl	Campari
⅔oz/2cl	passion fruit liqueur

Pour all ingredients into a shaker with ice. Shake. Strain into a shot glass.

BJ

Instruct the drinker to try and down this in one using no hands. Good luck!

1oz/3cl   Irish cream liqueur
1oz/3cl   Grand Marnier

Pour each ingredient, in the order listed, over the back of a barspoon into a shot glass. Garnish with a small dot of whipped cream.

Black Dream

There's nothing quite like a dark and dreamy night for sipping creamy shooters.

1oz/3cl   black sambuca
1oz/3cl   Irish cream liqueur

Pour the sambuca, then the Irish cream, over the back of a barspoon into a shot glass.

Blue Kamikaze

So named because the world takes on a blue hue as your taste buds self-destruct after a few of these.

⅔oz/2cl   vodka
⅔oz/2cl   blue curaçao
⅔oz/2cl   fresh lime juice

Pour all ingredients into a shaker with ice. Shake. Strain into a shot glass.

Brain Hemorrhage

This looks a bit gory, but it has an interesting sweet taste. And definitely goes right to your head!

⅔oz/2cl   peach schnapps
⅔oz/2cl   Irish cream liqueur
dash   grenadine

Pour the schnapps into a shot glass. Then, using a barspoon, float the Irish cream over the top. Pour the grenadine into the middle of the drink so it pulls the Irish cream down into the schnapps to create a diffused effect.

Brain

For those who enjoy the taste of smooth whiskey liqueur, orange, and cream.

1oz/3cl   Southern Comfort
½oz/1.5cl   triple sec/Cointreau
½oz/1.5cl   Irish cream liqueur

Pour each ingredient, in the order listed, over the back of a barspoon into a shot glass.

Bubble Gum

The combination tastes a little like bubble gum. You might well blow bubbles if you have too many!

1oz/3cl   melon liqueur
½oz/1.5cl   amaretto
½oz/1.5cl   heavy (double) cream

Pour all the ingredients into a shaker with ice. Shake. Strain into a shot glass.

Flatliner

Some drinkers swear this takes you almost to the Pearly Gates, just in time for the ethereal effects.

1oz / 3cl	sambuca
8 dashes	Tabasco sauce
1oz / 3cl	gold tequila

Pour each ingredient, in the order listed, over the back of a barspoon into a shot glass.

French Revolution

A rebellious recipe with a Gallic orange flavor balanced with a hint of citrus.

1oz / 3cl	Cointreau
½oz / 1.5cl	fresh lime juice
½oz / 1.5cl	fresh grapefruit juice

Pour the Cointreau into a shot glass. Pour the lime and grapefruit juices into a shaker with ice. Shake. Strain. Float the mixture on top of the Cointreau.

Golden Shot

A strong, creamy shooter with a touch of sweetness and the strength of vodka.

⅔oz / 2cl	Drambuie
⅔oz / 2cl	Irish cream liqueur
⅔oz / 2cl	vodka

Pour each ingredient, in the order listed, over the back of a barspoon into a shot glass.

Irish Charlie

A quick-fix creamy shooter with a minty flavor. A good digestif for after dinner.

| 1oz / 3cl | Irish cream liqueur |
| 1oz / 3cl | white crème de menthe |

Pour both ingredients into a shaker with ice. Shake. Strain into a shot glass.

Irish Flag

A creamy orange- and mint-flavored after-dinner shooter. Add green crème de menthe to please your taste buds.

⅔oz / 2cl	green crème de menthe
⅔oz / 2cl	Irish cream liqueur
⅔oz / 2cl	Grand Marnier

Pour each ingredient, in the order listed, over the back of a barspoon into a shot glass.

Kamikaze II

The addition of white rum takes this one step on from the original classic.

1oz / 3cl	vodka
⅓oz / 1cl	Cointreau
⅓oz / 1cl	white rum
⅓oz / 1cl	Rose's lime cordial

Pour all ingredients into a shaker with ice. Shake. Strain into a shot glass.

KGB 2

Wow. This digestif is not for the faint-hearted among us. It's rich and full of flavor.

⅔oz / 2cl   coffee liqueur
⅔oz / 2cl   Galliano
⅔oz / 2cl   cognac

Pour each ingredient, in the order listed, over the back of a barspoon into a shot glass.

Landslide

You'll feel yourself slip-sliding away on a sweet note after two or three of these.

⅔oz / 2cl   crème de bananes
             (banana liqueur)
⅔oz / 2cl   amaretto
⅔oz / 2cl   Irish cream liqueur

Pour each ingredient, in the order listed, over the back of a barspoon into a shot glass.

Melon Ball Shooter

A vibrant green color and a great combination, giving this a light fruity flavor.

⅔oz / 2cl   vodka
⅔oz / 2cl   melon liqueur
⅔oz / 2cl   fresh orange juice

Pour all ingredients into a shaker with ice. Shake. Strain into a shot glass.

Melon GT Slammer

The slightly bitter taste of tonic adds a great finish to the slightly sweet mixture.

⅔oz / 2cl   melon liqueur
⅓oz / 1cl   gold tequila
             tonic water

Pour all ingredients, except tonic water, into a shaker with ice. Shake. Strain into a shot glass. Top up with tonic water.

Mex Shooter

A hint of creamy green invades this interesting after-dinner chilled cocktail.

⅔oz / 2cl   melon liqueur
⅔oz / 2cl   vodka
⅔oz / 2cl   Irish cream liqueur

Pour all ingredients into a shaker with ice. Shake. Strain into a shot glass.

Midnight Joy

A deliciously creamy drink for the dark side of the night. Sip slowly to fully appreciate all the flavors.

⅔oz / 2cl   Irish cream liqueur
⅔oz / 2cl   white crème de cacao
⅔oz / 2cl   black sambuca

Pour each ingredient, in the order listed, over the back of a barspoon into a shot glass.

Opal Nera Café

An Italian-style cocktail the color of black opals and with the taste of coffee.

⅔oz/2cl	black sambuca
⅔oz/2cl	cold black coffee
⅔oz/2cl	heavy (double) cream

Pour the first two ingredients into a shaker with ice. Shake. Strain into a shot glass. Float the cream on top.

Ouzi Shooter

This is a strong mixture with an aniseed finish, balanced by a hint of sweetness.

⅔oz/2cl	vodka
⅔oz/2cl	pastis
⅓oz/1cl	fresh lemon juice
dash	gomme syrup

Pour all ingredients into a shaker with ice. Shake. Strain into a shot glass.

Parisian

Described by one cocktail connoisseur as "weird," there is a touch of the daring in this recipe.

½oz/1.5cl	Grand Marnier
½oz/1.5cl	kirsch
½oz/1.5cl	cognac
½oz/1.5cl	green Chartreuse

Pour each ingredient, in the order listed, over the back of a barspoon into a shot glass.

Pavlova Supreme

As sweet as the dessert named after the famous Russian ballerina.

| 1⅔oz/5cl | vodka |
| ⅓oz/1cl | crème de framboise (raspberry liqueur) |

Pour vodka into a shot glass. Float the raspberry liqueur over the top.

Psycho Tsunami

A great name for a superb cocktail the color of the deep ocean.

½oz/1.5cl	blue curaçao
½oz/1.5cl	fresh lime juice
½oz/1.5cl	frozen tequila
dash	Tabasco sauce

Pour each ingredient, in the order listed, over the back of a barspoon into a shot glass. The Tabasco sinks past the tequila to sit on the lime juice.

Rattlesnake

Lots of coffee flavor and a final powerful sting in this shooter named after the King of the Desert.

⅔oz/2cl	Kahlua
⅔oz/2cl	white crème de cacao
⅔oz/2cl	Irish cream liqueur

Pour each ingredient, in the order listed, over the back of a barspoon into a shot glass.

Red-Eyed Shooter

The delicious black-currant flavor brings the taste buds to life as it slips down.

1²⁄₃oz / 5cl	frozen vodka
¹⁄₃oz / 1cl	crème de cassis (black-currant liqueur)

Pour the vodka into a shot glass. Pour the créme de cassis over the back of a barspoon into the vodka to form an eye.

Slippery Nipple

This sensual shooter has gained a slightly risqué reputation since its creation.

¹⁄₃oz / 1cl	grenadine
²⁄₃oz / 2cl	white sambuca
²⁄₃oz / 2cl	Irish cream liqueur

Pour each ingredient, in the order listed, over the back of a barspoon into a shot glass.

Thriller

Perhaps this was created after the "Thriller in Manilla" boxing contest?

²⁄₃oz / 2cl	crème de fraises (strawberry liqueur)
²⁄₃oz / 2cl	Drambuie
²⁄₃oz / 2cl	overproof rum

Pour all ingredients into a shot glass and swirl to mix. Ignite the mixture, and let it flare a few seconds and then extinguish the flame. Sip carefully.

Vincent VG

Dedicated to the artist who cut off his ear under the influence of the French distilled spirit absinthe. Because this liqueur was illegal in America, Pernod is usually used as a replacement.

²⁄₃oz / 2cl	crème de framboise (raspberry liqueur)
¹⁄₃oz / 1cl	fresh lemon juice
²⁄₃oz / 2cl	Pernod

Pour the first two ingredients into a shaker with ice. Shake. Strain into a shot glass. Float the Pernod over the top.

Zulu

Drink enough of these and you'll feel as strong and tall as a tribal warrior.

²⁄₃oz / 2cl	grenadine
1oz / 3cl	gold tequila
dash	triple sec/Cointreau
dash	fresh lime juice
dash	mango purée

Pour the grenadine into a shot glass. Pour all other ingredients into a shaker with ice. Shake. Using the back of a barspoon, carefully float this mixture over the grenadine.

HOT DRINKS

⸺⸱⸻⸺

When the chill of winter's in the air, most of us want to hibernate in the comfort of home. The climate's just right for hot drinks.

These are simple mixtures, containing hot water, sugar, and a single spirit such as whiskey, rum, or brandy. Not every hot drink is a toddy, as the recipes in this section reveal.

In the Victorian era, a toddy was a hot drink taken to soothe the nerves or cure a chill. Today, it is something that adds zest when you are feeling a bit low. Toddies traditionally contain a slice of lemon peel and are often made with cinnamon, cloves, or nutmeg.

Mulled wines (hot wine, sugar, and spices, and perhaps brandy) are a favorite at Christmas. Be careful not to boil a mull, or the alcohol will evaporate.

Many modern hot drinks use coffee as a base, or rich hot chocolate: both should be freshly made, using quality ingredients to get the full flavor. Use fresh milk and fresh cream. When the recipe calls for spices, grate a nub of nutmeg over the top of the drink, and use fresh cinnamon sticks and cloves. Always serve these drinks HOT, not warm. These drinks are for wrapping your fingers around, which means using a heatproof toddy glass. To prevent a glass cracking, place a spoon in it while you pour in the hot mixture.

mulled wine (left), page 244, and **hot buttered rum**, page 242

Blue Blazer

Created by the legendary Jerry Thomas while he was at the bar of the El Dorado in San Francisco. Thomas was a star performer with this drink. He perfected the technique of lighting the whiskey and throwing the flaming liquid between two silver tankards. This act impressed President Grant of the United States so much he presented Thomas with a cigar.

Thomas was a man of principle—he refused to serve this drink until the thermometer fell below 50°F/10°C. Be careful when you attempt this drink and be sure to have a fire extinguisher handy.

1²⁄₃oz/5cl	whiskey
1²⁄₃oz/5cl	boiling water
1 barspoon	superfine (caster) sugar

Heat the whiskey in a small saucepan and pour into one tankard. Put the boiling water into the other tankard. Light the whiskey and, while it is flaming, pour the two liquids from one tankard to the other four times. This may seem difficult at first and practice is required before you perform this in front of guests. Serve sweetened with sugar. Garnish with a twist of lemon.

Black Stripe

This couldn't be more simple to make. It has all the qualities of a great restorative drink.

2oz/6cl	dark rum
1 tablespoon	clear honey
	boiling water

Mix the rum and the honey in a tankard. Top up with boiling water. Stir. Pour into a heatproof wine glass. Add a twist of lemon.

Buttered Applejack

Serves 4
A comforting cocktail for a cold winter's night.

1 quart/liter	clear apple juice
1oz/3cl	fresh lemon juice
1 teaspoon	grated nutmeg
1 teaspoon	cinnamon
4 slices	fresh gingerroot
2 teaspoons	grated orange zest
1 teaspoon	clear honey
1 tablespoon	butter

Combine all ingredients in saucepan and heat slowly. Do not boil. When hot, use a ladle to fill four individual heatproof toddy glasses. Garnish with a cinnamon stick to use as a stirrer.

Canadian Cocoa

This has a wonderful vanilla and chocolate milk flavor, with the additional sweetness of maple syrup.

⅔oz/2cl	Canadian rye whisky
⅔oz/2cl	dark rum
½oz/1.5cl	white crème de cacao
dash	maple syrup
	hot, frothy milk

Pour all ingredients, except milk, into a heatproof toddy glass. Stir. Add the hot, frothy milk. Stir. Grate fresh nutmeg over the drink.

Christmas Cheer

This recipe makes 30 glasses of cheer on a chilly winter's day.

4 bottles	red wine
16oz/48cl	water
6oz/18cl	dark rum
1	lemon
12	cloves
½ teaspoon	ground cinnamon

Stick the lemon with cloves and bake in the oven for 15 minutes at 350°F/180°C. Heat the wine, water, and rum. Add the cinnamon and a little grated nutmeg to the wine mixture. Float the lemon on top. Serve in heatproof toddy glasses.

Ciderific

A terrific, simple cider-based drink to lift your spirits. The cinnamon adds a spicy finish.

2oz/6cl	golden rum
4oz/12cl	cider
stick	cinnamon

Heat all ingredients in a saucepan and stir. Serve in a heatproof toddy glass. Add a few slices of apple in each drink.

Dot's Spicy Spot

A super fruity flavored combination with the strength of dark rum and calvados.

1oz/3cl	dark rum
1oz/3cl	calvados
2oz/6cl	white grape juice
2oz/6cl	cider
1 teaspoon	clear honey
stick	cinnamon
dash	fresh lemon juice

Gently heat all ingredients in a saucepan. Pour into a heatproof toddy glass. Add a slice of lemon stuck with cloves.

Firecracker

Serves 8
When you sip this warming
recipe, you feel reassured
that all is well!

1 bottle	red wine
16oz / 48cl	water
8oz / 225g	superfine (caster) sugar
2oz / 6cl	fresh lemon juice
4 sticks	cinnamon
4	cloves

Bring to a boil the water with the sugar, lemon juice, cinnamon, and cloves for five minutes. Add the wine and heat slowly to almost boiling point. Serve in heatproof toddy glasses.

Glühwein

This is a classic German-
style hot toddy. The wine is
more prominent in this rich
combination.

2 cubes	sugar
1 slice	lemon
1	cinnamon stick
8oz / 24cl	red wine

Boil all ingredients in a saucepan and serve as hot as possible. Serve in a heatproof toddy glass.

Hot Eggnog

This is a traditional Christmas
morning drink. Its origins are
unclear. The name could date
from the 17th-century English
habit of adding a beaten
egg to a small mug of strong
beer—called a "noggin."

1oz / 3cl	brandy
1oz / 3cl	rum
1	free-range egg
1 teaspoon	superfine (caster) sugar
	hot milk

Pour all ingredients, except milk, into a highball. Top up with hot milk. Stir. Grate nutmeg over the drink.

Hot Buttered Rum

A classic with a spicy finish,
this is a little fattening for
those on a diet, but worth
every mouthful.

1⅔oz / 5cl	dark rum
1 slice	soft butter
1 teaspoon	brown sugar
1 small	cinnamon stick
1 pinch	grated nutmeg
4 drops	vanilla extract
2oz / 6cl	boiling water

Mix the butter, brown sugar, cinnamon, nutmeg, and vanilla extract in a heatproof wine glass until creamed. Add the rum and the boiling water. Stir. Serve hot.

Hot Kiss

What more can I say about this drink? It brings on moments of creamy passion.

1oz / 3cl	Irish whiskey
½oz / 1.5cl	white crème de menthe
½oz / 1.5cl	white crème de cacao
4oz / 12cl	hot coffee
⅔oz / 2cl	heavy (double) cream

Pour the liqueurs and whiskey into a heatproof goblet. Add the coffee and stir. Finish with a layer of cream. Garnish with a dusting of chocolate powder.

Hot Scotch Toddy

The word "toddy" might come from "tarrie," a 17th-century word for a drink made from palm tree sap and drunk in the East Indies. Yet in 1721 the Scottish poet Allan Ramsey made a claim that it is derived from Tod's Well, a source of Edinburgh water.

1⅔oz / 5cl	Scotch
2⅓oz / 7cl	boiling water
⅓oz / 1cl	fresh lemon juice
3 dashes	Angostura bitters
1 teaspoon	clear honey
3	cloves
	twist of lemon

Pour the Scotch, boiling water, lemon juice, and Angostura into a heatproof toddy glass. Stir to dissolve the honey. Spear the cloves into the twist of lemon and add to the drink.

Irish Coffee

A soothing drink that was born at a freezing cold airfield at Shannon Airport, near Ireland's Atlantic Coast, just after the Second World War. The airport was a refueling stop for transatlantic aircraft, and while on the ground, the passengers were refueled by Irishman Joe Sheridan. He took the traditional Irish drink, whiskey in tea, and substituted coffee for tea to suit the Americans' tastes. Adding a thick whirl of lightly whipped Irish cream on top, and sugar, he served this in a stemmed glass to his customers.

The first Irish coffee was taken to San Francisco by the late writer Stanton Delaplane and served in 1952 at the Buena Vista bar at Fisherman's Wharf.

2 teaspoons	brown sugar
1¾oz / 5cl	Irish whiskey
3½oz / 10cl	hot coffee
⅔oz / 2cl	whipped cream

Pour the whiskey into a heatproof, large goblet. Add the brown sugar and stir. Add the hot coffee and stir with a teaspoon. Gently float the whipped cream over a barspoon to create a final layer. Do not stir. Serve while hot.

Irish Forty-Nine Coffee

Going speculating? There's much more cream in this than in a traditional Irish coffee.

1oz/3cl	Irish cream liqueur
1oz/3cl	Drambuie
	hot coffee
	whipped cream

Place a barspoon in a heatproof wine glass. Add the Irish cream and Drambuie, then fill with coffee. Stir. Float the cream over the top. Garnish with three coffee beans.

Italian Coffee

Coffee with a wonderful nutty flavor and a layer of whipped cream brings the evening to a fine end.

1oz/3cl	amaretto
2/3oz/2cl	coffee liqueur
	hot coffee
	whipped cream

Place a barspoon in heatproof toddy glass. Add the amaretto and coffee liqueur. Fill with coffee. Stir. Float the cream over the top. Garnish with three coffee beans.

Midnight Snowstorm

A combination of chocolate and mint flavors all wrapped up in a creamy concoction.

1²/₃oz/5cl	white crème de menthe
	hot chocolate
	whipped cream

Pour the crème de menthe into a heatproof toddy glass. Top up with hot chocolate and float the whipped cream over the top.

Mulled Wine

Serves 8
This is best made just a few hours before you want to serve it. Always use a quality dry red wine as a base for this delicious soul-warmer.

1 bottle	dry red wine
1²/₃oz/5cl	brandy
1²/₃oz/5cl	Grand Marnier
2 teaspoons	superfine (caster) sugar
3 teaspoons	clear honey
2oz/6cl	fresh orange juice
2oz/6cl	fresh lemon juice
1	cinnamon stick
few	cloves
few	star anise
2	bay leaves

Put the spices together in a small cheese-cloth spice bag. Place in a saucepan with the red wine, brandy, and Grand Marnier. Add the sugar and honey. Stir until both are dissolved. Add the juices. Simmer for 1¹/₂ hours, stirring from time to time. Serve in a heatproof wine glass. Garnish with a slice of lemon with cloves pressed into the peel.

Razzamatazz

This is dark and full of luscious, rich berry flavors, with a dominance of coffee sipped through the creamy top layer.

1oz / 3cl	crème de framboises (raspberry liqueur)
½oz / 1.5cl	crème de cassis (black-currant liqueur)
½oz / 1.5cl	coffee liqueur
	hot coffee
	whipped cream

Pour the liqueurs into a heatproof toddy glass. Add the coffee. Stir. Top up with whipped cream. Garnish with a few small blackberries.

Sensual Sip

I like the combination of brandy and Kahlua with chocolate in this recipe.

1oz / 3cl	brandy
1oz / 3cl	Kahlua
	hot chocolate
	whipped cream

Pour the brandy and Kahlua into a heatproof toddy glass. Add the hot chocolate to three-quarters full. Stir. Float the whipped cream on top. Stir with a chocolate stick. Be quick about it, because it will melt.

Snow Bunny

A delectable orange and chocolate flavor comes to the fore as you stir this.

1⅔oz / 5cl	Grand Marnier
	hot chocolate
	cinnamon stick

Pour the Grand Marnier into a heatproof toddy glass. Add the hot chocolate. Stir with a cinnamon stick for the full flavor.

Tom and Jerry

A hot drink invented by "Professor" Jerry Thomas in 1852 at the Planter's House Bar, St. Louis, Missouri. He refused to serve it before snowfall.

1	free-range egg
1⅓oz / 4cl	dark rum
½oz / 1.5cl	brandy
1 teaspoon	superfine (caster) sugar

Beat the egg yolk and the egg white separately, then combine in a heatproof toddy glass. Add the spirits and sugar. Fill with boiling water. Grate fresh nutmeg over the drink.

CALABRESE CLASSICS

———eↄↄ———

The cocktail recipes in this section have been created to be enjoyed at any time of the day, anywhere, be it by the pool or in the early evening at home. You may be surprised by some of the ingredients— but hey, that's what makes the difference! For me, a great drink is the perfect balance of texture, flavor, and visual appeal.

It's about which single flavor harmonizes with another, and the secret is to understand that simplicity rules. It is also an adventure into the realm of a hundred flavors. So it is important to understand that the final combination is not a single taste, but the taste of everything combined.

Each of these unique recipes features layer upon layer of flavors designed to please a refined palate. Try them and see how your senses react!

spicy fifty, page 260

Always chill a cocktail glass in the freezer before use.

Absolute Love

Pisang Ambon is based on the recipe of an old Indonesian liqueur made with exotic herbs and fruits.

1oz / 3cl	lemon vodka
½oz / 1.5cl	Pisang Ambon liqueur
½oz / 1.5cl	limoncello
½oz / 1.5cl	fresh lemon juice
	bitter lemon

Pour all ingredients, except bitter lemon, into a shaker with ice. Shake. Strain into a highball filled with ice. Top up with bitter lemon. Add a stirrer and serve with a straw. Garnish with a slice of star fruit.

Amalfi Dream

Here's the cocktail I drink when I want to dream of going home in the summer.

1⅔oz / 5cl	vodka
⅔oz / 2cl	limoncello
⅓oz / 1cl	fresh lemon juice
4 to 5	fresh mint leaves

Pour all ingredients into a shaker with ice. Shake vigorously. Strain into a cocktail glass, letting mint fragments slip through to create a layer on top of the drink. Garnish with a spiral of lemon.

Anouchka

Named after a beautiful Russian guest who requested something strong and sweet.

3oz / 9cl	vodka
⅓oz / 1cl	crème de mûre
	(blackberry liqueur)

Pour the vodka and crème de mûre into a mixing glass with ice. Stir and strain into a cocktail glass. The drink will be a clear and delicate lilac color.

Bimbi

This cocktail was named after one of my regular female guests with a penchant for schnapps.

1⅔oz / 5cl	vodka
⅓oz / 1cl	prunelle schnapps
⅓oz / 1cl	Cointreau
handful	fresh raspberries

Pour the chilled vodka, schnapps, and Cointreau into a shaker with ice. Add the raspberries. Shake vigorously to break down the berries. Strain into a cocktail glass. Garnish with two raspberries and a sprig of mint on a cocktail stick.

Blood Transfusion

A drink designed to clear your head if you are suffering from a hangover.

1oz/3cl	vodka
1oz/3 cl	sherry
1oz/3cl	Fernet Branca
5oz/15cl	tomato juice
1oz/3cl	fresh lime juice
2 dashes	Worcestershire sauce
pinch	celery salt

Fill a highball with ice cubes. Pour the vodka and sherry over the ice first. Add the tomato and lime juices, then celery salt and Worcestershire sauce. Stir. Float a layer of Fernet Branca on top.

It will either cure you, or increase the pain! The rest of the drink will sort out your head and make you forget the night before. Good luck!

Blue Lychee

A well-balanced combination of sweet and sour flavors, plus the unique flavor of lychee liqueur.

1oz/3cl	vodka
1/3oz/1cl	lychee liqueur
2/3oz/2cl	apple juice
2 dashes	blue curaçao
1/3oz/1cl	fresh lime juice

Pour all ingredients into a shaker with ice. Shake. Strain into a cocktail glass.

Blushing Fran

Enjoy—my daughter Francesca did, on her 18th birthday!

1½oz/4.5cl	vodka
½oz/1.5cl	Campari
½oz/1.5cl	framboise liqueur (wild strawberry)
½oz/1.5cl	elderflower cordial
1/3oz/1cl	fresh lemon juice
½ slice	fresh pineapple
2 thin slices	red chili pepper

Cut the pineapple into chunks and place in the bottom of a shaker. Muddle to extract the juice. Add remaining ingredients and ice. Shake sharply. Double strain into sugar crusted cocktail glass. Garnish with a small red eye chili pepper sitting on the edge of the glass.

Bolton Cocktail

This is named after singer Michael Bolton, who came to the bar one night and wanted a drink, but left it to my imagination.

1 2/3oz/5cl	vodka
1/3oz/1cl	peach schnapps
2/3oz/2cl	raspberry purée
1/3oz/1cl	fresh lemon juice
1 teaspoon	clear honey

Pour all ingredients into a shaker with ice. Shake vigorously to combine honey with the other ingredients. Strain into a cocktail glass. Garnish with a few raspberries in the middle of the drink so when you have drunk it all, the raspberries will be left, soaked with flavor. Garnish with a small wedge of lime.

Bond Cocktail

This combines the two favorite drinks of author Ian Fleming's literary character James Bond—vodka and champagne.

1²⁄₃oz / 5cl	vodka
²⁄₃oz / 2cl	champagne
¹⁄₃oz / 1cl	Pernod
1	sugar cube

In preparation, place both the vodka and a cocktail glass in the freezer for about three hours.

Pour the vodka into the glass. Slowly pour the champagne on top. Soak the sugar cube with Pernod. Drop it into the glass. Stir gently.

Breakfast Martini

I created this drink in 1997, inspired by my wife Sue's insistence that I should partake of an English breakfast. Since then its fame has spread around the world and is now a modern classic.

1²⁄₃oz / 5cl	gin
¹⁄₂oz / 1.5cl	Cointreau
¹⁄₂oz / 1.5cl	fresh lemon juice
1 teaspoon	medium-slice orange marmalade

Pour all ingredients into a shaker with ice. Shake. Strain into a cocktail glass. Squeeze a thin twist of orange on top (this gives it that extra bouquet of orange) and garnish with a thin spiral of orange.

Campari Nobile

This unique bittersweet cocktail won me the title of Bartender of the Year in 1993.

²⁄₃oz / 2cl	vodka
²⁄₃oz / 2cl	Campari
¹⁄₃oz / 1cl	limoncello
3¹⁄₃oz / 10cl	combined fresh orange and raspberry juices
	bitter lemon

Pour all ingredients, except the bitter lemon, into a shaker with ice. Shake. Strain into a highball with ice. Top up with bitter lemon. Stir. Garnish with five raspberries and a sprig of mint on top of the drink, plus a twist of orange on the rim. Serve with a straw and a stirrer.

Champagne Wonder

This was created for the inimitable songwriter and singer Stevie Wonder during one of his visits to the bar.

6	raspberries to purée
²⁄₃oz / 2cl	pineapple juice
²⁄₃oz / 2cl	fresh orange juice
2 dashes	amaretto
	champagne

Make the raspberry purée by mashing the raspberries with a barspoon through the strainer over the bowl. Pour the pureé into the shaker. Add the rest of the ingredients, except the champagne, and shake. Strain into the chilled champagne flute and top up slowly with champagne. Make a slit in the bottom of a strawberry and sit it on the rim.

Chocolate Affair

An intriguing combination of flavors that makes you want to lick your lips. Chocolate, almond, and coffee flavors and the kick of the cognac are bound by the cream.

1oz / 3cl	chocolate liqueur
½oz / 1.5cl	Tia Maria
½oz / 1.5cl	cognac
½oz / 1.5cl	amaretto
½oz / 1.5cl	heavy (double) cream

Pour all ingredients into a shaker with ice. Shake. Strain into a cocktail glass. Garnish with a thin chocolate stick.

Christmas Pudding-tini

A cocktail for a festive occasion that combines the chill of a martini with the warmth and flavor of a Christmas plum pudding!

2oz / 6cl	chilled gin
1 teaspoon	brandy
1 teaspoon	white crème de cacao
sherry glass	sambuca
few	tiny Christmas puddings

Pour all ingredients, except sambuca, into a mixing glass filled with ice. Stir. Strain into a cocktail glass. Spear a mini christmas pudding and dip into a small sherry glass of sambuca. Light it and drop into the cocktail. Eat the pudding and then enjoy the cocktail.

Cinnamon Warmer

Multiply the recipe by the number of people if you make this for a few friends.

1¼oz / 3.5cl	calvados
½oz / 1.5cl	dark rum
3⅓oz / 10cl	clear apple juice
⅔oz / 2cl	fresh lemon juice
3 thin slices	fresh gingerroot
1 teaspoon	clear honey
3	cloves
1	cinnamon stick
	lemon and orange peels

Pour all ingredients, except the spices, into a saucepan and heat slowly. Place the spices in a muslin cloth, tie the top in a knot, and place spices in the saucepan. Float a few twists of lemon and orange rind in the mixture. When warm, not boiled, pour into a heatproof glass.

Cupid's Corner

Named for all those who sit in an alcove in the Library Bar, hidden from view.

1oz / 3cl	cognac
1oz / 3cl	Chambord liqueur
1oz / 3cl	heavy (double) cream
dash	grenadine

Pour all ingredients into a shaker with ice. Shake. Strain into a cocktail glass. Garnish with a small drop of cream in the middle of the drink. With the tip of a cocktail stick, make the outline shape of a heart. Try this once or twice before serving to friends. It is easy!

Easter-tini

Created to celebrate the rite of Easter, with a chocolate flavor to please the sweet-toothed among us!

1²/₃oz / 5cl	vodka
²/₃oz / 2cl	white crème de cacao
⅓oz / 1cl	Cointreau
dash	sambuca

Pour all ingredients into a shaker with ice. Shake. Strain into a cocktail glass. Garnish with a tiny chocolate egg dropped in the drink.

Euphoria

I created this drink for the launch of Euphoria Men, by Calvin Klein. Fresh–Addictive–Sexy, it has it all!

1½oz / 4.5cl	vodka
½oz / 1.5cl	fresh lemon juice
½oz / 1.5cl	framboise liqueur
	(wild strawberry)
½oz / 1.5cl	Parfait amour liqueur
2	fresh purple basil leaves

Pour all the ingredients into a shaker filled with ice. Shake sharply to extract the flavor from the basil and double strain into a chilled cocktail glass. Garnish by lightly spraying a fresh purple basil leaf with Euphoria Men Cologne and place on top of the drink. This will give a wonderful aroma before you encounter the drink.

Femme Fatale

Named after the actress Milla Jovovich, one of the most beautiful women I know!

1²/₃oz / 5cl	vodka
²/₃oz / 2cl	crème de framboise
	(raspberry liqueur)
½oz / 1.5cl	fresh lemon juice
½oz / 1.5cl	fresh orange juice
1 teaspoon	clear honey
handful	fresh raspberries

Pour all ingredients into a shaker with ice. Shake vigorously to break down the raspberries. Strain into a cocktail glass. Garnish with two raspberries and a small sprig of mint on a cocktail stick. Set this across the glass.

Fig Supreme

The delicate flavor of fresh figs—my favorite summer fruit—combines well with the aged tequila. Its extra time in the cask provides a superb underlying woody taste.

2oz / 6cl	aged tequila
½oz / 1.5cl	fresh lime juice
½oz / 1.5cl	Grand Marnier
dash	grenadine
1	ripe, dark fig, peeled
	and diced

Place all ingredients into a shaker with ice. Shake sharply to break down the figs. Pour into a cocktail glass, letting some ice cubes fall into the glass. Garnish with a wedge of fig.

femme fatale (left) and **godfrey**

GG

Created for Geoffrey Gelardi at the Lanesborough Hotel, this cocktail has a spicy melon and ginger flavor.

1oz/3cl	gin
⅔oz/2cl	melon liqueur
⅓oz/1cl	blue curaçao
⅔oz/2cl	fresh lemon juice
	ginger ale

Pour all ingredients, except ginger ale, into a shaker with ice. Shake. Strain into a highball filled with ice. Top up with ginger ale. Stir. Garnish with a wedge of lemon on the rim. Serve with a stirrer.

Galloping Gasp

The combination of flavors present in one mouthful produces an intriguing drink.

1oz/3cl	cognac
⅔oz/2cl	ruby port
⅔oz/2cl	Cointreau
⅓oz/1cl	anisette

Pour all ingredients into a mixing glass with ice. Stir. Strain into a cocktail glass.

Garlic Affair

An off-the-wall combination guaranteed to keep the vampires at bay. It has warmth, sweetness, a hint of sharpness, and a whiff of spice, plus the unusual ingredient, garlic.

1½ oz/4.5cl	Cognac VSOP
½oz/1.5cl	apricot brandy
½oz/1.5cl	fresh lemon juice
1	small clove garlic
	ginger beer

Gently crush the garlic to release flavor in the bottom of a shaker. Add remaining ingredients, except the ginger beer. Add ice. Shake. Strain into a highball glass filled with ice and top up with the ginger beer. Stir. Garnish with a wedge of lime.

Godfrey

Created after a gentleman who has as much of a passion for cognac as I do!

1⅔oz/5cl	cognac
½oz/1.5cl	Grand Marnier
½oz/1.5cl	crème de mûre
	(blackberry liqueur)
4	blackberries

Pour all ingredients into a shaker with ice. Shake vigorously to break down the berries. Strain into a cocktail glass. Or, pour directly into an old-fashioned glass filled with ice cubes. Garnish with a blackberry and a sprig of mint on a cocktail stick.

Hemingway Hammer

This is a combination of a Martini cocktail and a Daiquiri. Powerful, sharp, and soft, pale blue in color, it is like the ocean off Cuba.

⅔oz/2cl	vodka
⅔oz/2cl	white rum
⅓oz/1cl	blue curaçao
⅓oz/1cl	extra dry vermouth
⅓oz/1cl	fresh lime juice

Place all ingredients into a shaker with ice. Shake. Strain into a cocktail glass. Garnish with a wedge of lime.

Honeypie

Dedicated to one of my guests, who used to greet me with "Hi, honeypie."

1oz/3cl	white rum
1oz/3cl	cognac
1 teaspoon	clear honey
⅔oz/2cl	heavy (double) cream

Pour the rum and cognac into a mixing glass filled with ice. Stir. Strain into a cocktail glass. Shake the cream and honey sharply in a shaker with ice to blend them together. Float this mixture over a barspoon on top of the rum and cognac mixture. Squeeze a twist of orange zest (zest facing the drink) to let a teardrop of orange into the drink. Garnish with a Cape Gooseberry on the side of the glass.

Hurricane Marilyn

Created while I was in the British Virgin Islands just after Hurricane Marilyn had devastated the area.

⅔oz/2cl	Pusser rum
⅔oz/2cl	white rum
⅓oz/1cl	Canadian whisky
⅓oz/1cl	Cointreau
2⅓oz/7cl	cranberry juice
2⅓oz/7cl	guava juice
⅔oz/2cl	fresh lemon juice
2 dashes	grenadine

Pour all ingredients into a shaker with ice. Shake. Strain into a highball filled with ice. Garnish with a sprig of mint set in the top of a strawberry and a slice of kiwifruit on the rim next to it. This is a drinker-friendly cocktail!

John Daniels

Inspired by a line from one of my favorite movies, Scent of a Woman.

1⅓oz/4cl	Jack Daniel's whiskey
⅔oz/2cl	amaretto
⅓oz/1cl	fresh lemon juice
	ginger ale

Put the whiskey, amaretto, and lemon juice into a shaker with ice. Shake. Strain into a highball with ice and top up with ginger ale. Garnish with a slice of orange dropped in the drink.

Lady Hunt

Created for Caroline Hunt, founder of the Rosewood Hotels & Resorts Group. The taste is similar to a whiskey sour, but more mellow because of the Tia Maria and amaretto.

1⅓oz / 4cl	malt whisky
½oz / 1.5cl	Tia Maria
½oz / 1.5cl	amaretto
⅔oz / 2cl	fresh lemon juice
1 teaspoon	egg white powder

Pour all ingredients into a shaker with ice. Shake to create a froth. Strain into a cocktail glass. Garnish with a maraschino cherry and a slice of orange on a cocktail stick.

Lanesborough Cocktail

Created as a magical champagne cocktail to drink when celebrating even the smallest victory!

⅓oz / 1cl	Grand Marnier
⅔oz / 2cl	passion fruit juice
⅔oz / 2cl	cranberry juice
	champagne

Pour the juices and Grand Marnier into a shaker with ice. Shake. Strain into a chilled flute and fill with champagne. Garnish with a strawberry—take out the green stem and replace it with a tiny sprig of mint. Make a slit in the bottom of the strawberry and sit it on the rim.

Le Délice du Library Bar

Created for a breathtakingly beautiful woman who walked into the bar when it was busy—and turned everybody's head!

½oz / 1.5cl	amaretto
½oz / 1.5cl	peach purée
½oz / 1.5cl	cranberry juice
½oz / 1.5cl	fresh orange juice
	champagne

Pour all ingredients, except champagne, into a shaker with ice. Shake. Strain into a chilled flute. Top up with champagne. Garnish with a stem of red currants sitting on the rim.

Macmartini

Created for one of the Library Bar regulars who was enamored with the color of the Indian Ocean.

1⅔oz / 5cl	gin
⅓oz / 1cl	blue curaçao
⅓oz / 1cl	melon liqueur
1 teaspoon	champagne

Pour all ingredients, except champagne, into a shaker with ice. Shake. Strain into the cocktail glass. Gently float the champagne on top.

Maestro

This cocktail is my name sake! A wonderful combination of sweet, sour and earthy flavors, this is a unique cocktail!

1½oz / 4.5cl	vodka
2/3oz / 2cl	crème de fraise (strawberry liqueur)
½oz / 1.5cl	fresh orange juice
½ barspoon	maple syrup
½ barspoon	aged balsamic vinegar (min. 8 yrs)
2	fresh strawberries

Muddle the strawberries in the bottom of a shaker. Add remaining ingredients with ice. Shake sharply. Double strain into a chilled cocktail glass. Garnish with half a strawberry sitting on the edge of the glass, then drop a dash of balsamic vinegar onto the strawberry.

Maiori Magic

If you want to satisfy a thirst, this is the drink to do it. A slightly bitter flavor comes from the Campari.

1⅓oz / 4cl	Campari
2/3oz / 2cl	limoncello
2/3oz / 2cl	fresh lemon juice
	tonic water

Pour the Campari directly into a highball filled with ice. Add the limoncello and lemon juice. Top up with tonic water. Stir. Squeeze a wedge of lime over the drink and then drop it in the drink.

Marked Man

A true Soprano's cocktail, a mix of American and Italian breeding! Full of vigor and enough spice to last the night!

1½oz / 4.5cl	Maker's Mark bourbon
½oz / 1.5cl	Campari
½oz / 1.5cl	limoncello
½oz / 1.5cl	orange juice
3–4	fresh mint leaves
1 slice	fresh ginger

Muddle the ginger in the bottom of a cocktail shaker. Add remaining ingredients and ice. Shake sharply to allow the mint to be broken into segments. Strain into a chilled champagne flute. Allow some of the mint segments to go through the strainer. Garnish with fresh ginger cut into thin strips to sit on the edge of the glass.

Meg's Mania

Created for one of the Library Bar guests who is fond of champagne and saké.

1⅔oz / 5cl	vodka
⅓oz / 1cl	saké
⅓oz / 1cl	cranberry juice
1oz / 3cl	fresh lime juice
	champagne

Pour all ingredients, except champagne, into a shaker with ice. Shake. Strain into a champagne flute. Top up with champagne. Stir. Make a lime spiral with a zester. Place this on the rim of the glass and let it trail down the side.

Midnight Temptation

The idea of these flavors together inspired me to create this harmony of apricot liqueur and coffee with port.

1oz / 3cl	apricot brandy liqueur
⅔oz / 2cl	ruby port
⅔oz / 2cl	heavy (double) cream
⅔oz / 2cl	Kahlua

Pour the apricot brandy, port, and cream into a shaker with ice. Shake. Strain into a cocktail glass. Gently float the Kahlua on top.

Moulin Magic

A strong drink that has an equally strong red color. It's also full of mystery.

1⅔oz / 5cl	gin
⅔oz / 2cl	Pernod
⅔oz / 2cl	crème de cassis (black-currant liqueur)
2oz / 6cl	cranberry juice
2oz / 6cl	fresh orange juice

Pour all ingredients into a shaker with ice. Shake. Strain into a highball filled with ice. Garnish with a stem of red currants on the rim.

Oriental Martini

Here's an intriguing mix of vodka and saké that guarantees a flavor thrill. Be wary of having too many.

1⅔oz / 5cl	vodka
⅔oz / 2cl	saké
⅔oz / 2cl	Yuzu juice (a Japanese lime)
few slices	fresh gingerroot

Pour all ingredients into a shaker with ice. Shake. Strain into a cocktail glass. Drop a few thin slices of ginger into the drink.

Peta's Passion

Dedicated to a friend whose passion for life often carries her away into another realm.

1⅔oz / 5cl	tequila
2⅓oz / 7cl	apple juice
1oz / 3cl	fresh lime juice
1 teaspoon	superfine (caster) sugar
1⅔oz / 5cl	passion fruit juice

Pour all ingredients into a shaker with ice. Shake. Strain into the highball filled with crushed ice. Scoop out the pulp of the passion fruit and lay it on top of the drink: it gives it a piquant aroma. Serve with a stirrer.

Purple Sweetheart

This cocktail is a wonderful color and was created for a woman with as colorful a personality.

⅔oz / 2cl	vodka
⅔oz / 2cl	white rum
⅓oz / 1cl	Parfait Amour
⅓oz / 1cl	Cointreau
handful	blueberries
dash	peach schnapps
dash	champagne

Pour all ingredients, except champagne, into a shaker with ice. Shake. Strain into a cocktail glass. Float the champagne over the drink. Garnish with a few blueberries on a cocktail stick set across the glass.

Red Earl

This cocktail was created for Earl Spencer, brother of the late Diana, Princess of Wales.

1¾oz / 5cl	vodka
2 to 3 slices	fresh gingerroot
handful	fresh raspberries
⅔oz / 2cl	limoncello

Slice the fresh gingerroot thinly. Place in the shaker. Muddle firmly with the end of the barspoon. Add the raspberries, limoncello, and vodka. Then add ice cubes. Shake to let all flavors combine well. Strain into a goblet. Garnish with two raspberries and a sprig of mint on a cocktail stick across the glass.

Sal's Sinner

Created to bring out the devil in you and spice up the hours between after-dinner and bed.

⅔oz / 2cl	cognac
⅔oz / 2cl	green crème de menthe
⅔oz / 2cl	white crème de cacao
⅔oz / 2cl	heavy (double) cream
2 dashes	Tabasco sauce

Pour the crème de menthe and white crème de cacao into a mixing glass with ice. Stir. Strain into a cocktail glass. Pour the cream and cognac into a shaker with ice. Shake. Gently float this mixture over the back of a barspoon to lay it on top of the green mixture. Add the Tabasco sauce. Garnish with a slim chocolate mint stick.

Sky Dog

Created for a media guest who loved Margaritas and asked me to create a Margarita with a twist.

1⅓oz / 4cl	silver tequila
½oz / 1.5cl	Cointreau
½oz / 1.5cl	fresh lime juice
½oz / 1.5cl	cranberry juice
½oz / 1.5cl	pink grapefruit juice

To prepare a cocktail or Margarita glass, rub a wedge of lime around the rim to moisten it. Dip the rim into a saucer of fine salt. Pour all ingredients into a shaker with ice. Shake. Strain into the glass. Garnish with a wedge of lime.

Snap, Crackle, and Drop

Just like the name, it will play with your taste buds. I have to say that I even impressed myself with this one!

1½oz/4.5cl	tequila riposado
7–8 dash	Angustura bitters
4–5 twists	freshly ground black pepper
	lime wedge

Stir Angostura bitters and pepper on a saucer until it turns to a paste. Coat one side of a lime wedge with the paste. Pour the tequila into a shot glass and place the lime on top with the pasted side uppermost. The lime should be bitten before taking a sip of the tequila.

Snowstorm

Created while waiting for a white Christmas, this is a winter survival kit cocktail with a creamy mint flavor and a hint of almonds.

1oz/3cl	vodka
½oz/1.5cl	limoncello
½oz/1.5cl	white crème de cacao
⅓oz/1cl	Orgeat (almond) syrup
1oz/3cl	heavy (double) cream

Pour all ingredients into a shaker with ice. Shake. Strain into a cocktail glass. Garnish with a stem of red currants dipped in lemon juice and then in superfine (caster) sugar. This gives a shimmery effect to the cocktail.

Spice Sensation

A great digestif with a wonderful peppery nose and a dry, spicy finish. Each sip presents the palate with one amazing taste after another.

1oz/3cl	cognac
½oz/1.5cl	yellow Chartreuse
½oz/1.5cl	Bénédictine
½oz/1.5cl	Cointreau
2 dashes	Angostura bitters

Pour all ingredients into a mixing glass with ice. Stir. Strain into a cocktail glass.

Spicy Fifty

This cocktail was inspired by the opening of my bar Salvatore at Fifty, sadly no longer open. It has a delicate fragrance, sweet and sour flavors, and a spicy after-kick. The bar may be gone, but like its reputation the drink lives on!

1⅔oz/5cl	Stolichnaya vanilla vodka
½oz/1.5cl	fresh lime juice
½oz/1.5cl	Bottlegreen elderflower cordial
⅓oz/1cl	Monin honey syrup
2 thin slices	chili pepper

Pour all ingredients into a shaker filled with ice. Shake. Strain into a chilled cocktail glass. Garnish with a red eye chili on the rim of the glass.

Summer Scene

All the flavors of exotic fruit combined with the delicious flavor of white rum!

1⅓oz/4cl	white rum
⅓oz/1cl	blue curaçao
2⅓oz/7cl	mango juice
2⅓oz/7cl	pineapple juice
⅔oz/2cl	Rose's lime cordial
⅓oz/1cl	fresh lemon juice

Pour the pineapple, mango, and lemon juices and lime cordial into a highball filled with ice. Stir until a coral color develops. In a mixing glass, pour the white rum and blue curaçao and stir until well combined. Pour this mixture over the back of a barspoon so it floats on the fruit juices. Garnish with a slice of star fruit on the rim. Serve with a stirrer and two straws.

Sweetheart

This is an aperitif with a delicate hint of bitter orange and sweet lemon, and named after my daughter, Francesca.

1oz/3cl	vodka
1⅓oz/4cl	Aperol
⅔oz/2cl	limoncello
⅔oz/2cl	fresh lemon juice
3⅓oz/10cl	cranberry juice

Put all ingredients into a shaker with ice. Shake. Strain into a highball filled with ice. Garnish with a stem of red currants on the rim of the glass, beside a small sprig of mint.

Sweet Sue

Created for my wife, Sue, the perfect companion after dinner!

1oz/3cl	cognac
½oz/1.5cl	Kahlua
½oz/1.5cl	Frangelico (hazelnut liqueur)
½oz/1.5cl	limoncello
½oz/1.5cl	heavy (double) cream

Pour the cognac, Kahlua, and Frangelico into a mixing glass with ice. Stir quickly. Strain into a cocktail glass. Pour the limoncello and cream into the shaker. Shake. Float this creamy mixture over a barspoon to create a layer over the cognac mixture. Using a peeler, grate shavings of semisweet or milk chocolate directly over the glass onto the creamy layer.

Telegraph Alert

A long and refreshing drink with ginger to keep you alert; lemon for sharpness balanced by the sweetness of honey.

1⅔oz/5cl	vodka
2⅓oz/7cl	apple juice
2⅓oz/7cl	cranberry juice
⅔oz/2cl	fresh lemon juice
4 slices	fresh gingerroot
1 teaspoon	clear honey

Pour the juices, vodka, and honey into a shaker with ice. Add the ginger. Shake. Strain into a highball filled with ice. Garnish with a thin wedge of apple.

Titanic Blue Fizz

For all lovers who would like a champagne-based after-dinner drink. This is my own witchcraft potion.

1oz/3cl	Galliano
½oz/1.5cl	Strega
½oz/1.5cl	blue curaçao
1oz/3cl	champagne

Pour the Galliano and Strega into a mixing glass with ice. Stir. Strain into a cocktail glass. Pour the champagne and blue curaçao into a mixing glass with fresh ice. Stir. Then gently float this over the drink. Garnish with a thin slice of star fruit set on the rim.

Tropical Spice

This is a really exotic combination of spicy rum and fruit juices. One sip of this and you'll find yourself in limbo land.

1⅓oz/4cl	gold rum
⅔oz/2cl	Cointreau
1⅓oz/4cl	fresh orange juice
1⅓oz/4cl	papaya juice
⅔oz/2cl	fresh lime juice

Place all ingredients into a shaker with ice. Shake. Strain into a goblet filled with ice. Garnish with a layer of orange slice, a slice of lime, and a cherry in the middle on a cocktail stick across the glass. Serve with a straw.

Truffle Martini

A fascinating, earthy flavor infuses the vodka in this special Martini.

1 bottle	vodka
1	whole black truffle, thinly sliced
few slices	fresh gingerroot
1⅔oz/5cl	grappa
dash	champagne

Place the thinly sliced black truffle in a bottle of vodka. Add the slivers of fresh ginger and grappa. With the cap firmly on, shake the bottle to combine the ingredients. Place in the freezer for one week to let the flavors infuse. To make one cocktail: almost fill a cocktail glass with the infused vodka. Top up with a dash of champagne.

Va Va Voom

An interesting combination producing a taste that races along!

1½oz/4.5cl	vodka
½oz/1.5cl	passionfruit syrup
1½oz/4.5cl	apple juice
½oz/1.5cl	lime juice
6	fresh mint leaves

Pour all ingredients into a shaker filled with ice. Shake sharply to break down the mint. Pour over crushed ice, allowing the mint to pass through the strainer, into a highball glass. Garnish with apple fan and 1 sprig of mint.

Velvet Rosa

This is named after my mother, who lives in Maiori, Italy. It reflects her bubbly, gentle, and loving nature.

²⁄₃oz/2cl	white rum
¹⁄₃oz/1cl	peach schnapps
1oz/3cl	cranberry juice
	champagne

Pour all ingredients, except champagne, into a shaker with ice. Shake. Strain into a champagne flute and top up with champagne. Stir quickly to bring the effervescence into play. Garnish with a small and delicate red rose petal.

Wake-Up Cure

In this modern variation of the classic Bloody Mary, I added a touch of champagne in memory of the night before!

1oz/3cl	vodka
²⁄₃oz/2cl	Cointreau
¹⁄₃oz/1cl	fresh lemon juice
3¹⁄₃oz/10cl	tomato juice
	champagne
	Tabasco sauce
pinch	celery salt
pinch	superfine (caster) sugar

Pour all ingredients, except champagne, into a shaker with ice. Shake. Pour into a highball filled with ice to about three-quarters full. Top up with champagne. Stir. Garnish with a wedge of lime.

Wiggle It All About

Be warned about this cocktail! It can make the body do weird things, like wiggle around the dance floor.

1²⁄₃oz/5cl	bourbon
²⁄₃oz/2cl	Cointreau
2¹⁄₃oz/7cl	guava juice
2¹⁄₃oz/7cl	pineapple juice
dash	grenadine

Pour all ingredients into a shaker with ice. Shake. Strain into a highball filled with ice. Garnish with a wedge of pineapple and a maraschino cherry.

Wonderland

This summertime cocktail has a delicious fruity flavor with a rum base.

1²⁄₃oz/5cl	white rum
¹⁄₂oz/1.5cl	cherry brandy
¹⁄₃oz/1cl	fresh lemon juice
dash	peach schnapps
handful	blackberries

Pour all ingredients into a shaker with ice. Shake vigorously to break down the blackberries. Strain into a cocktail glass. Garnish with two blackberries on a cocktail stick, with a small sprig of mint in the center. Set this across the glass.

NON-ALCOHOLIC

There's so much freshness in these drinks, with raspberries, strawberries, blueberries, and cranberries, each alive with rich color and flavor, particularly the citrus varieties. The juices made from them contain the individual fragrances . . . the nose is so intense that it heightens all of your senses.

The secret of making a good, non-alcoholic cocktail is in being able to disguise the fact that the drink has no alcohol, yet still making it sexy. The combination of juices still gives you the sharp, sweet, spicy, and creamy flavors that excite your palate. The various textures combine to make it look good as well. It doesn't disappoint you; it still teases your taste buds.

tropicana, page 273

TWO TIPS

"Fill the glass" means to fill to three-quarters, leaving space for a mixer.

Always fill the glass with ice cubes unless otherwise stated, again, to about three-quarters full.

These drinks ensure people can drive home safely with their children.

The number of fresh (or long-life) juices available today, in either a carton or a bottle, and the fact that nearly everyone has a blender and/or a juicer in the kitchen, make the non-alcoholic drink an attractive option for social occasions.

These days, there is also more emphasis on looking and feeling healthy, and drinking exotic combinations of fresh fruit juices is a great way to achieve this new lease of energy. Once you learn about the vitamin content of each fruit—either A, C, D, E, or the B group—you can learn how to combine them to give you the essential daily vitamins you need to carry on your hectic lifestyle. Specific fruits have a secret energizing content and when you combine these, you can create powerful and tempting potions.

With my recipes, they not only look wonderful, but taste divine, too! There is just as much pleasure in creating a non-alcoholic drink as there is in creating one with a spirit—and you can make each cocktail suitable for individual palates by adding or subtracting the amount of various ingredients.

So, think fruits, spices, and herbal extracts for cocktails that easily pass themselves off as the real thing.

Allegria

The name means "happiness" in Italian. This drink is refreshing—and has only 78 calories.

half	ripe mango, peeled, cut and diced
1²⁄₃oz / 5cl	carrot juice
1²⁄₃oz / 5cl	pineapple juice
1²⁄₃oz / 5cl	fresh orange juice
²⁄₃oz / 2cl	fresh lemon juice
	still mineral water

Put the mango pieces in the blender, add the other ingredients, except water, a scoop of ice cubes, and blend. Using the lid to stop the ice tumbling into the glass, pour the mixture into a goblet filled with fresh ice. Fill to three-quarters. Add the water to dilute the mixture a little. Stir. Garnish with a slice of orange and a maraschino cherry. Serve with a straw.

Carrot and Cranberry Cocktail

A nutritious cocktail that's easy to make and very refreshing.

4oz / 12cl	carrot juice
2oz / 6cl	cranberry juice
2 teaspoons	clear honey

Pour all ingredients into a shaker with ice. Shake well to let ingredients combine well. Strain into a highball filled with ice. Garnish with stem of red currants on the rim.

Coconut Affair

Full of texture and flavor.

1oz / 3cl	coconut cream
1½oz / 4.5cl	fresh orange juice
1½oz / 4.5cl	pineapple juice
6	fresh strawberries diced
½oz / 1.5cl	double cream

Blend all ingredients until smooth. Add 1 scoop of crushed ice and blend again. Serve in a large wine glass. Garnish with half a strawberry on the rim of the glass.

Coconut Grove

If I had been at the famous nightclub during Frank Sinatra's reign, I would have created this cocktail for him.

3¹⁄₃oz / 10cl	pineapple juice
1²⁄₃oz / 5cl	coconut cream
1²⁄₃oz / 5cl	fresh pink grapefruit juice

Place ingredients into a blender with a scoop of crushed ice. Blend for 10 seconds and pour into a colada glass. Garnish with a thin segment of grapefruit and a spiral of orange. Serve with a straw.

Cracker

So called because it is a cracker! It's very simple to make and delicious to sip.

1²⁄₃oz / 5cl	cranberry juice
1²⁄₃oz / 5cl	pineapple juice
1²⁄₃oz / 5cl	passion fruit juice
1²⁄₃oz / 5cl	grapefruit juice
	7UP

Fill a highball with ice. Add the pineapple, passion fruit, and cranberry juices. Finally, add the grapefruit juice. Top up with 7UP Stir. Garnish with a slice of lime. Serve with a straw and a stirrer.

Cranpina

An interesting combination of tart berries with sweet pineapple juice and two citrus fruit juices makes a refreshing cocktail.

2¹⁄₃oz / 7cl	cranberry juice
2¹⁄₃oz / 7cl	pink grapefruit juice
2¹⁄₃oz / 7cl	pineapple juice
1oz / 3cl	fresh orange juice

Fill a highball glass with ice cubes. Pour the first three ingredients into the glass. Stir. Add the orange juice—it will sink slowly down the glass as you drink it, but will look amazing when you first serve the cocktail.

Forest Fizz

Imagine the juices oozing from these berries. That's what this drink tastes like.

handful	fresh blueberries
handful	fresh blackberries
6 to 8	fresh raspberries
¹⁄₃oz / 1cl	fresh lemon juice
1 teaspoon	superfine (caster) sugar
	club soda

Place the berries in a blender with the lemon juice. Sprinkle the sugar over the berries. Blend until smooth. Strain the mixture through a nylon strainer or a fine cheesecloth into a highball filled with ice. Top up with soda. Stir.

If you can, use blueberry soda to give this a better flavor. Garnish with a selection of berries on a cocktail stick across the drink and a sprig of mint on top in the middle. Serve with a straw.

Ginger Alert

A drink designed to give your system a wake-up call, this has a fusion of ginger and apple flavors.

3¹⁄₂oz / 10cl	clear apple juice
1²⁄₃oz / 5cl	clear pear juice
²⁄₃oz / 2cl	fresh lemon juice
1	small piece fresh gingerroot
	ginger ale

Pour the apple, pear, and lemon juices into a shaker with ice. Grate the ginger into the shaker. Shake well to infuse the ginger flavor. Strain into a highball with ice. Top up with ginger ale. Stir. Garnish with a wedge of apple. Serve with a straw.

Ginger Zest

All of the exotic flavors of the Orient are in this spicy and healthy cocktail.

2⅓oz/7cl	fresh carrot juice
2⅓oz/7cl	tomato juice
1 teaspoon	clear honey
1oz/3cl	fresh lemon juice
2 to 3 slices	fresh gingerroot
dash	Worcestershire sauce

Place the ginger into a shaker. Muddle to release the essence, then pour in all ingredients. Add a scoop of ice cubes. Shake for 10 seconds.

Pour into a highball, letting the ice fall into the glass as well. Garnish with a red and a yellow cherry tomato, each cut in half, and speared by a cocktail stick, with a leaf of basil between them.

Island Surfer

The combination of these two colorful fruits and juices produces a smooth-textured drink full of flavor.

2⅔oz/8cl	fresh mandarin juice
1⅓oz/4cl	pineapple juice
1	kiwifruit, peeled and diced
4	strawberries, diced

Put all ingredients into a blender. Blend until smooth. Add a scoop of crushed ice and blend again. Pour into a large goblet. Garnish with a slice of kiwifruit. Serve with a straw.

Kiwi Punch

Serves 10
A little beauty from the Southern hemisphere with a green hue that will remind all Kiwis of home.

12	kiwifruit
1⅔oz/5cl	kiwi syrup
2oz/6cl	fresh lemon juice
2 bottles	alcohol-free wine
1 quart/liter	7UP or club soda

Peel and blend the kiwifruit and strain through cheesecloth to collect the juice. Or use an electric juicer; then you will not need to strain the liquid. Add the sugar to the mixing bowl. Pour the alcohol-free wine into a punch bowl and mix in the kiwifruit and sugar mixture. Add the 7UP or soda (this gives a drier taste). Garnish with a few slices of peeled kiwifruit and small strawberries afloat in the punch. Serve in wine glasses.

Lanesborough Cooler

This is popular with guests at the hotel when they arrive back after a frantic day and need a refreshing drink.

1oz/3cl	Orgeat (almond syrup)
⅔oz/2cl	fresh lemon juice
1oz/3cl	fresh lime juice
	7UP

Fill a goblet with ice cubes. Add the syrup and juices. Fill with 7UP. Garnish with a wedge of lime in the glass.

Lilac Beauty

If you can't find fresh berries, use frozen and thaw them beforehand.

2 tablespoons	low-fat plain yogurt
2⅓oz/7cl	white grape juice
handful	fresh blueberries
handful	fresh blackberries

Combine all ingredients in a blender until smooth. Strain into a goblet. Garnish with one or two berries on top of the drink. Serve with a straw.

Magic Moment

You really want to catch the moment these ingredients come together for a full burst of flavor. It's very simple to make. And very easy to drink more than one . . .

3½oz/10cl	red or white grape juice
⅔oz/2cl	fresh lemon juice
⅔oz/2cl	strawberry syrup
	club soda

Pour the juices and syrup into a highball filled with ice. Top up with soda. Stir. Garnish with a few grapes sitting on the rim of the glass. Serve with a straw.

Mangococo

Exotic flavors with a smooth edge.

1½oz/4.5cl	mango puree
1	fresh passion fruit
1oz/3cl	coconut cream
2oz/6cl	passionfruit juice

Scoop out the passion fruit into a blender; blend all ingredients with crushed ice until smooth. Pour into highball glass. Garnish with a cape gooseberry on the rim of the glass and serve with a straw.

My Mint Tea

Serves 2
My wife, Sue, likes to drink this sitting in the garden room on a hot afternoon. This is a very good digestif, soothing to the stomach.

bunch	fresh mint
1 quart/liter	boiling water
1oz/3cl	fresh lemon juice
1 teaspoon	lavender honey

Put the mint leaves in a heatproof pitcher and pour the boiling water over them. Add the honey and lemon juice. Stir to infuse the ingredients. Leave to cool naturally. When cool, remove the peppermint leaves. Pour the liquid into two highballs filled with ice. Add a sprig of fresh mint and a slice of lime.

On the Beach

Where else do you want to go on a sultry summer's day? Once there, this will quench your thirst.

quarter	ripe yellow melon, diced
handful	raspberries
3⅓oz / 10cl	fresh orange juice
⅓oz / 1cl	fresh lime juice
dash	grenadine
	7UP

Pour all ingredients into a blender. Blend for 10 seconds without ice, then add a scoop of ice. Blend again. Pour into a goblet filled with ice. Top up with 7UP. Stir. Garnish with melon balls and raspberries spiked on a cocktail stick across the glass. Serve with a straw.

Prairie Oyster

This is a piquant pick-me-up for the morning after the night before.

1 teaspoon	olive oil
3 dashes	Worcestershire sauce
1	free-range egg yolk
	salt
	ground black pepper
2 tablespoons	tomato ketchup
dash	white-wine vinegar

Rinse a wine glass with the olive oil and discard the oil. Add the tomato ketchup and the egg yolk. Season with the Worcestershire sauce, wine vinegar, and salt and pepper. Close your eyes and drink in one gulp. Serve a small glass of iced water on the side.

Pussyfoot

A pleasant fruit drink, enriched by egg yolk, for those who like to drive home after a party.

5oz / 15cl	fresh orange juice
1oz / 3cl	fresh lemon juice
1oz / 3cl	fresh lime juice
1	free-range egg yolk
2 dashes	grenadine

Pour all ingredients into a shaker with ice. Shake. Strain into a highball filled with ice. Garnish with a slice of orange and a maraschino cherry on a cocktail stick.

Red Apple Fizz

Crisp apples make the best juice, and combine their flavor with sweetness and bubbles, and you have a tempting fizz.

1oz / 3cl	fresh apple juice
dash	passion fruit syrup
dash	grenadine
	ginger beer

Pour the juice, passion fruit syrup, and grenadine into a highball filled with ice. Stir. Top up with ginger beer. Stir. Serve with a stirrer.

Sangrita

Serves 10
This is a traditional Mexican
drink that wakes up your
taste buds. Prepare at least
two hours before you plan
to serve it at a party.

35oz/105cl	tomato juice
16oz/48cl	fresh orange juice
5 teaspoons	clear honey
3oz/9cl	fresh lime juice
pinch	salt
1	chili, finely chopped
½ teaspoon	white onion, finely chopped
	ground black pepper
10 drops	Worcestershire sauce

Pour all ingredients into a mixing bowl. Stir well. Place in the refrigerator to chill for about two hours. Then strain into a large glass pitcher. Serve in wine glasses.

Sensation

This perfect combination
of sharp, sweet, and spicy
flavors creates a taste
sensation.

3½oz/10cl	tomato juice
1⅔oz/5cl	passion fruit juice
1⅔oz/5cl	fresh carrot juice
⅓oz/1cl	fresh lemon juice
1 teaspoon	clear honey
3 to 4 dashes	Worcestershire sauce

Pour all ingredients into a shaker filled with ice. Shake well to combine honey. Pour the mixture into a highball filled with ice. Garnish with a cherry tomato and a sprig of basil.

Summer Sunset

Serves 4
A refreshing drink full of
vitamins and energy—the
papaya contains medicinal
qualities—to take you through
the day, whatever you may
be doing.

half	yellow melon
half	papaya
half	mango
6	strawberries
7oz/20cl	passion fruit juice
7oz/20cl	peach juice
1	lemon, cut in half
1oz/3cl	fresh orange juice
3 dashes	grenadine

Scoop out the seeds from the fruit and discard. Dice the fruit. Put it into a blender and add the passion fruit and peach juices. Add a squeeze of lemon and the grenadine. Blend for 10 to 15 seconds. Add two scoops of ice cubes and blend again to chill the drink. If preparing a day in advance, do not add ice until ready to serve.

Fill four highballs with ice and fill each three-quarters full. The drink will be pale red.

The final touch: using a barspoon, float the fresh orange juice over the top. It will sit on top of the juices and gradually drizzle its way in fine strands to the bottom of the glass. Garnish with a small sprig of fresh mint set in the top of a strawberry. Serve with a straw.

Tropicana

All the exotic tastes of the tropics are combined in this creamy summer cocktail.

1oz / 3cl	coconut milk
2⅓oz / 7cl	pineapple juice
2⅓oz / 7cl	mango juice
1	small banana, peeled and diced

Place all ingredients into a blender and blend for a few seconds. Add a scoop of crushed ice. Blend again. Pour into a goblet. Serve with a straw and garnish with a Cape Gooseberry set on the rim.

Virgin Caipirinha

A Brazilian name for the most popular cocktail usually made with cachaça. This gives you all the flavors without the alcohol kick!

half	lime, diced
half	small lemon, diced
half	small orange, diced
1	sugar cube
	ginger beer

Place the fruit in the bottom of a mixing glass. Add the sugar cube and a dash of ginger beer. Muddle to release the juices. Strain into an old-fashioned glass filled with crushed ice. Top up with ginger beer. Garnish with a sprig of mint on top of the drink. Serve with a straw.

Virgin Colada

This is a commonly requested coconut-flavored cocktail. It's really a Piña Colada without the rum!

4oz / 12cl	pineapple juice
2oz / 6cl	coconut cream
	crushed ice

Pour the pineapple juice into a blender. Add the coconut cream. Blend for a few seconds. Add the crushed ice and blend again. Pour into a colada glass. Garnish with a wedge of pineapple and a maraschino cherry. Serve with a straw.

Virgin Lea

An award-winning cocktail that's a perfect combination of sweet, spicy, and sharp flavors in one sip.

4oz / 12cl	tomato juice
1⅔ oz / 5cl	passion fruit juice
half	yellow bell pepper, sliced
1 teaspoon	clear honey
2 dashes	Worcestershire sauce

Place the pepper slices in a blender and add the juices. Blend for 10 seconds at low speed. Add honey, Worcestershire sauce, and ice cubes. Blend at high speed for 10 seconds. Pour through a strainer into a highball filled with ice. Garnish with a cherry tomato speared with a sprig of basil. Sit a cherry tomato on the rim. Serve with a straw and a stirrer.

Virgin Mary

A truly spicy pick-me-up you can drink as a tonic when you feel the need for one.

5oz / 15cl	tomato juice
1oz / 3cl	fresh lemon juice
2 dashes	Worcestershire sauce
	salt and ground black pepper
dash	Tabasco sauce
1 stick	celery

Pour the tomato juice into a highball filled with ice. Season to taste with the spices. Stir well. Add the celery stick to use as a stirrer.

White Sandy Beach

I created this when I was in Little Dick's Bay in the British Virgin Islands, which has a beautiful fine white sandy beach. Paradise! This is a wonderful combination of a colada with a banana texture.

3⅓oz / 10cl	pineapple juice
1⅔oz / 5cl	coconut cream
1	small ripe banana, sliced

Place all ingredients into a blender with a scoop of crushed ice. Blend. Pour into a colada glass. Garnish with a three slices of banana on a cocktail stick sitting across the glass. Add a sprinkle of nutmeg to finish the drink. Serve with a straw.

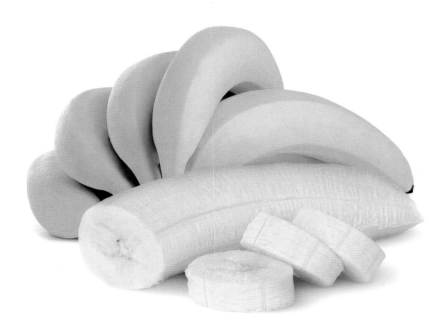

general index

index of drink names

Note: Page numbers in indicate photographs.

acknowledgments

The author would like to thank everyone who made this book possible. It was a mammoth task and a great team helped me put it together. Firstly, to my publishing duo, Lincoln Boehm and Charles Nurnberg, a great thank-you. To Lynn Bryan, thanks. Thanks also to Limelight Management. To the team of bartenders at The Library Bar: George, Fabrizio, Stevan, Matteo, Jack, Fiore, and Sophia: many thanks for being there. To all other bartenders (including Jerry Mignot, Dick Bradsell, and Dale deGroff) whose recipes I selected, thanks!

The BookMaker would like to thank Dartington, Riedel, and WaterfordWedgwood for their kindness in loaning glassware, as well as Christofle, Thomas Goode, and Harrods.

CREDITS

26 Baccarat; 28 Iittala tumbler; 37 Lalique water glass and Dartington cocktail glass; 46 Dartington cocktail glass; 56 Lalique tumbler; 72 LSA old-fashioned glass and Dartington cocktail glass; 93 far right, Lalique; 102 Dartington cocktail glass and Margarita glass; 106 left, Thomas Goode crystal highball, right, Kosta Boda highball; 112 Eliche water glass by Salviati, from Harrods, and Eliche old-fashioned glass; 122 Stuart cocktail glass and Thomas Goode highball; 132 Salvatore's cocktail glass; 143 Dartington cocktail glass and small private cocktail glass; 152 Christofle highball and old-fashioned glasses; 167 Christofle 3000 cocktail glass; 173 left, champagne flute, Eliche by Saviati from Harrods, and right, champagne flute, Kawali by Christofle; 188 both John Rocha for Waterford Crystal highball; 202 Dartington Rachel pitcher and Edinburgh crystal tumbler from Harrods; 214 Dartington tumbler and cocktail glass; 228 Conran shot glass and Orrefors liqueur glass; 238 LSA hot toddy glass and Jerry's Home Store mulled wine glass; 253 left, Thomas Goode Italian water goblet and right, Lalique old-fashioned glass; 264 Lalique water glass.